OLD TESTAMENT PLAYS

OLD TESTAMENT PLAYS

by

LAURENCE HOUSMAN

JONATHAN CAPE
THIRTY BEDFORD SQUARE
LONDON

Palestine Plays
FIRST PUBLISHED 1942

Samuel the Kingmaker
FIRST PUBLISHED 1944

Old Testament Plays
FIRST PUBLISHED 1950

Dewey Classification
822.91

PRINTED IN GREAT BRITAIN IN THE CITY OF OXFORD
AT THE ALDEN PRESS
BOUND BY A. W. BAIN & CO. LTD., LONDON

CONTENTS

INTRODUCTION

THIS re-issue, under a new title, of all the author's plays based on Old Testament history has the added interest that the stage version and title of *Jacob's Ladder* have been substituted for the earlier version. The running commentary on Jacob's character, from two Voices (more heard than seen), to right and left of the stage, was put in while the play was in actual rehearsal by the Old Vic Company. And this added so greatly to it effectiveness, that it has been retained for all future use, and is the only version licensed for stage-presentation.

If the author's exposure of the fictitious uprightness of *Samuel The King Maker's* character shocks any readers of that play, he invites their attention to the documentary evidence in support of it, provided in the introduction. Only if they can refute *that* have they any right to be shocked.

ABRAHAM AND ISAAC

PREFACE

THE history of the Israelites is the history of an extraordinarily God-conscious people; and the Old Testament is very largely a record of the long process of trial and error by which they arrived finally at a conception of God to which Christianity was able to attach itself. But that conception was only arrived at gradually and with difficulty, after many mistakes by the way. And because those mistakes became embedded in their Scriptures, and were vouched for as 'the Word of the Lord', Christianity, when it took over the Bible as the inspired Word of God, took over its defects as well as its excellencies – the misses as well as the hits; and as a result (even down to the present day) Bibliolatry has been one of the greatest hindrances to Christianity: it has perpetuated many superstitions which would otherwise have died a natural death, and has imposed on the mind of each rising generation, as matter for unquestioning belief, things which the religious mind of today finds spiritually distasteful.

The reluctance of our theologians to throw over these vain beliefs has been largely responsible for the increasing neglect into which 'holy scriptures written for our learning' (and from which there is so much to learn) have fallen during the last two generations. Sound moral feeling, quite as much as intellectual scepticism, has caused modern thinkers to regard as no longer worthy of respect a system of miraculous intervention which turns God into a showman performing tricks for the delectation of a small favoured tribe, providing it with short cuts to victory over its enemies, and special visitations of plague, pestilence, or famine whenever its rulers behave badly. Such a process of alternate coddling and bullying is no true education for man or nation: it only produces spoiled children; and until their

11

later prophets taught them better, the children of Israel were thoroughly spoiled children. Having decided that they were 'the Chosen People', they wrote their history in terms of tribal megalomania; and, as a consequence, ostentation and favouritism became divine attributes; and their extravagant taste for miraculous intervention, often on quite trivial occasions, has obscured the meaning and lessened the spiritual value of many a beautiful Old Testament story.

The best one can do for them today, to restore the respect they have lost, is to eliminate these useless excrescences. And so, in the Plays which here follow, the story is given without the miracle. The deep heart-searchings of Abraham to find in it the mind of God required the outside intervention of no Angel. The wrestling of Jacob with his shifty, time-serving conscience was an inward and solitary one. Micaiah's parable of the Lying Spirit – Jonah's of the Whale – belong to the prophetic technique of their day; and the puzzled inquiry which I put into Jonah's mouth, 'Is it not strange, Shemmel, that to make men believe the truth we prophets have to tell lies?' has its application even in the present day. Why is it that these old stories of miracle are still so insistently regarded, not as inventions quite natural in their day, but as religious truths which must not be questioned?

I cannot help feeling, therefore, that if these Plays cause offence to any, it is the surer proof that pious hindrance still stands in the way of a right understanding of what an old Quaker quaintly described as 'the better side of God's character'.

L. H.

SCENE I

For the right setting of this play there is no need that scenery or costume should be correct either as to date or locality; indeed, better not; for although Eastern in origin, it retells a story so deeply human in its appeal that wherever it has become known, it has taken a native colouring in the minds of its readers So, in the form in which it is here presented, there has been no attempt to preserve the archaic and biblical character of the original, but only to express in simple everyday language the painful heart-searchings of a rather primitive mind seeking to discover the Will of God in the terms of a command coming from without; and, in agonized obedience to that supposed Will, finding at last that the Will of God is truly within the heart of man, and in no other place.

(*In a plain tent-like interior sits* ABRAHAM, *sunk in deep dejection. He is now an old man, but his mood makes him look much older than he is; strength seems to have gone out of him. He wears the dress of one who lives on the land—an owner of flocks and herds, but also a worker.* SARAH, *his wife, enters from the inner tent, carrying a pail and a milking-stool. On her way out she stops, looks at him, puts down pail and milking-stool, and goes towards him.*)

SARAH Abram, what's the matter?

ABRAHAM Matter? Nothing.

SARAH What's worrying you?

ABRAHAM *You.*

SARAH It's you that's worrying *me*, Abram. You've got something on your mind It's as if ye'd done a crime.

ABRAHAM I've done no crime! God keep me from it; that's all I ask.

SARAH Well, sure He will. What's tempting ye to it?

ABRAHAM Maybe 'tis God. Quit asking!

SARAH Abram, I can't let it be. This last week, how much have ye slept o' nights? I've heard ye get up from your bed, and kneel down and pray; and I could hear the sound of it, but not the words. And after all your praying, you groaned as though it had brought you no comfort, and you've come back to bed, and there ye have lain, sighing your heart out; and never a wink of sleep have ye had, nor I either – thinking, but not daring to speak to you, for *you* not speaking to *me*. What is it, Abram?

ABRAHAM Nothing I can tell you, Woman; it's a trouble that's come to me from the Lord – if 'tis the Lord that's tempting me. Maybe He'll let me know in His own good time. But He's told me nothing yet. Quit asking!

SARAH (*with a sigh, giving it up*) Well, it's no use my going on about it, if you won't tell me anything.

ABRAHAM No use at all. We'll just leave it at that.

SARAH While I make some better use of myself.

(*She picks up pail and stool, then turns to him again, and inquires cheerfully:*)

How have things gone in the field today?

ABRAHAM Well – all well.

SARAH Isaac's getting to be a real help to you now, isn't he?

ABRAHAM Yes; he is that.

SARAH He's getting a big lad.

ABRAHAM Yes; so he is.

SARAH Growing so fast, he'll soon be a man.

ABRAHAM So you think he'll soon be a man?

SARAH Why yes; he almost looks it now; so tall as he is for his age, and so strong.

ABRAHAM Aye; tall and strong – a fine lad; and we so late in the making of him.

SARAH Yes; God was good to us, Abram, when He gave us such a son to our old age. If he goes on like he is, he'll soon be able to take things over for you. Why don't you let him now for a bit — just as a trial? For you're older now for your age than you used to be.

ABRAHAM Yes; older for my age now.

SARAH And you're tired.

ABRAHAM Aye; tired I am.

SARAH And it's because you won't give yourself enough rest. That's what's the matter; that's what has made you so out of heart these last days.

ABRAHAM Out of heart, you say? I've too much heart in me: that's what's the matter with me. I wish I'd no heart at all. 'Twould be easier then.

SARAH What would?

ABRAHAM Nothing . . . everything!

SARAH You are talking daft, Abram.

ABRAHAM Yes, Woman; I'm talking daft. I don't want to talk.

SARAH Then I'll go and milk the goats for better company.

(She goes out; ABRAHAM remains seated; he bows his head into his hands, and groans. Presently he raises himself and lifts his hands in supplication.)

ABRAHAM O Lord, what is the truth of this thing ye're telling me to do? Let me know, let me see Thy Face; and if I know that it *is* Thy telling, I will do it, though it be to the death. But if Thou show me *not* Thy Face, how am I to know that it is Thy telling? All is darkness now; no light. Lord, show me Thy light!

(He pauses, but seems to get no answer; with a hope-less gesture he rises and turns towards the door. ISAAC enters. ABRAHAM stands and looks at him:

something in his look causes the lad to hesitate, a little shy in his greeting.)

ISAAC Hullo, Father. Here I am back.

ABRAHAM Isaac, have you done your work? Have you brought in and penned all those sheep I told you?

ISAAC Yes, Father.

ABRAHAM Where had you been gone that I lost sight of you?

ISAAC Only up on hill, Father.

ABRAHAM What did you go there for?

ISAAC Just to look out – and see.

ABRAHAM See what?

ISAAC Whatever was to see – further away where the world begins. I'd like to see the world, Father. Here at home one sees so little; never any change – all days the same.

ABRAHAM D'you want change, Isaac?

ISAAC Yes, sometimes. And from top of the hill one sees more of the world than down here. That's why I go there.

ABRAHAM And what did you see – this time?

ISAAC I saw a great company of travellers, going south; all their beasts with loads on them. Who were they? . . . Where were they going, Father?

ABRAHAM Merchants, my son, from foreign parts, maybe; going from city to city to find sale for their merchandise.

ISAAC What are cities like, Father?

ABRAHAM Like nothing you've ever seen; streets and streets of houses all shut up in walls . . . full of people, thousands of 'em, rich and poor, with their kings to rule over them, and their temples set up to false gods.

ISAAC What is a false god, Father?

ABRAHAM One that deceives his worshippers, telling them lies, making them do wicked things.

ISAAC Are there many of them?

ABRAHAM Aye; the world is full of them – more than a man can count. And all going strong.

ISAAC Why strong, Father?

ABRAHAM Because the hearts of men are evil – and what their false gods tell them to do, they wish to do. Aye, they like doing it well. But when it's the true God that speaks, He tells you to do hard things: – hard, hard.

ISAAC How many true Gods are there?

ABRAHAM There's only one true God, my son.

ISAAC Your God, Father?

ABRAHAM Aye; my God and your God.

ISAAC But *I* don't know Him, Father. What's He like? Have you ever seen Him?

ABRAHAM No man can see God, Isaac.

ISAAC Then how do you know He's there at all – anywhere?

ABRAHAM You hear His voice speaking.

ISAAC But how do you know that it's *His* voice, if you've never seen Him?

ABRAHAM If you heard my voice from far off, calling to you, my son, you'd know 'twas me.

ISAAC Yes, Father; because I've heard your voice other times, when I've seen you.

ABRAHAM If you'd been born blind, my son, you would still know my voice. Man has been born blind to the ways of Heaven; but he knows the Voice of God speaking in his heart.

ISAAC But has God ever spoken in mine, Father?

ABRAHAM I don't know, my son. Maybe you're so young that He hasn't spoken to you yet. But when a hard thing comes for you to do that you know you've got to do, then it'll be God speaking.

ISAAC Why must it be a *hard* thing, Father?

ABRAHAM Because God is much greater than man – and

wiser. And God's ways not being man's ways, man finds it hard. . . .

(*This talk is too hard for* ISAAC *to follow. He moves towards the door, and stands looking out. His Father watches him.*)

ABRAHAM So you like change, you say? And you like going up a hill . . . Then I've a bit of news for you . . . To-morrow you'll be going with me to a place where God tells me He wants us to go . . . to a hill much higher than yon; aye; more than a hill, a mountain — Mount Moriah, they call it. We are going right up to the top of it, you and I. You'll have a large look from there on the world lying down beneath you, and the world out away beyond, further than ever you or I'll have feet to go. You'll see a lot from up there — that you'll never see again . . . And you'll like to go there — won't you?

ISAAC Yes, Father. I'll like to go up there. I shan't want ever to come down again . . . But why are we going, Father? What shall we have to do when we get there?

ABRAHAM We shall do what God wants us to do. Leave that to Him. Ask me no more.

ISAAC How far is it?

ABRAHAM A three days' journey, my son.

ISAAC That's further than I've ever been.

ABRAHAM Yes; much further it'll be.

ISAAC Oh, I wish tomorrow were come! . . . Why couldn't we start today, Father?

ABRAHAM There's no need to hurry. Tomorrow will be time enough. The day'll keep.

(*He goes to the door, stands looking out, and speaks only to himself.*)

Down goes the sun . . . This day's over . . . I have made the Lord's will to be mine.

(*He goes out.* ISAAC *stands puzzled.*)

ISAAC Why is he so sad? He says God has told him; but he doesn't want to go. How funny!

(*Enter* SARAH *carrying her pail of milk.*)

Mother! Have you heard? Did you know? Has Father told you?

SARAH Told me what, child?

ISAAC We are going away, Mother: he's taking me with him – a three days' journey to somewhere I've never been: to a great high mountain, Mother; we are going right up to the top where one can look out and see all the world. Just think of that!

SARAH (*setting down her pail*) I think your Father is out of his senses, Isaac. What for does he want to go climbing mountains at his age? There's no sense in it.

ISAAC Oh, yes, there is, Mother. He says it's a hard thing to do, but that God told him. And that's why.

SARAH God told him?

ISAAC Yes, Mother; he says that if anything is hard to do, you must do it; because doing hard things is God's will.

SARAH Well, if it's only a hard thing God wants him to do, he could just as well have done it at home: he might have stood on his head – or something a bit harder maybe, if that didn't satisfy him. You know, Isaac, God is not making your Father happy; he's not treating him right. Night after night he can't sleep: gets up out of his bed, goes off and prays, and comes back more miserable than he went. It's not reasonable praying to a God who does that to you. He'd better try a change, I think. There's plenty of other gods to choose from.

ISAAC But you can't change from the true God to a false god, Mother.

SARAH How does he know he's got the true God? You've

only his word for it. Men all think they've got the true God, whichever it is: but whether they have or no, that's not left for a woman to say. When I married your Father, his God became my God; and had I married someone else 'twould have been a different one; so there's where I leave it . . . Ah, but you're not listening to a word I say – just like your Father – always dreaming.

ISAAC No; I was only thinking, Mother.

SARAH Thinking what?

ISAAC Of the world.

SARAH Eh? What of it?

ISAAC I want to see it.

SARAH Well, you've only to look round.

ISAAC More of it. What I see here's nothing.

SARAH No, only what's going to be your life and what's made it: the sheep and the goats, and the cattle and the serving men; and your Father and Mother. We're nothing – or we'll not be much longer.

ISAAC (*protesting*) Oh, Mother!

SARAH And because your Father's taking you a journey, where you'll see new things, you're happier than I've ever been able to make you, for all the care I've had of ye. Well, it's natural, I suppose, that you should want to see the world, and what it's like, and all that's in it – the good and the bad. What are you most wanting to see?

ISAAC I don't know, Mother. Things . . . places . . . people.

SARAH People – ah, ye mean women . . . Young maidens, with eyes looking at you, eh? Now isn't that true, Isaac?

ISAAC How did you know, Mother?

SARAH Mothers don't have to know, when their sons begin to be men . . . Well, who is she?

ISAAC I don't know, Mother: I shall never know . . . 'Twas a month ago, when those travellers came by, and stopped, and asked for their water-skins to be filled. There was one with them; she wore a veil; and when she put it aside, I saw one of her eyes – only one, Mother. And I've been seeing that eye of hers ever since – sleeping and waking.

SARAH Aye; it's begun for you! And now, till you've seen the other eye and all the rest – of her, or of another – you're never going to have peace.

ISAAC I don't want peace, Mother; I want life. Peace isn't life.

SARAH No? Maybe you're right. Anyway peace isn't your Father's life; though it's peace he should be having now he's so old. You know, Isaac, I shouldn't wonder if it isn't to please you that he's doing this, taking you to the top of a mountain just for you to see what you call the world. For he was always a yielding man; and you could make him do wrong things if you went on at him long enough . . . Ah, I did that once. And I remember (after he'd done it), he made himself think 'twas the Lord's will and not mine as had made him. Seems he liked better to think 'twas the Lord had made him do what was wrong, than that his wife should have made him. Ah, that's like a man. For so being 'twas the Lord's will – made it right . . . But it wasn't.

ISAAC What was it, Mother?

SARAH I'll tell you. I was sorry for it, after; but 'twas too late then. There was a woman here named Hagar. Your Father had had a son by her; thirteen years before you were born that was. I'd wished for it to be, having no son of my own. But when you came I was jealous; for Ishmael was a fine lad, and your Father was fond of him. And because I feared he'd be fonder of him than ever he'd be of you, and would put him first, maybe, I made him send both of 'em away. He didn't want to, but I would have it. And when he'd done it, then he said 'twas the Lord's will. That's your Father's way; when he's done something he didn't want to do he thinks 'twas God made him do it. So

21

now he tells you 'tis God sending him off to this mountain he's got to climb when he's no longer the strength for it; but I think it's for you he's doing it, because it pleases you. And you do want to go?

ISAAC Yes, Mother.

(*While she has been speaking* ABRAHAM *enters, and stands listening.*)

SARAH To go away and leave your poor old Mother alone.

ISAAC But I'm coming back, Mother.

SARAH Oh yes, you're coming back; but you'll come back with your head so full of all the things you've seen that there'll be no keeping you. Aye; it's what a mother has to learn, and to bear – having given all her care and all the love of her heart to the son she's borne, she has to give him up – and let him go to another. Aye, she may keep her old man, till both be grey; but a woman is ever widowed of her sons. And I'll forgive the woman that takes you from me that you may have joy of her, and children of your own. But if God took you from me, Him I would never forgive.

ABRAHAM Woman, you are speaking wickedly.

SARAH Yes, Abram, I'm speaking wickedly, but I'm speaking truth. For if God dealt so with me, He'd be no God of mine; nay, though He were your God, He should not be mine!

ABRAHAM You don't know what you're saying, Woman: you don't know what you're saying! And this is my word to you, and my command – that you speak not another word, lest God strike you dead. Get in!

(SARAH, *frightened, runs in to the the inner tent.*)

ISAAC What did Mother mean, Father?

ABRAHAM Nothing . . . Woman's words . . . Man has no right, Isaac, to make God do man's will. If he did, man would be his own God. We live to do *His*, not ours. (*He*

22

goes to the door, and stands looking out.) Come here to me, Isaac . . . See yonder sun setting; see it go. Some day you'll see it set for the last time.

ISAAC I shall see it rise again tomorrow, Father.

ABRAHAM Aye, tomorrow, maybe, you'll see it rise; and the next day and the next. But a day will come after, when you'll not. Our lives are in God's hands, Isaac – yours *and* mine. If God would take my life this day, surely I would be thankful – for a great mercy it would be! (*It begins to get dark.*) Go in, my son, to your Mother, and be kind to her; be very kind. Tomorrow, we start early; when the sun rises we start on our way.

> (ISAAC *goes in.* ABRAHAM *stands motionless. It gets darker and darker.*)

Oh, the black sunrise it'll be! Shall I ever see sunrise again? No light to the darkness of my days will ever come to me now . . . Only the darkness of the grave!

SCENE 2

> (*On the top of Mount Moriah is a low hillock; on it a stone roughly shaped like an altar. Dawn has hardly begun; it is still twilight.* ABRAHAM *enters, followed by* ISAAC, *bearing a load of wood. He halts and looks round.* ISAAC *stands looking at him for some time, in silence, then speaks.*)

ISAAC Are we there, Father?

ABRAHAM Aye; we're there. We've no further to go now. This is the very place. 'Twas here He told me we were to come.

ISAAC What are we here for?

ABRAHAM For a meeting.

ISAAC Who with?

ABRAHAM With God.

ISAAC With God? Am I going to see God, Father?

ABRAHAM I don't know, my son. But if, after this day, there's any life in you, you'll be seeing God better than I, maybe.

ISAAC You talk strange, Father.

ABRAHAM Aye, for a strange thought has come to me. I would to God now that you were not my son.

ISAAC What are you looking like that for, Father? Are you angry with me? Have I done anything wrong?

ABRAHAM Only by being born, my son.

ISAAC Why was I wrong to be born, Father?

ABRAHAM There's some born that better hadn't been born. I was one; now you're another.

ISAAC What do you mean, Father?

(ABRAHAM *seats himself, and draws* ISAAC *towards him.* ISAAC *sits at his knee.*)

ABRAHAM Listen, my son. You know that all your life I've cared for you, and loved you, and done all for you that a father could do. Do you remember one day when I saved your young life, when you'd fallen down into a pit; and three days you were lost to us. And I came and found you and drew you out again?

ISAAC Yes; I remember, Father.

ABRAHAM If now I asked your life of you, would you give it me?

ISAAC My life, Father?

ABRAHAM If I asked you to give me the life I saved, would you give it me?

ISAAC If it was to save your life, Father.

ABRAHAM I said not to save *my* life. I said, if I asked it, would you give it me?

ISAAC I would wish to give it you, Father, if I had the courage for it.

ABRAHAM Have courage, my son; for the day may come soon . . . Listen again, son. If there was one that had cared for me all my life, as I have cared for you – that had saved my life as I saved yours, but more times than one; if He came and asked of me my life, should I not give it Him?

ISAAC Yes, Father.

ABRAHAM And if He came, and asked – not *my* life, but yours, should I not give it Him?

ISAAC Why should he ask mine, Father?

ABRAHAM I do not know why. But if He *did* ask it –

ISAAC He? Who is it you mean, Father?

ABRAHAM I mean God. There's none other that could ask it – only God.

ISAAC How would He ask? Would you hear Him speak?

ABRAHAM Aye; as I have heard Him speak often – before. Day in, day out, I could not get away from Him; could not get Him out of my mind, out of my heart – always there – speaking. Ever asking me – did I love Him? Was I ready to do anything He told me to do – *was* I? So – the better to satisfy Him, and my own mind – I began to think of all the things I *would* do for Him. 'Yes,' I said. 'Yes, and yes; Lord, I would do that, and I would do that, and I would do that – aye, willingly – if it were Thy will I should do it' . . . But that wasn't enough for Him. (*His face becomes terrible.*)

ISAAC Father!

ABRAHAM For one day the thought came to me, all of a sudden, of one thing I would *not* do for Him. And then I knew that was the very thing He would have me do.

ISAAC How did you know it?

ABRAHAM My heart told me. For there, in my heart, was

25

the wickedness – that I hadn't the will to serve Him in that thing, in that one thing . . . And because I hadn't the will for it, sure and certain I knew then that it was His Will.

ISAAC What was it, Father?

ABRAHAM A sacrifice, my son

ISAAC What sort of a sacrifice?

ABRAHAM Blood; the blood of a lamb.

ISAAC That's no great thing, is it, Father?

ABRAHAM In God's eyes maybe not . . . maybe not. As God sees we cannot see – poor mortals as we be. So, here we be come to the place, and this the appointed time for the lamb to be slain . . . We've no further to go now.

ISAAC But, Father, though we have the wood and the fire for kindling, where is the lamb?

ABRAHAM God has provided the lamb, my son.

ISAAC Then it's not yours, Father?

ABRAHAM No, not what I can call mine – everything that is mine being His . . . Unbind the wood, my son. Aye; and give me the rope. Now lay the wood. There's a stone that you can lay it on. For a stone has no heart, so the heart of it won't break, as mine'll break when the fire's lighted, and the sacrifice, with its life gone out, laid on it.

ISAAC (*stopping*) Father, you frighten me.

ABRAHAM Aye; and if 'twere not the Lord's will, I'd tell you now to run for your life – for your dear life; for 'twas not to *you* that the bidding came – only to me. And because when word of it came, piercing my heart, so that my heart breaks and bleeds – so, surely, I know that 'tis only God can have laid this bidding on me – to do His will . . . Stand up, my son, stand up, and let me bind you. And for pity of your Father's heart that's breaking, stand still and do not strive. (*He starts binding him.*)

ISAAC But why are you binding *me*, Father?

ABRAHAM Because 'tis the Lord's will.

26

ISAAC But are you going to kill *me*, Father? Am I the lamb?

ABRAHAM Aye: you are the lamb, my son.

ISAAC And killing me, do you do God's will, Father?

ABRAHAM Killing you – I do – His will.

ISAAC Willingly, Father?

ABRAHAM Aye – God helping me – willingly.

ISAAC Then He knows, Father!

ABRAHAM Knows what?

ISAAC That your will is to do His Will . . . If He knows *that* – what more does He want, Father? . . . What more does He want?

> (ABRAHAM *raises himself, and stands rapt in the revelation that has come to him. Slowly the light of dawn grows brighter.* ISAAC *kneels at his feet.*)

Oh, do not hold me bound! I too am willing, Father!

ABRAHAM (*lifting his hands*) O God, God, hast Thou heard? 'Twas the lamb that spoke, not I: but surely he spoke truth. If with my whole heart I have been willing to serve Thee – to the death, and have not withheld my son, my only son, from Thee, then is my truth known unto Thee, and my condemnation is over, and Thy reproof has gone from me. O Searcher of hearts, what more dost Thou need? Is not life dearer to Thee than death? Is not *my* son Thy son? Aye, plainly now, in light, not in darkness, Thou speakest to me again. I have heard Thee with the hearing of my ear, but now mine eye seeth Thee.

ISAAC You see God, Father?

ABRAHAM I see God.

ISAAC Where?

ABRAHAM In the land of the living, in the heart of man whom He hath made. We are His children and He careth for us. In Him we live . . . In Him there is no death. Thou wast my Father, when I was ignorant of Thee. I wake in

Thy likeness, and am satisfied. For Thou art the God not of the dead but of the living. And from Thee comes no darkness but light!

> (*The sun rises, and shines fully upon him. He stoops, looses* ISAAC *from his bonds, raises him, and stands holding him embraced. And presently they will hear the bleating of a ram caught in a thicket; and an alternative sacrifice will present itself, and be thankfully accepted as a sign that the controversy between* ABRAHAM *and his God is over.*)

SCENE 3

> (*In the tent* SARAH *stands waiting and looking out. It is near the end of the day; the sun is setting.* ABRAHAM *comes slowly in, rather weary upon his feet; he carries his travelling-pack in his hand.*)

SARAH (*a little hard of tone*) Well, Abram: so you are back, are you?

ABRAHAM I am – back.

SARAH I'd been hoping, maybe, you'd give up, and come back sooner.

ABRAHAM You shouldn't have done, Woman.

SARAH No: I suppose I shouldn't have given it a thought, as 'twas no affair of *mine*. Well; you've had your outing; and I hope it's done you good.

ABRAHAM It has done that. Here, Woman – take this!

> (*He hands over his bundle.*)

SARAH Ah! but it's tired you out; I can see that.

ABRAHAM Aye . . . But it's good to be tired after doing what's been so well worth doing.

SARAH (*dryly*) Well, if you like to think so! (*Then relenting.*) But there! I'm sorry I spoke sharp to you. Sit down, Abram, and rest yourself.

ABRAHAM No, I'll go in, I'll go right in; and lie down for a while. (*He moves to the inner door.*)

SARAH Where's Isaac? What's *he* doing?

ABRAHAM He's out there with the ass, stabling her for the night. He'll be with you in a minute.

(*He moves to the door. Meanwhile* SARAH *has undone the bundle.*)

SARAH Why, Abram! Whatever made you take your holy robes with you? You didn't need *them* on top of the mountain, did you?

ABRAHAM I did, Woman.

SARAH What for?

ABRAHAM That's no concern of yours, Woman. I'd reason for it, you needn't doubt. Have you never heard of a holy mountain – aye, holy to God? (*He goes in.*)

SARAH Holy? Oh, it's that God of his that's always leading him astray. I wish he'd get another!

(*Enter* ISAAC.)

ISAAC Well, Mother, here I am back!

SARAH Aye, back at last; and time too. Aren't you going to give your Mother a kiss? (*He kisses her.*) D'you think I haven't missed you, all the long days you've been away?

ISAAC Only six, Mother.

SARAH Seemed more like a month to me, left here all alone, with all the pens to see to, and the milking to do; and every night lying awake, thinking of your old Father, and him not fit to go anywhere – the state he was in – so low and out of spirit as he was.

ISAAC He's all right now, Mother.

SARAH Say what you like; but he was looking well-nigh
worn out when he came in just now. And he's gone in to
lie down: which he wouldn't, if he was feeling as 'all right'
as you say he is.

ISAAC It's been a hot day and a long journey. But when
we were going he seemed never to sleep at all. Now – these
last three days, he's slept well. The first night, coming
back, he was off before ever I was. I lay and watched him for
hours.

SARAH What kept you awake?

ISAAC (*evasively*) Oh, just thinking; and wondering what
it would be like to be old and wise and good like him. In
his sleep, he put his hand over me, and I lay in his breast.

SARAH Aye; he loves you well, Isaac.

ISAAC He does, Mother.

SARAH Well, tell me, now, all that you've been doing.
Your Father's so shut up he won't tell me anything. Where
is it you've been?

ISAAC (*avoiding her eye*) To the top of a mountain.

SARAH Ah! 'twas there he said he was going when he first
talked of going away. And I said – at his age, whatever for?
'To do something hard', he says. And when I said – why
couldn't he do that at home? he'd no answer except some
foolishness about the ways of God not being the ways of
man . . . And what did you do when you got there?

ISAAC (*who is finding this difficult*) Oh . . . we sat down,
and rested.

SARAH Well – and then?

ISAAC And then we talked – and looked at the view.
(*This gives him something to talk about.*) 'Twas a fine view,
Mother, right up over the world; you could see for miles
and miles. Down below us, in the valleys, 'twas all dark,
for 'twas early; the sun hadn't risen.

SARAH (*astonished*) You went up before the sun was
risen?

ISAAC Yes, Mother.

SARAH Why?

ISAAC Because we wanted to get to the top, and see the view.

SARAH Before sunrise?

ISAAC Yes; it's the best time for it, just when the sun rises. It makes everything so clear.

SARAH Well – and then?

ISAAC Then we came down again.

(*But this is not going to satisfy* SARAH; *the more she thinks of it, the less does she find in it.*)

SARAH D'you mean to tell me you only went up to see the view?

ISAAC (*reluctantly*) No, Mother, of course it wasn't only to see the view. 'Twas to make a burnt-offering for a sacrifice.

SARAH What had you to sacrifice?

ISAAC A ram.

SARAH You didn't take a ram *with* you?

ISAAC No, we found it. 'Twas there caught in a thicket.

SARAH (*puzzled*) Well, but did you *know* you were going to find it?

ISAAC No, Mother; it just so happened 'twas there.

SARAH Well, it's being only a woman, I suppose, and having no understanding, as your father is always saying; but this beats *me*. I can see no sense in it! You went up to make a sacrifice, and you didn't take the sacrifice with you? Then how did you mean to make it? What of?

ISAAC That's what *I* said, Mother. I asked him. And Father said that God would provide the lamb.

SARAH The lamb? Just now you said 'twas a ram.

ISAAC 'Twas a young ram, Mother. Anyway, it wasn't any older than I am now.

SARAH 'Twould need no *young* ram to be that.

ISAAC (*trying to satisfy her*) Well, this *was* a young ram, Mother.

SARAH And so, you made a sacrifice of it?

ISAAC Yes, Mother – Father did.

SARAH (*taking up the robe from the opened bundle*) Oh, so that's why! I was wondering how ever there came to be blood on it! If you hadn't told me, I might have thought your Father had done a murder, and was afraid to tell me of it. For when he went in just now, it seemed like as he didn't want to talk to me about it. Ah, well! men's ways aren't women's ways, and never will be. We shall never understand them, not if we were to stand on our heads to do it . . . And now, I'll go and be getting you something to eat, for you must be hungry.

ISAAC Yes, Mother; I'm very hungry.

> (SARAH *goes off to get the meal. Presently through the curtain over the inner door*, ABRAHAM *looks out cautiously to see if the coast is clear.* ISAAC *gives him a gesture of reassurance.* ABRAHAM *comes in.*)

ABRAHAM Has your Mother been asking you things, Isaac?

ISAAC Yes, Father.

ABRAHAM (*apprehensively*) What have you told her?

ISAAC Only so much as she could understand, Father.

ABRAHAM How much was that?

ISAAC About the ram, Father; and the sacrifice. I saw her looking at those blood marks; so I told her what was the cause of them.

ABRAHAM Aye, you've a wise heart, and an understanding mind, Isaac. There's things a woman hasn't the mind for; so being, it's better to leave them not said . . . And your old Father – what have you in your mind about him, Isaac?

ISAAC Understanding, Father.

ABRAHAM God bless you for that, Isaac. Surely 'twas one
Father that went up the mountain, 'twas another that came
down. But *that* your Mother would never understand; she'd
always have it against me. It's a great doubt I have, Isaac,
that she'd never look at me the same, did she know what had
been in my heart to do, before God made His meaning clear
to me. She's a good woman, is your Mother, and a good wife
to me has she been. But she loves you better than she
loves me.

ISAAC Why do you think that, Father?

ABRAHAM 'Tis natural, my son. A woman's child is of
her own flesh and blood; the bearing is hers, and all the
travail, and the pain, and the joy that comes after. And that
being the way of it, she'd find it hard – maybe – if she
knew – not to think ill of me.

ISAAC She shall never know from me, Father. There's
no need.

ABRAHAM (*much relieved*) You're a good son to me, Isaac.
God's blessing be on you.

(SARAH *comes in, and begins laying the table with the
meal.*)

SARAH Ah! so you're up again, Abram. Are you rested?

ABRAHAM I've had all the rest I need for now. And
please God, this night I shall have more – and, in my
dreams, peace.

SARAH Then now, maybe, you'll be ready for a meal.

ABRAHAM I *am* ready, Woman.

SARAH (*as she lays the table*) There's not much that I've
got for you; not knowing when you'd be coming back.

ABRAHAM It's enough, Woman.

SARAH I'd have had more for you yesterday, had you
come then – soon enough. 'Twas near noon when four
travellers came to the door wanting food and drink; so I

killed the kid for them, and what they could not eat, I gave them to take away.

ABRAHAM Had they come with so little food of their own?

SARAH Ah. So it would seem; for they'd come off in haste, fleeing for their lives.

ABRAHAM Where did they come from?

SARAH Zoar, the hill-city, so they told me. 'Twas a man with his wife and his two children.

ABRAHAM And fleeing for their lives, you say?

SARAH Yes, from the gods of that city, and their own people, where they'd been born and bred. 'Twas a strange tale, and hard to believe; but it sounded true. They've a god there called Moloch.

ABRAHAM Aye, Moloch, one of their false gods.

SARAH And when they make a feast for him, they cast lots for those that shall give their children for a burnt sacrifice – 'to pass through the fire to Moloch' is their word for it. Well, this time 'twas on one of their sons the lot had fallen, a fine lad – the same age as Isaac, he was. So, in the very dead of night, before the feast day, they got up, secretly, and came safe away. And they'll never be able to go back they say. They'd be all put cruelly to death, because they would not give their god what he required of them . . . Is your God like that, Abram?

ABRAHAM No; He is not like that, Woman.

SARAH Well, that's a good thing to know– that He'd never wish you to do a thing like that.

ABRAHAM Aye; it's a good thing to *know*, Woman. But maybe, a man, for lack of understanding, might think that He *did* wish it.

SARAH If He did, He'd be no God o' mine. I'd find me another.

ABRAHAM You cannot choose God to your own liking, Woman. There's only one true God, and true He is, but hard to find, man being so slow of understanding. But when you *have* found Him, you know that He is the one true God, and that there is none like Him in all the world.

SARAH And you've found Him?

ABRAHAM Aye: I've found Him – or He's found *me;* and dark and difficult was the way. Mighty and merciful is He: slow to anger, and of great goodness.

(SARAH *goes out to fetch the last dish for the meal. Father and son sit silent, looking at each other.* SARAH *returns and sets the dish down.*)

SARAH There! that's the best I can do for you. (*She starts helping them.*)

ABRAHAM Wait, Woman, wait! Would you have us eat without first asking a blessing?

(SARAH *sits down.* ABRAHAM *rises.*)

God be merciful to us, and bless us, and shew us the light of His countenance, and be merciful unto us. That His way may be known upon earth, and His saving health among all nations.

Let the people praise thee, O Lord: yea, let all the people praise thee.

Then shall the Nations rejoice and be glad, and the far Nations shall run unto Thee. Then shall the earth bring forth her increase; and God even our own God shall give us His blessing. God shall bless us: and all the ends of the world shall fear Him. Thus shall the man be blessed that feareth the Lord. Yea, he shall see his children's children: and peace upon Israel.

(*Having ended the blessing* ABRAHAM *sits down.*)

ISAAC Who is Israel, Father?

ABRAHAM I know not, my son. The word just came to me. And though I see not the end thereof, now I see the beginning of his day, and I am rejoiced because of it: and in Him my heart is glad.

> (*In the first part of the blessing* SARAH *and* ISAAC *have joined. While it is being said the light of day dies slowly; it becomes almost dark. At the end of the blessing* SARAH *goes out, and brings in a lamp just before the scene closes.*)

JACOB'S LADDER

A Play in Three Acts

For the staging of this play, two CHORUS SPEAKERS *are seated, one on each side of the stage, slightly raised, within the framework of the Proscenium. It is intended that they should be heard rather than seen; and should speak as commentators rather than as actors, except in the two scenes where Jacob is wrestling with his conscience.*

PROLOGUE

CHORUS ONE

> This is the story of Jacob,
> The man with the smooth face,
> Who obeyed his Mother
> Cheated his Brother,
> Deceived his Father.
> Received a Blessing,
> Dreamed a dream, the most famous in history,
> And, out of his dream (here is the mystery)
> Founded a race.

CHORUS TWO

> Jacob wasn't a good man
> To judge by the tale that's told of him;
> And he didn't behave well,
> When greed or fear took hold of him.
> But Jacob had this to his credit,
> Though his character wasn't alluring:
> He'd grit; he stuck to his job;
> He was patient, faithful, enduring.

CHORUS ONE

> To his weakness came strength by meekness;
> And he showed such wise discretion,
> That the promised land of his fathers
> Was given him for a possession.
> Out of his seed grew a nation,

In Canaan came they to dwell –
Twelve tribes of one generation –
The children of Israel.

CHORUS TWO

These were the children of Jacob,
The man with the smooth face,
Who obeyed his Mother,
Cheated his Brother,
Deceived his Father,
Received a Blessing.
Dreamed a dream, the most famous in history,
Followed the dream, and founded a race.

THE SCENE OPENS

CHORUS ONE Here, in his tent, by the well of Sheba, sits
Isaac, the father of Jacob – waiting.

ACT I

SCENE I

(*He is old and feeble, and the sunlight coming through the open door of the tent seems to trouble him. He tries to rise, but finds the effort too much for him. He calls – waits a few moments then calls again.*)

ISAAC Rebekah . . . Rebekah.

REBEKAH (*a little impatiently*) Coming! Coming!

(*Presently she enters, and stands waiting for him to speak.*)

Here I am, Isaac . . . What d'you want me for?

ISAAC Close out the light. It's hurting my eyes.

REBEKAH (*as she does so*) It's always those eyes of yours now, Isaac. They're getting worse.

ISAAC They *are* – worse *and* worse.

REBEKAH Suppose, now, I was to make you a soothing ointment – would you have me put it on?

ISAAC An ointment? What would you make it of?

REBEKAH Let me see, now – what was it? (*She begins to count off on her fingers*). The fat of an adder, the egg of a tortoise, the flesh of a snail, the blood of a toad, and the spittle of a goat . . . Now was that all? Aye, that was all.

ISAAC Sounds good. Where did you hear of it?

REBEKAH When I was a child, I heard a wise woman telling my Mother of it. My brother Laban had weak eyes when he was born; It's in the family, you know – weak eyes: but that cured them. Well, what d'you say to it, Isaac?

ISAAC (*wearily*) Oh, you can try it. If it does me no good, it won't do me any harm – going blind as I am now.

(ISAAC *sighs heavily.*)

41

REBEKAH There's something fretting you, Isaac. What is it?

ISAAC Where's Esau? It's many days now since he's been home to see me.

REBEKAH It takes a wiser than me to say where Esau may be these days, now that he's gone and taken to wife that daughter of Beeri, the Hittite.

ISAAC Aye, taken a wife: taken a wife! He should not have done it. Would I not have found him a wife from among my own people?

REBEKAH Ah, you've thought of it too late, Isaac. But Esau was always one for going his own way. Not like Jacob. 'Tis he that's had all the care of things since you've been past work; Esau only remembers to come home now when he's hungry and wants me to feed him.

ISAAC He brings his meat with him. I would like well to have another taste of his venison now, Rebekah. Aye a great strong fine lad is my son Esau – my son Esau.

REBEKAH Jacob's a better.

ISAAC He's not, Woman! And remember this – Esau is our first-born.

REBEKAH Aye, by just two minutes – no more. And how much does first-born count, when they be twins? If I'd lain on my other side for it, Jacob might have come first.

ISAAC The first-born is the chosen of the Lord, Woman. The doing is His, not yours.

REBEKAH A man may think so; but a woman knows more about the 'doing' than he does. If 'twas the man that had the bearing of them, first-born would be the end of it: there'd be no second. Two were enough for me.

ISAAC You speak foolishly, Woman. I would we had more children, not fewer. Shall two be enough to fulfil the Lord's promise to our father Abraham – that his seed should possess the earth? I've my doubt of it.

REBEKAH Leave it to Him, Isaac. If He made the Promise,
'tis for Him to keep it – not you. And maybe, when Jacob
marries, he'll have more children, with more fear of the
Lord in them, than ever Esau will have by that Hittite
woman. Is our God's Blessing and Promise to go to *them*?
What have you to say to that, Isaac?

ISAAC Maybe the fault was mine, for not finding him a
wife of his own people.

REBEKAH Then the sooner you find one for Jacob, the
better ... I've been thinking about that, Isaac. My
brother Laban has two daughters, Leah and Rachel,
neither of them married yet. If Jacob were to wed one of
Laban's daughters, wouldn't that please you?

ISAAC It would please me well.

REBEKAH Then why waste time about it? You are getting
old, Isaac.

ISAAC Yes; I'm getting old; it's time I made my will, I'm
thinking.

REBEKAH Made your will? – Made up your mind, you
mean? What about it?

ISAAC About all that, when I go, I must leave to others.
We've two sons, and each must have his portion. But to
Esau I must give first.

REBEKAH If you give Esau the flocks and the cattle, you'd
better see that he has Jacob to look after them. *He* won't.
And if he won't, what right to them has *he*? Jacob has a
better.

ISAAC I will do with mine own as I will, Woman. The
Promise and the Blessing which God gave to my father
Abraham must go where God meant it to go. My Father
did not divide the Blessing between me another; neither
will I divide it from Esau, my first-born. Say no more,
Woman! I know 'tis on Jacob that *your* heart is set. But
Esau is my first-born: for him was the Promise made, and
the Blessing that goes with it.

43

REBEKAH Well, if God's way is man's way, you may get it to your liking; or you may not.

ISAAC Give me a hand, Rebekah. Your talking has tired me. I will go in, and rest. Send word to Esau that I want him. Tell him to come soon.

> (REBEKAH *helps him from his seat, and leads him to the inner chamber. Then she returns, and hitches back the tent-flap. Outside is level evening light. She stands looking out; presently she beckons.*)

REBEKAH Jacob . . . Jacob . . . come here!

> (JACOB *comes in, and stands wiping off the sweat of his labour from his face and his bare shoulders.*)

Your Father says we are to send and fetch Esau. He wants him for something.

JACOB D'you know what it is, Mother?

REBEKAH About 'making his will' he calls it. What can that mean?

JACOB Something to be done, maybe, that he thinks Esau will do better than I should. Well, if he likes to think so – !

REBEKAH Yes; but listen, Sh! Don't speak loud (*she points*) . . . Esau, he says, is to have the Promise and the Blessing; for being the first-born. And your portion will be to serve your brother Esau, with just what little's left over for your own. How'll you like that, Jacob?

JACOB 'Twill be no change, Mother. As I have served my Father all these years, and got nothing for it; so I shall serve *him*, and get no more.

REBEKAH It's not fair, Jacob.

JACOB No, Mother, it's not fair. But first-born *is* first-born; there's no getting away from it . . . not with Father, anyway: Is my supper ready?

REBEKAH Yes, Jacob. Come in! It's all ready and waiting.

JACOB (*pausing*) There's that goat out there, that I took the kid from, waiting to be milked. She's crying for it.

(*Outside the bleating of a goat is heard.*)

JACOB I can get my own supper, Mother, if you'll see to the goat.

(*He follows her in.*)

CHORUS ONE See! Here comes Esau.
CHORUS TWO The First-born.
CHORUS ONE The First-born.

(ESAU *enters. He flings down his weapons, and sits down, exhausted.* REBEKAH *comes back, carrying a bowl and a milking-stool.*)

REBEKAH Why, Esau! What brings you here?

ESAU Just a pair of feet, Mother – too tired to go a step further. It's been a hot day; and many hours I've been out in it.

REBEKAH Ah! you don't always manage to get a kill do you? Hunting'll never make you a rich man, Esau.

ESAU I've no wish for it. I want to be free. Where is Father?

REBEKAH He's gone in to lie down. (ESAU *makes to get up and go to him.*) Don't go to him now; he'll be sleeping.

ESAU How's the old man getting on?

REBEKAH Just that way, Esau – getting old.

ESAU Mother, haven't you got anything for me to eat? I'm nigh famished.

REBEKAH Ah, you should have come sooner. I've just given Jacob all there is for his supper.

ESAU Haven't you any bread?

REBEKAH Not till I do a fresh baking. But out yonder's a goat wants milking – if you like to get yourself some of that . . . I'll go and tell Jacob you're here. (*She goes in, and is heard calling to* JACOB.)

ESAU (*calling after her*) Don't trouble about him and me, Mother . . . 'Tis a warm welcome my Mother gives me! Milk for a starving man's belly! Milk!

CHORUS ONE Had you brought venison, Esau, your welcome would have been warmer.

(JACOB *enters, carrying a large porringer, from which he is eating, and doesn't trouble to stop for more than a word now and again.*)

JACOB Hullo, Esau. (*He takes up a spoonful and blows on it.*)

ESAU Hullo, Jacob . . . Say! What have you got there?

JACOB What I'm eating, you mean? (*He clears the spoonful.*) My supper.

ESAU What is it?

JACOB Lentils.

ESAU Jacob – you might let me have some of it   I could do with it!

JACOB Ah! So can I. I've worked for it. You haven't.

(*He goes on slowly eating; takes a spoonful, blows to cool it, then swallows it.*)

ESAU I'm your brother, Jacob; well-nigh starving, I am! And to see you there, eating – !

JACOB (*sarcastically*) Gives you an appetite, eh? But it doesn't make you want to be *me*, does it, Esau? – you being the first-born.

ESAU What's that to do with it? If I'd got here a bit sooner, we should have been sharing it now.

JACOB Oh? Should we? Why?

ESAU Wouldn't Mother have given me my portion of it?

JACOB You go and ask her now, if I'm to give *you* what

she's given *me*. If she tells me to, I'll do it. There's a fair offer.

ESAU (*bitterly*) And a safe one, sure enough! You were always Mother's favourite.

JACOB And you're Father's.

ESAU What good does that bring me?

JACOB It will some day – you being the first-born.

ESAU Anything I get from being the first-born I'd let you have now for that mess of pottage.

(JACOB *stops eating.*)

JACOB Would you?

ESAU (*angrily*) Yes, I would! (JACOB *starts eating again.*)
CHORUS TWO There's a chance for you, Jacob!

ESAU But not if you go on eating it!

(JACOB *quite stops eating now.*)

JACOB Your birthright for this pottage you say? You'd give it me?

ESAU I would! But I don't see *you* giving something for nothing.

JACOB (*bitterly*) To get my Father's love would be something.

ESAU That's not my birthright. I get that for being the better man.

JACOB And I – who do the work – get none of it . . . Well, leave out the love, then. For *this*, will you give me the rest?

ESAU I will – if you want it.

JACOB Honest?

ESAU More honest than *you'll* ever be, Jacob! (*Then, as* JACOB *seems doubtful.*) D'you want me to swear to it?

JACOB We may as well have it clear, while we are about it.

ESAU Out with it, then! What am I to say?

JACOB Say this: So help me God –

ESAU So help me God –

47

JACOB For this mess of pottage which he now gives me –

ESAU For this mess of pottage which he now – sells me –

JACOB Aye; 'sells', if you like ... I sell to my brother Jacob –

ESAU I sell to my brother Jacob –

JACOB My birthright.

ESAU My birthright.

JACOB To all which, as first-born.

ESAU To all which, as first-born.

JACOB Is now, or shall ever be mine –

ESAU Is now, or shall ever be mine –

JACOB To be his only, from this day forward.

ESAU To be his only, from this day forward.

JACOB So help me God.

ESAU I've said that already!

JACOB All right; so long as you remember you *have* said it. There you are, then!

CHORUS ONE 'Tis a hard bargain you've made, Jacob.

CHORUS TWO With a hungry brother.

(*He gives* ESAU *the pottage.* ESAU *begins eating ravenously.* JACOB *stands watching him for a while.*)

JACOB Make the most you can of it, Esau; don't burn your mouth with it: it won't run away. Neither will it last as long as you might wish it to. What I've got from you – though it leaves me hungry today – may last better.

CHORUS ONE We live and learn, Jacob; we live and learn!

JACOB You've done a foolish thing, Esau. You'd better know it.

ESAU Oh? Does that please you?

JACOB Well, don't say I didn't tell you. If you lose by it, it's yourself you must blame – not me. So long!

(*He takes up the milking-stool, and turns to go.*)

ESAU Where are you going now?

JACOB To get myself some milk from yon goat – to make up for my lost supper.

ESAU Milk's no fit drink for a *man*! to my thinking.

JACOB It suits me well enough.

ESAU Aye, it would!

CHORUS TWO That's one to Esau, Jacob.

(JACOB *goes; then comes back to say*.)

JACOB Mind now! Never you blame *me* for what you've done today – selling me your birthright.

(*He goes*.)

ESAU (*shouts after him with good-humoured contempt*) I won't, Jacob, I won't! I've something here that I like better.

CHORUS ONE So Esau sells his birthright for a mess of pottage – and *cares* not.

(*He laughs and goes on eating the pottage.* ISAAC *comes through from the inner chamber. He moves feebly, uncertain of step with his hands out as though feeling his way*.)

CHORUS TWO Here comes old Isaac.

ISAAC Is that Esau I hear? . . . Ah, my son, my son! (*Father and son embrace*.) 'Tis Esau come back to me.

ESAU (*tenderly*) Sit down, Father; sit down.

(*He makes* ISAAC *sit down, and kneels before him.* ISAAC *reaches out, and strokes his face and hands*.)

ISAAC Aye, aye, this is Esau – the rough hands and the hairy face! By the touch and the smell of him I know 'tis my son Esau.

ESAU Why, surely, Father; you don't need eyes for that! We haven't forgotten each other yet.

ISAAC Esau, have you brought something? . . . Any venison?

ESAU No, Father. Today I've had no luck. But I'll try again tomorrow. You shall have it, Father.

ISAAC Why have you been away from me so long, Esau? What have you been doing with yourself?

ESAU Marrying, Father. I've take the daughter of Elon, the Hittite, to be my second wife.

ISAAC Oh, my son, my son! Why hast thou taken wives of the daughters of Canaan? Wherefore didst thou not wait till I had found thee a wife from mine own people?

ESAU I waited long, Father.

ISAAC Long? I was near twice your age, Esau, before my Father gave me your Mother, Rebekah, to wife. Forty years old I was then.

ESAU Forty! Ah! my blood's hotter than yours, Father; I could not have waited till I was forty.

(*Meanwhile* REBEKAH *has entered, and, behind* ESAU, *stands listening.*)

ISAAC So now you've taken two wives from a strange people. I cannot be glad of it. And the fault was mine.

ESAU Oh! don't let it trouble you, Father. Find me another wife of your own people. Has not your brother Ishmael got daughters?

ISAAC Aye, that is a good thought! You shall marry a daughter of Ishmael; and by her you shall have sons to whom shall come the Promise and the possession. Listen, Esau! There is a great blessing waiting for you: God's blessing – not mine, though by my mouth shall it be spoken. God gave it to Abraham, my Father; he gave it to me, to give to you, and to your son's sons after you! 'Tis God's promise that this land shall be yours, Esau; and you the father of a great nation; and all your brethren and kinsmen shall serve you.

ESAU (*on the track*) Did Jacob know of that Father?

ISAAC Your Mother knew. Maybe she's told him.

ESAU (*sure of it*) Aye, maybe she did!

ISAAC It has been waiting for you; and now the time for it has come. For, see now, I am old, and I know not the day of my death . . . Tarry with me this night; and tomorrow, when it is day, take your spear and your bow, and go out into the field, and fetch me venison, and make a savoury meat of it such as I love. And I will eat of it, as I ate with my father Abraham when he gave the Blessing to *me*. Come in with me, my son. Tonight you shall lie near me, so that, if I wake, I may know that Esau my son has come back to me . . . Take me to bed, for I am weary.

> (ESAU *raises his Father tenderly, and leads him to the inner chamber.* REBEKAH *crosses, stands listening for a while, then goes to the door and calls softly.*)

REBEKAH Jacob!

CHORUS TWO Jacob, your Mother is calling you.

> (*The Scene closes.*)

SCENE 2

> (*The same; morning of the next day.*)

CHORUS ONE Now night has passed, and day has come.

CHORUS TWO Esau is away hunting; Isaac is still sleeping.

CHORUS ONE And here is Rebekah teaching Jacob his lesson.

JACOB But Mother, he'll know I'm not Esau, when I'm close to him. He sees well enough for that.

REBEKAH No, he won't, Jacob. You leave that to me. I know what I'm doing.

> (*As she speaks she is mixing something on a small platter.*)

JACOB What have you got there, Mother?

REBEKAH The ointment for your Father's eyes.

JACOB (*puzzled*) To make him see *better*?

REBEKAH It will – when I take the bandages off again. Not while it's on, though.

JACOB Oh! . . . I see!

REBEKAH So now you know . . . And there's another thing I've thought of. Maybe your Father will kiss you; so you must have a beard, and hairy arms, Like Esau . . . I've put the kid on to stew; where's the skin you took off it?

JACOB It's there, outside, Mother.

REBEKAH Then bring it along in; I've a use for it.

JACOB But, Mother, how are you going to make the kid taste like venison?

REBEKAH Oh, there's not much to choose between a kid and venison that's fresh. I've pleased your Father before now, giving him kid, and calling it venison. There's only one thing that's troubling me – your voice: it's not so full and deep as Esau's. You must try to make it more like. Say as little as you can; and leave the talking to me. How long has Esau been gone?

JACOB He was off at day-break.

REBEKAH Had you any word with him?

JACOB I spoke to him . . . but he didn't answer . . . went past as if I wasn't there.

REBEKAH Had you been quarrelling yesterday?

JACOB (*doubtfully*) No, Mother; not quarrelling.

REBEKAH Then what do you make of it?

JACOB I don't know, Mother; it frightens me . . . It means that I must be gone before he comes back . . . When he finds out, maybe he'll want to kill me . . . I don't think we'd better do it, Mother.

REBEKAH You go and get me that skin, Jacob.

(JACOB *goes*; REBEKAH, *still at her mixing, stands looking after him. A sound from within makes her peep through the curtains.* JACOB *returns carrying the skin.*)

Your Father's beginning to wake up. You go in and have a word with him.

JACOB (*nervously*) I – I'd rather not, Mother.

REBEKAH You do it. Say you're just off to your day's work; then he'll have you off his mind for when 'Esau' comes. For he won't want *you* to be here then – not while he's giving everything to *Esau.*

JACOB We must hurry, Mother. Esau may get his kill sooner than you reckon for.

REBEKAH I'm not one to waste time, Jacob. I'll see you're safe off before *he* comes. Your pack shall be ready for you; and food for the way. It's a three days' journey to Padan-aram, where your Uncle Laban lives now.

(*She takes the goat-skin from Jacob.*)

Ah, I can make a nice beard for you out of this, and something for your arms too. Now, go in to your Father.

JACOB (*still reluctant*) Must I, Mother?

(REBEKAH *settles the matter by drawing open the door-curtain of the inner chamber, and calling:*)

REBEKAH You awake, Isaac?

ISAAC (*within*) Yes; I'm awake.

REBEKAH Here's Jacob coming in to see you.

(*She motions for* JACOB *to enter, and goes off with the goat-skin.* JACOB *approaches, but stays at the door.*)

JACOB Good morning, Father.

ISAAC Why have you not gone to your work yet?

JACOB I've but just come back from it, Father. I've been out for two hours.

ISAAC Where's Esau?

JACOB Gone off somewhere.

ISAAC Since when?

JACOB Oh, a long time back.

ISAAC Ah! good! . . . Was that new well you dug the other day worth the finding?

JACOB Yes, there's been enough in it since to water all the flocks. The old one's drying up.

ISAAC Then 'twas a good thing you found it.

JACOB Yes, Father.

ISAAC 'Tis a gift the Lord has given you, Jacob. Some day you may have good cause to be thankful for it – if ever there's a drought.

JACOB Maybe, Father.

ISAAC Well, get to work; I won't have you be idle. And tell your Mother I want her.

(JACOB *goes and calls.*)

JACOB Mother. Father wants you.

(*He goes, practising softly to himself, 'Father, here is your venison.'* REBEKAH *enters and goes in to* ISAAC.)

ISAAC Rebekah, get me up.

REBEKAH Won't you lie a bit longer, Isaac? It's early for you to be getting up.

ISAAC I want to be up – to be ready for when Esau comes back.

REBEKAH But he won't be back for a long time yet.

ISAAC How do you know, Woman? If the Lord finds it for him, he'll not be long.

REBEKAH The Lord didn't find it for him yesterday. He was hunting all day, and got nothing.

ISAAC Aye, but today he will not come back empty-handed. For this is the day which the Lord has chosen for the giving of the Promise and the Blessing – to Esau my first-born – *and to no other.*

54

REBEKAH Have it your own way, Isaac. I'll say no more about it . . . I'll be back to you soon. (*She goes.*)

ISAAC (*fondly to himself*) Esau, my son, Esau.

(*The Scene closes. As it opens again* REBEKAH *is leading in* ISAAC; *she guides him to where he is to sit.*)

REBEKAH There! Sit down, and I'll make you comfortable.

(*She punches and rearranges the pillow behind his back; then brings a low foot-stool.*)

And put your feet up on that.

ISAAC The light is too strong in my eyes, Rebekah.

REBEKAH It won't be in a minute, when I've put on the ointment. I've got it all ready for you. (*She goes and gets the platter.*) Now, lean back your head, and shut your eyes. It's not going to hurt you. (*She begins to put on the ointment.*) This cured my brother Laban, and it's going to cure you. You'll be seeing ever so much better when I take off the bandage again.

(*She starts putting on a bandage.*)

ISAAC What are you putting on a bandage for, Rebekah?

REBEKAH Because, if I didn't, it would all run off when you sit up again . . . There! Now you be patient, Isaac! and don't you go taking it off till I tell you. (*She lets him sit up.*)

ISAAC How long have I got to keep it on?

REBEKAH Only for an hour or two.

ISAAC I shan't be able to see Esau when he comes.

REBEKAH You'll see him better afterwards.

ISAAC Shall I?

REBEKAH Why, yes! Isn't that the very reason why I've done it – so you could see better?

ISAAC You are good to your old man, Rebekah.

REBEKAH Am I?

ISAAC Though sometimes I'm cross with you.

REBEKAH Oh, that doesn't mean anything.

ISAAC No? . . . Yes, sometimes, when you go trying to put Jacob before Esau — Esau, our first-born.

REBEKAH Oh, that's over and done with now. After today, I'll say 'tis the Lord's will that you've given the Blessing where you *have* given it . . . Once given, there'll be no taking it away, will there, Isaac?

ISAAC No, 'tis the Lord's Blessing: and what He gives He takes not away.

(*And now* JACOB *can be seen, waiting for the moment when he is to enter.*)

REBEKAH Well, everything's ready now; and you won't have long to wait either. I've got a surprise for you, Esau's here now.

(*Silently she makes the signal to* JACOB.)

ISAAC Now? Come back?

REBEKAH Aye, he's been back these two hours.

ISAAC The venison? Has he got me the venison?

REBEKAH Yes, and here he is bringing it.

(JACOB *comes in carrying bread and wine, and a bowl of stewed venison. He is wearing a false beard of goat-skin; and on his hands and arms strips of it have been fastened.*)

Come in, Esau, come in! Your Father is waiting for you.

JACOB (*doing his best to be Esau*) Father, I have brought you your venison.

(REBEKAH *takes the bowl, and sets it beside* ISAAC.)

ISAAC Ah! Esau! How have you found it so quickly, my son?

JACOB The Lord brought it to me, Father.

ISAAC (*doubtfully*) Is that Esau speaking? It sounds more like Jacob.

REBEKAH Why, of course, it's Esau. How could it be Jacob? Jacob is out yonder in the field . . . Your hearing has gone like your eyes, Isaac. He didn't sound to *me* like Jacob . . . And here's your venison waiting for you.

ISAAC (*impatiently*) Oh, leave it leave it, Woman, and go! I will not eat till I have given the Blessing. The Blessing must come first.

(REBEKAH *goes out.*)

Come near, my son, and let me feel you, that I may know surely that you are Esau, my first-born . . . Aye, surely, surely, this is Esau; this is not Jacob. No, no, this is not Jacob. Truly you *are* my son – Esau?

JACOB Yes, Father.

ISAAC Aye, for though the voice be like the voice of Jacob, the hands are Esau's. Come near now, and kiss me. . . .

(JACOB *kisses him.*)

Ah! the smell of my son is as the smell of a field that the Lord has blessed. Kneel down, my son, kneel down. The Promise and the Blessing which God gave to my father Abraham, and which He gave to me, I give to thee, and to thy seed for ever. People shall serve thee; nations shall bow down to thee. Thou shalt be lord over thy brethren, their sons, and their sons' sons shall bow down to thee. Cursed be every one that curseth thee, and blessed be he that blesseth thee. (*He rises.*) God Almighty bless thee, and make thee fruitful, and multiply thee, that thou mayest be a multitude of people, and inherit the land wherein now thou art a stranger . . . All that He gave me to give is thine; and none shall take it from thee . . . (*He sits down exhausted; after a while he speaks.*) Hast thou brought me any wine, Esau?

JACOB Yes, Father.

ISAAC Give it me. First I will drink of thy wine; then I will eat of thy venison. And my soul shall be glad because of thee.

> (JACOB *pours out wine, and gives it to him. While* ISAAC *is drinking,* REBEKAH *returns in haste, carrying* JACOB'S *pack. In dumb show she bids him be gone;* ESAU *is returning.* JACOB *takes his pack, and runs to the door; but it is too late. He starts back, and hides himself behind the tent-door.* ISAAC, *having drunk the wine, holds out the empty cup.*)

Here, Esau, take this, and give me my venison.

> (REBEKAH *takes the cup from him, picks up the bowl, and starts feeding him.*)

ISAAC Ah! good, good; that is good!
ESAU (*outside*) Father!

> (ESAU *enters, carrying a small deer on his shoulder.*)

ESAU I have brought you your venison.
CHORUS TWO Now, Jacob, run – run for your life!

> (*Behind his back* JACOB *slips out and is off.* REBEKAH *puts down the bowl, runs to the door, wringing her hands as she sees him go. Then, unable to face the discovery, she goes out after him.*)

ISAAC (*starting up*) Esau! That is Esau's voice! Esau!

> (*He tears the bandages from his eyes. He sees that it is* ESAU.)

Ah, my son, my son! Thou hast come too late! Thy brother Jacob has been, and stolen away the Blessing.
ESAU Stolen it, Father?

ISAAC Aye! for here in my blindness he brought me wine and venison; I ate and I drank. And the Promise and the Blessing which were for thee, I have given to him.

ESAU Well was he named Jacob; for now twice has he supplanted me; first my birthright; and now *thy* Blessing.

ISAAC Your birthright?

ESAU Aye! Sold for a mess of pottage! He owes me nothing for that. But honest buying and selling wasn't good enough for him. Stealing was better!

ISAAC Oh, that I might now put a curse upon him that I have blessed!

CHORUS TWO Put no curse on him, Isaac; he has put it on himself; wherever he goes, Fear, like his own shadow, will go after him.

CHORUS ONE Fear of the man that he is; fear of the brother he has wronged.

ISAAC Oh, Esau, my son, my son! the Blessing has gone from thee!

ESAU Have you but *one* blessing to give, Father? Has not every son the right to a father's blessing? It's no promise I'm asking for – only your blessing; not God's – *yours*, Father.

ISAAC You shall have that, my son, though poor must be the Promise that goes with it. Lay thy head upon my knee, and I will give it thee.

(ESAU *kneels*; ISAAC *lays his hands on his head in blessing.*)

This is thy Father's blessing, and his word that God shall make true. Possessions shall not be thy portion, nor riches thy inheritance. Thy dwelling shall be in the field, and the dews of heaven shall fall on thee. Thou shalt live by the sword, and do service to thy Brother; till a day come when thou shalt have power, and shalt break his yoke from off thy neck.

ESAU When that day comes, Jacob will have cause to fear me!

ISAAC Nay, nay! I charge thee, lay no hand on him. For now God has given him the Promise and the Blessing. We must not fight against God, my son.

CHORUS ONE That fight will be Jacob's; for a poor thing is Jacob.

CHORUS TWO Aye! if God make anything of *him*, God will do well.

ISAAC Where is your Mother, Esau?

ESAU Out yonder.

ISAAC Call her.

(ESAU *goes to the door and calls.* ISAAC *sits waiting. After a while* REBEKAH *enters, fearful, but resolute.*)

ISAAC Rebekah.

REBEKAH Yes, Isaac.

ISAAC *You* did this.

REBEKAH Yes, Isaac.

ISAAC You blinded me, so as to deceive me.

REBEKAH Yes, Isaac.

ISAAC Surely for this God will punish you.

REBEKAH Yes, Isaac. I shall never see Jacob again . . . But it *was* good for your eyes, wasn't it, Isaac? You do see better now.

ISAAC Yes, Woman, I see better now! Get in!

(*She goes in weeping.*)

CHORUS ONE There goes Rebekah to learn the cost,
Of the wrong she did for the son she has lost.
Through years of waiting, sorrow, and pain.

CHORUS TWO She will never see Jacob again.

(*A dark rocky defile, desolate and solitary – a place of echoes. An owl calls: its cry is repeated.*)

CHORUS TWO And now, where Jacob has gone,
            We follow . . . What is this place?
CHORUS ONE This is Bethel.
CHORUS TWO And here comes Jacob.

(JACOB *enters footsore and weary. An owl calls.* JACOB *starts in fear, and halts.*)

JACOB What is that? . . . Who called?

(*The call is repeated.* JACOB *claps his hands, and cries 'Shoo!' As he speaks an echo is heard answering him three times.*)

I don't like this place; no, I don't like it! (*. . . don't like it!*)
But here must I stay this night. (*. . . this night.*) For I am
weary and can go no further. (*. . . no further.*) (*He takes off his pack and throws it down. He sees water running from a cleft in the rock.*)
Ah, water! Here's water at last! (*. . . at last!*)

(*He is about to drink, when he hears footsteps. He shrinks back in fear. A grey-hooded figure enters from behind, stops, and stands facing him as he turns.*)

JACOB Who are you?
THE VOICE Why do you want to know who I am?
JACOB You've been following me.
THE VOICE Following you? We have but been going the same road.
JACOB (*doubtfully*) I seem to know – your voice.
THE VOICE Whose voice – Jacob?

JACOB (*startled*) How did you know who I am? Tell me your name! Who are you?

THE VOICE My name is – Fear. But my voice is Jacob's voice.

JACOB Why are you here?

THE VOICE You brought me, Jacob. I am your own fear – the fear you have of your brother Esau.

JACOB Why should I fear him? Have I not the Promise and the Blessing?

THE VOICE From whom?

JACOB From God.

THE VOICE Your Father is not God, Jacob.

JACOB God gave it to *him*.

THE VOICE And from him you *stole* it.

JACOB Esau sold it to me.

THE VOICE Did he *know* what he was selling?

JACOB He said that he did not – care.

THE VOICE Then why are you now – so afraid of him?

JACOB (*resolutely*) I am *not* afraid. You are an evil spirit! . . . Go from me! Leave me!

THE VOICE I am yours to obey . . . When you have lost sight of me, make sure that I *have* gone. We shall meet again – Jacob.

> (*He goes,* JACOB *stands listening as the sound of his footsteps grows fainter.*)

JACOB (*speaking low*) He goes – away, away . . . I hear him no more. (*Then louder, in sudden relief.*) He's gone! (. . . *gone!*)

THE VOICE *Not* gone, Jacob.

> (JACOB *stands rigid, fighting his fear. After a pause* THE VOICE *speaks again.*)

Hadn't you better – run away?

JACOB Whither should I run? Where else can I go?

THE VOICE Surely, anywhere but here: the world is wide.
Isn't it easier to run from Fear than to stay where Fear is?

JACOB Then – God helping me – I will do the harder
thing. I will stay where Fear *is*.

THE VOICE Well said, Jacob. So – this time – I leave you
– to yourself . . . Farewell: Sleep well, Jacob – and wake!

CHORUS TWO Under your head a stone, your bed bare
ground;

Alone, with darkness round you, sleep,
sleep sound –

and dream.

JACOB Gone! Help has come to me! I am no longer
afraid! . . . Water, and rest, and sleep – here's all I need.

(*Having drunk, wrapping his cloak round him, he
lies down. Then in a voice scarcely heard:*)

Sleep . . . sleep!

CHORUS ONE So now to weary body and weary feet,
Comes blessed sleep, and folds him from his
fears;

And here tonight Blessing and Promise
meet.

As, in a dream, he sees the coming years. . . .

CHORUS ONE Jacob.

JACOB Yes?

CHORUS ONE Are you asleep?

JACOB Yes.

CHORUS ONE And is your mind at ease?

JACOB Yes.

CHORUS ONE And is your heart at rest?

JACOB Yes.

CHORUS ONE Have you no fear for what may fall this
night?

JACOB No fear.

CHORUS ONE Nor what tomorrow may bring? . . . No fear?

JACOB No fear.

(Again the owl calls: an echo answers. Silence follows. There comes a soft radiance, and in the air a low vibration is heard. Very faintly the vibration begins to have music in it.)

CHORUS TWO Jacob is dreaming his dream;
     And in his dream, he beholds
     A ladder set up on the earth,
     And the top of it reaches to Heaven;
     And on it the Angels of God
     Go up, and come down.
     And lo, the Voice of the Lord:
     'Here am I, Abraham's God,
     And Isaac, your Father's – to whom
     (For them and their seed for ever)
     Promise I gave, and Blessing;
     And that, which to them I swore
     By Myself, I take not away.
     Therefore to thee will I give
     This land whereon now thou liest:
     To thee and thy seed I give it.
     And I will be with thee, and keep thee,
     Whithersoever thou goest,
     And bring thee again to this land
     In safety at last.

CHORUS ONE And Jacob wakes, and answers . . .

JACOB Surely the Lord was in this place, and I knew it not, how dreadful is this place. This is the House of God, and yonder is the gate of Heaven. Now therefore let this stone, O Lord, be a witness between Thee and me this day, of the Promise and Blessing which thou hast given me. And if Thou wilt be with me, and keep me in the way that

I must go, and give me bread to eat, and raiment to put on, and will bring me again in peace to my Father's house, then surely will I know that Thou art God, and will have no other God but Thee.

CHORUS ONE Bargain noted. Anything else, Jacob?

JACOB And of all that Thou shalt have given me in that day, and always thereafter, faithfully will I give back to Thee, Lord, if it please Thee, one-tenth.

CHORUS TWO One-tenth.

JACOB Always one-tenth, never less.

CHORUS TWO Never less.

JACOB So help me God, and all the Angels of the dream that I have dreamed this night.

CHORUS TWO That you have dreamed this night.

JACOB One-tenth, did I say? Now was that too much. No, not if He keeps His word to me. But quite enough . . . ?

CHORUS TWO Quite enough.

JACOB Quite enough.

CHORUS TWO Quite enough.

(*Jacob picks up his pack, and goes.*)

CHORUS ONE And who has any right to say one word against Jacob for that prudently measured promise which so accurately represents what good average human nature reckons to be the right and proper amount of interest (short of usury) due to God for all the material benefits it has received from Him?

CHORUS TWO Aye. Why did you laugh? Was not Jacob, in this matter, the exemplar and guide of all the ages that came after, both under the Mosaic, and also the Christian dispensation, even to the present day?

CHORUS ONE So there goes Jacob, to make his fortune,
Jacob follows the Dream;
We follow Jacob.

CHORUS TWO To the house of Laban, his uncle . . .
Here is Laban.

> (LABAN *is sitting at a small table with a money-bag
> open before him; from this he counts out the sum of
> money which he reckons to be due to the* HERDSMAN
> *whom he is now dismissing from his service. Against
> the wall stand three* TERAPHIM.)

LABAN (*laying the money on the table*) Two, four, six,
eight, ten . . . There! Take your wages, and go!

> (*The Man takes up the money and counts it.*)

HERDSMAN This is not enough, Master. This is not the
wage I bargained for.

LABAN You did not do the work I bargained for. You
will get no more . . . That last well that you dug was too
shallow to hold water, and has now run dry.

HERDSMAN You never complained of it till now. I could
have dug it deeper had you told me. A bargain's a bargain.

LABAN Yes; and while *you* did not keep it, I had to keep
you . . . Off with you! Go!

HERDSMAN May all the Gods curse you! May the day
come when someone cheats *you* as you have cheated *me*!

> (*Exit* HERDSMAN.)

LABAN Cheat *me*? He'd have to be a clever fellow to
cheat *me*.

> (*He ties up his money-bag; then, as he goes to put it
> away, he stops, and turns to his three* TERAPHIM.)

No, no; you wouldn't curse me, would you? It wouldn't
pay you. Beor, Ashera,[1] Shamem, how are you today? Well?

----
[1] Ashĕra, *not* Ashēra.

Don't pay any attention to what that man said. He has never done anything for you; and for me did his work so ill that I have had to get rid of him . . . Shamem be good enough to ask Baal-zebub to let us have more rain. It is wanted badly – the wells are running dry. And also, will he be good enough not to send a plague of locusts upon our crops as he did last year. Do this for me, and I will pay you handsomely. Beor, 'tis now the breeding season; will you see to it that the ewes have more twins born among them than happened last year? For every three score of twins they bear you shall have one as a thank-offering . . . Ashera, will you be graciously pleased, as soon as maybe, to find a husband for my daughter Leah? No one has yet asked for her; for she is not comely as is Rachel her sister; and until she is married Rachel must not. Do this, and I will reward you suitably . . . Will you, also, do your best between you, to find me a better servant than the last one; and if you can send after him the curse which he left for me, I shall be more than ——

> (*He is just about to add 'satisfied', when* RACHEL *enters. Followed by* JACOB.)

RACHEL Father, here is Cousin Jacob.

LABAN Who's he? Never heard of him.

RACHEL He say that Aunt Rebekah has sent him.

LABAN Oh? Has she? I thought she had forgotten us.

JACOB (*politely intervening*) Indeed no, Uncle. She sends you her love and greeting.

LABAN Oh! does she? Well, being your Mother's son, I make you welcome. Sit down and rest. You look tired.

JACOB I *was* tired, Uncle; but now the pleasure of seeing you for the first time, and also Cousin Rachel, and being so kindly welcomed though I come uninvited, has already refreshed me.

LABAN Well; sit down, sit down!

(JACOB *looks about him, but can see no seat humble enough, so kneels down, and sits upon his heels.*)

CHORUS ONE That was clever of you, Jacob.

LABAN So, your name's Jacob, is it? Any brothers?

JACOB I have one brother, named Esau.

LABAN And which are you – the elder or the younger?

JACOB My brother Esau is the elder.

LABAN And your Mother, how is she?

JACOB She was quite well, thank you, Uncle, when I left her.

LABAN And your Father – is he still alive?

JACOB Yes; but he is old and feeble; and does not always know what he is doing. He gave me his Blessing when I asked for it; but he did not know that I was going. It was my Mother sent me.

LABAN And how long have you come for?

JACOB As long as you will have me, Uncle; if I can be of any use to you.

LABAN Well, what can you do?

JACOB I can herd, and milk, and shear; I can sow, and reap, and plough. Also I can find water.

LABAN Oh? Are you a water-diviner?

JACOB Yes, Uncle.

LABAN Well, if you can do all those things, I might find a use for you. Rachel, go and fetch bread and wine, for your Cousin Jacob to refresh himself after his long journey.

(*As* RACHEL *goes,* JACOB *turns his head and looks after her.*)

LABAN (*observantly*) Yes; a pretty wench, isn't she?

JACOB (*adoringly*) She is beautiful.

LABAN So you know how to work, eh?

JACOB Yes, Uncle.

LABAN You call yourself a good worker?

JACOB That will be for you to say, Uncle.

LABAN And you know how to find water, you say?

JACOB Yes, Uncle.

LABAN Well, a good thing to know, that is. For in this land wells are hard to find, and they soon run dry.

(RACHEL *returns, bringing bread and wine.*)

Help yourself, Jacob. And you can leave us now, Rachel. Jacob and I have got to talk business.

(*Again, as she goes,* JACOB *turns to look after her; and* RACHEL *looks back at him.*)

LABAN Well, if you like to stay, Jacob, there's work here for you. But though you be one of the family, I don't expect you to do it for nothing. What wages do you want?

JACOB I want no wages, Uncle.

LABAN No wages?

JACOB Your daughter Rachel is very beautiful, Uncle; and I think that already she looks at me with favour. For your daughter Rachel I am willing to serve you without wages.

LABAN How long?

JACOB You name the time, Uncle.

LABAN For seven years? Eh?

JACOB If you will keep her for me so long.

LABAN Well, there's no reason why you shouldn't have her as well as any other man, Jacob, you being your Mother's son; so long as you put in good work, so that I don't lose by it. But listen, Jacob; Rachel is my younger daughter; I have another named Leah. It is not well for the younger to marry before the elder. Now, if you will take Leah instead of Rachel, you need not serve seven years for *her*.

JACOB You are very kind, Uncle; but it is only for Rachel that I would serve you without wages. If you will promise me Rachel, I will serve for her seven years.

LABAN It would be a better bargain for you to take the other, Jacob. And you've not seen her; you might like her as well – or better.. (JACOB *shakes his head*.) Well, I don't mind owning that Rachel is the fairer of the two. Poor Leah has tender eyes – always has had, ever since she was a child.

JACOB For that, Uncle, I know a good remedy of my Mother's, which she used on my Father's eyes just before I left. It did them good; perhaps it might do good to Leah's eyes also.

LABAN It might. What was it?

JACOB The fat of an adder, the egg of a tortoise, the blood of a toad, the flesh of a snail, and the spittle of a goat.

LABAN Sounds good! I seem to have heard it before. It did your Father's eyes good, you say?

JACOB Oh yes. It made him see *much* better. The ointment was still upon his eyes when he blessed me; and he could not see whether it was me or Esau that he was blessing. But afterwards he saw much more plainly. How much good it has done him since, I do not know.

LABAN Well, you seem to me, Jacob, to be a wise and prudent young man – of good understanding. And so long as you do as well with your hands as you seem to do with your head, I shan't lose by it if I let you serve me – seven years, you say? – with Rachel at the end of it. Well, the offer was yours; I take it. I have your promise?

JACOB Yes, Uncle. I promise now that, God helping me, I will serve you well and faithfully, as you shall require of me; and for this I ask no wage, but at the end of seven years you shall give me the hand of your daughter Rachel in marriage.

LABAN That's settled then.

(LABAN *gives* JACOB *a friendly pat on the shoulder; then turns, and bestows on his three* TERAPHIM *a nod*

of recognition for service rendered. At the door
RACHEL'S *voice is heard; and she enters, followed by*
LEAH.)

RACHEL Father! . . . Please, may we come in, Father?

LABAN Yes, come in Rachel; come in!

RACHAEL I've brought Leah. She wants to see Cousin
Jacob.

CHORUS ONE Take a good look at him, Leah. He takes a
lot of knowing.

CHORUS TWO But he's worth it.

(JACOB *makes an inclination of respectful salutation*
to LEAH, *who peers at him short-sightedly, but says*
nothing.)

RACHEL Is Jacob going to stay with us for long, Father?

LABAN Jacob is going to stay – for seven years.

RACHEL Seven years! . . . And then?

LABAN Then someone is going to be married.

RACHEL Oh!

(*Evidently, to* RACHEL, *this means something; but to*
LEAH *nothing.* RACHEL *stands looking at* JACOB *with a*
pleased smile. LEAH *turns away.*)

CHORUS TWO Rachel looks pleased.

CHORUS ONE Take care, Rachel, take care! Your Father
doesn't always mean what you think he means.

LABAN Leah, take your Cousin Jacob to the room over the
granary. The man who had it has gone.

(*Exit* JACOB *and* LEAH, *to one side.* LABAN *goes out on*
the other.)

CHORUS TWO For better acquaintance, eh, Laban?

CHORUS ONE But it's no good, Laban; Jacob is not going
to fall in love with Leah.

RACHEL Thank you, beautiful Ashera! Bless you! It was all your doing; *you* brought him. And when he marries me – seven years is a long time to wait, Ashera; couldn't you shorten it? . . . Anyway, when he does, I promise and vow that, wherever I go, I will take you with me, and serve you as you deserve to be served. And whatever you tell me to do –

(LEAH *re-enters.*)

LEAH What are you doing there, Rachel?

RACHEL I was asking Ashera . . . I was asking Ashera to find a husband – for *both* of us.

LEAH Only one for the two?

RACHEL Oh, no! One each, of course. I wouldn't like to have to share – anyone – with you.

LEAH (*sourly*) Wouldn't you?

RACHEL Besides, you are the elder; so *you* must be married first.

LEAH I've waited long enough.

RACHEL Waiting doesn't matter – much, so long as you get the right one in the end.

LEAH But it matters if you get no one.

RACHEL Oh, you'll get somebody some day. Trust Ashera for that! . . . Dear, divine, beautiful Ashera, good-bye! . . . Remember!

(*She leaves the* TERAPHIM, *and goes and sits down by* LEAH.)

Leah . . . what do you think of Cousin Jacob?

LEAH Why should I think anything of him?

RACHEL Well, as he is going to be here for seven years, it does rather matter whether one likes him or not.

LEAH (*listlessly*) D'you like him?

RACHEL I think so. Yes; he seems to me so different from any man I've ever seen before.

LEAH How is he different?

RACHEL Well, when I first met him he was so polite, and deferential, and obliging – lifting away the stone off the well for me – which I couldn't have done myself. And when he asked if I knew where Laban lived, there was such a lost sheep look about him; and his voice was so sad and sorrowful. And when he heard that Laban lived here and was my Father, all at once he broke down and cried.

LEAH Cried?

RACHEL Yes, for joy. I've never seen a man cry before – not like that. He cried so beautifully that, at last, I kissed him . . . I mean, I let him kiss me.

LEAH You call that modest?

RACHEL I couldn't help it, Leah. And, after all, as we *are* cousins, why shouldn't he?

LEAH D'you mean to go on kissing him?

RACHEL I don't know . . . I haven't thought about it.

LEAH Then don't. (*Pause.*) Thread that needle for me, Rachel.

RACHEL (*sighing as she does so*) Seven years is a long time, Leah.

LEAH What for?

RACHEL Anything . . . In seven years such a lot of things might happen that one didn't expect, and didn't want to happen.

LEAH Yes; and in seven years something that you *did* expect might *not* happen after all. I've left off expecting anything . . . You'd better do the same. It's safer.

RACHEL If one didn't expect *something*, life wouldn't be worth living.

LEAH Maybe it's not. Here am I – I'm older than you; I've lived longer; but living longer hasn't made me happier. And, if it hasn't, what's the use of living?

RACHEL It depends on the use you make of it. If you don't it's your own fault.

LEAH (*passionately*) My fault? My fault? It's not my fault that I was born half-blind – and so plain that no one wants to look at me!

(*She breaks down and cries.*)

RACHEL Hush! Hush! Here's Jacob.

(JACOB *enters, as far as the door; there stops politely to inquire.*)

JACOB Dear cousins, I hope I'm not intruding. May I come in? What is Leah crying for?

RACHEL Her eyes, Jacob. She can't see well; she never could; and now they're getting worse.

JACOB Then don't cry any more, Leah. I know a good cure for them.

LEAH What is it?

JACOB Now, let me see if I can remember . . . The fat of an adder, the egg of a tortoise, the flesh of a snail, the blood of a toad, and the spittle of a goat.

LEAH It sounds silly.

JACOB You mustn't think it silly, Cousin Leah, or it won't do you any good. You must have faith in it.

LEAH What's faith?

CHORUS ONE Yes, Jacob, what is faith?

JACOB Faith means being certain – having no doubt that something you want will come true, if you believe in it enough. On my way here I had a dream which is going to come true because I have faith in it. If I hadn't, it would remain just a dream, and nothing more.

RACHEL A dream? What was it? Tell us, Jacob.

(JACOB *sits down by* RACHEL, *away from where* LEAH *is sitting; and it is to* RACHEL, *not* LEAH, *that he tells his dream.*)

74

JACOB It was a very holy, beautiful dream. I could not have dreamed it for myself; and that's how I know it must have come from the Lord God of my Fathers, and that it is going to come true . . . There, in my dream, I saw a ladder set up from the earth, and its top was so high that it reached to Heaven. And there were Angels on it, going up, and coming down again.

RACHEL Angels? What were they like?

CHORUS TWO Yes, what were they like, Jacob?

CHORUS ONE Jacob is a business man, remember.

JACOB They were like rich merchants, Rachel – for they were carrying on their shoulders all the riches of the world – bags full of silver, and gold, precious stones, boxes of spice, bales of silk, vessels of beaten brass, coffers of ivory and sandalwood; so many I could not count. Every one, as he came down, brought treasure with him, and then went up to fetch more. And as I watched I heard the voice of the Lord God of my Fathers calling to me out of Heaven, and saying, 'All this that thou seest shall be thine. Also the land whereon now thou liest I will give to thee and to thy seed after thee for a possession.'

RACHEL Oh! what a wonderful dream, Jacob.

JACOB Yes; and it's going to come wonderfully true, because I've got the faith for it – even though now I haven't a penny of my own.

RACHEL Oh, Jacob, I do think you are the most wonderful man in the world!

JACOB Not yet, Rachel; but I'm going to be. For that dream to come true, I shall have to wait many years. For the next seven years I am to be your Father's servant – getting no wages for it – only my keep, nothing more. But when the seven years are over, and I go back to my own land again, I shall be one of the richest men in the world – no, I shall be the richest; for then I shall have what I want most of all . . . How will you like that, Rachel?

RACHEL (*wistfully*) I don't know, Jacob. Of course, I would *like* you to be rich; but it may take such a long time that I shall never see it happen. Couldn't you have another dream, Jacob, that won't take so long to come true?

JACOB Another? Perhaps all my dreams will take long to come true . . . Suppose I were to tell you one that I have not yet dreamed; but that I'm going to dream?

RACHEL How can you know what the dream will be, if you haven't dreamed it yet?

JACOB Because I've the faith for it, Rachel . . . I'm going to dream of a man who went a long journey, with nothing in the world of his own – except faith. And one day he saw a woman – very beautiful she was – so beautiful that there was nothing he desired so much in all the world as to marry her. But because he was poor and homeless, he had to wait; with only the promise that at the end of seven years, she should be his wife. And because of the great love he had for her, the seven years seemed only a few days . . . That is the dream I am going to dream, Rachael. I'm going to dream it for seven years . . . And, Rachel – to make it come true, aren't two dreams better than one? Suppose you were to dream too.

(RACHEL *gets up, and goes across to* ASHERA.)

RACHEL Oh, Ashera! Ashera! Dear, beautiful, divine Ashera; make me dream too!

JACOB Rachel, what *are* you doing?

LEAH (*sarcastically*) She's making believe, Jacob, that she's got faith; and that something is going to happen . . . But it *won't*, Rachel.

(*Outside the voice of* LABAN *is heard calling.*)

LABAN Jacob . . . Jacob.
JACOB Yes, Uncle?

76

LABAN Come along, and start work. I can't have you idling.

JACOB Coming, Uncle.

(*Exit* JACOB.)

LEAH You little silly!

CHORUS TWO So Laban has got you, Jacob; you've met your match at last.

CHORUS ONE It will be twenty years before Jacob gets free again. Twenty years.

(*The Scene closes.*)

ACT II

SCENE 1

CHORUS TWO And now seven of those twenty years have passed. For seven years Jacob has served Laban — seven years for the Promise and the Blessing.

CHORUS ONE Laban's promise, not God's, Jacob.

CHORUS TWO And now it is the night of the Bridal.

CHORUS ONE And look! There stands the Bride.

(*We are still in the House of* LABAN. *Nightfall is beginning, and while* ZILPAH *and* BILLAH, *the two handmaids, are giving the finishing touches to her bridal array,* LEAH *submits with lack-lustre indifference, heavy and downcast.* LABAN *stands looking on, till his attention is distracted by* RACHEL, *who shakes herself, stamps and utters whimpering cries of rage.*)

LABAN Rachel, go in! Go in, I tell you! Go in!

RACHEL But Father, why is it Leah? Why is it Leah? It was to be *me*. Jacob was to marry *me*.

LABAN It is Leah, because in this country it is not done to give the younger in marriage before the first-born.

RACHEL Why couldn't Leah have married someone else?

LABAN Because no one else would have her. If I could have found her another husband I would have done so. As I couldn't, she's got to marry Jacob.

(RACHEL, *with a squeal of rage, goes all claws for* LEAH.)

LABAN (*angrily*) Rachel, stop it! . . . You must learn to obey your Father. For a maiden living in her Father's

78

house, his voice is as the voice of God. So you do as I tell you. When Leah is married, we'll soon find a husband for *you*.

RACHEL I want Jacob!

LABAN You can't have Jacob . . . Take her away in, and see that she doesn't come out again until after the marriage is over.

RACHEL (*struggling, as the two maids remove her*) Ashera! Ashera! Ashera!

LABAN Leah, my daughter, I've done the best for you I could. What on earth are you crying for?

LEAH When he finds out – Jacob will hate me.

LABAN Jacob is no fool. He knows how to take what's given him, and make the best of it.

LEAH But Father, loving Rachel as he does, he'll never love me.

LABAN Love isn't everything, Leah; it's short, and it wears out. Presently he'll have children by you. Children count. Aye, Jacob has it greatly in mind to have sons to come after him, and to bear his name. For Jacob has a fine belief in himself, and in what the Lord God of his Fathers is going to do for him . . . Draw down your veil, Daughter, and don't take it off this night. Tomorrow will be time enough. Do this; obey your Father; and all will be well. (*Music is heard approaching.*) Hark! They are bringing the bridegroom. Go in, my daughter, go in, that I may have you brought out to him, as a bride should be, when he comes to ask for you.

> (LEAH *goes in.* LABAN *turns and makes a salutation to the three* TERAPHIM.) ·

Holy ones, prosper us in what we are about to do, and let this marriage be fruitful.

> (*Outside the door the procession has halted. The* GROOM'S MAN *enters; and with due formality, the marriage ceremony begins.*)

GROOM'S MAN Sir we have, here without, a kinsman of yours, named Jacob. Is it your pleasure to receive him?

LABAN Tell him he is welcome. Bid him come in.

(*The* GROOM'S MAN *goes to the door, and speaks to* JACOB *outside.*)

GROOM'S MAN The master says you are welcome. He bids you to come in.

(JACOB *enters, followed by the* MUSICIANS.)

LABAN The blessing of all the gods be upon thee, Jacob. Wherefore are thou come?

JACOB With the blessing of the Lord God of my Fathers I come to have of thee the hand of thy daughter Rachel in marriage. For all the service I have rendered thee this shall be my recompense. I ask no more.

LABAN If I grant thee thy request, and give thee my daughter in marriage, dost thou promise that thou wilt not go from her, nor send her away from thee, to take any other in her place?

JACOB I will not go from her, or send her away from me, nor will I take any other in her place.

LABAN And wilt thou care for her, and cherish her, and be a faithful husband to her all the days of her life; and make her the mother of thy children?

JACOB I will keep her, and care for her, and cherish her, and be a faithful husband to her all the days of her life; and make her the mother of my children.

LABAN Then Jacob, I will grant thee thy desire, and give thee my daughter to wife. She is here within waiting. I will have her brought to thee.

(LABAN *claps his hands. The two* HANDMAIDS *enter.*)

My daughter – is she ready?

ZILPAH Yes, Master.

LABAN Bring her!

> (*The two* HANDMAIDS *withdraw, and return leading* LEAH *by the hand. She is now wearing a veil which covers her from head to foot.*)

LABAN My daughter, here has your kinsman Jacob come seeking to make you his wife, according to my promise which I made to him. You are willing to be his wife?

LEAH Yes, Father.

LABAN You will serve, honour, and obey him in all things, as a wife should do?

LEAH Yes, Father.

LABAN You will be faithful to him, and comfort him, and stay by him, all the days of your life?

LEAH Yes, Father.

LABAN Then, Jacob, to thee I give this my daughter. She is thy wife.

> (LABAN *joins their hands.*)

JACOB Why is she now so veiled; Father?

LABAN It is the custom of my people, Jacob; for if thou look upon thy virgin in the night, while the gods of my house are sleeping, evil may befall, and she may be taken from thee. Tomorrow, when it is full day, thou shalt look upon her, and know her for thy wife. Have patience. It will not be long . . . Farewell, Jacob my son; farewell, my daughter. May the Gods look favourably upon you, and bless you, and make you fruitful.

> (*As* JACOB *leads* LEAH *to the bridal chamber the* MUSICIANS *begin singing.* LABAN *makes towards the three* TERAPHIM *a gesture of respectful salutation; and goes softly out.*)

BRIDAL SONG

Arise, my love, arise!
Call, and I will come unto thee!
Among the hills and the valleys I sought thee.
Now have I found thee.
The dews of night fall on thee;
The stars of night shine on thee;
In the abundance of thy beauty,
In the shelter of night,
I will find comfort and rest.

> (*As the* MUSICIANS *sing, night falls; the scene fades
> slowly; the song dies softly away.*)

I come, O my Beloved, I come!
Thou hast opened to me the gate of thy garden.
In the darkness the flowers thereof give forth their
fragrance.
Lo, the flowers, the flowers that I have gathered;
I have come to lay them in the sweetness of thy breast.
Let the day go down, and let the night be long,
And let all the hours of the night be turned to song!

CHORUS ONE As Promise and Blessing were given to thee,
Jacob, which were meant for another, so now has Laban
rewarded you in like kind.

CHORUS TWO As you deserved, Jacob.

CHORUS ONE Sleep well – and wake.

> (*The scene darkens, till presently a cock crow is heard
> followed by bird-song. Gradually light returns.*)

CHORUS ONE The wedding night is over. Hark to the
birds!

CHORUS TWO And here comes that old bird, Laban.

LABAN (*to the* TERAPHIM) Holy Ones, I trust that you have

seen to it that, in there, all is well; and that, having done their duty by each other, there has been no –

(*From within comes a cry of rage.*)

Ah, my poor Leah, my poor Leah!

(*He goes up to the* TERAPHIM, *and speaks to them confidentially.*)

You see now what's happened: He has found out that it isn't Rachel. And it's all your fault, you know; if only you had provided another husband for Leah, this unpleasantness need never have come about.

(*Enter* JACOB *in hot temper.*)

JACOB Oh! Why have you done this? Why have you lied to me? What have I done that you should so deceive me?

LABAN (*soothingly*) It had to be, Jacob. There was no other way.

JACOB You promised me Rachel! All these seven years I served you for Rachel. Why have you given me Leah instead of Rachel?

LABAN (*saying his little piece*) In this country it is not done to give the younger before the first-born. Leah will make you a good wife, Jacob; she has more sense than Rachel, more submission and obedience. Surely, 'twas a good bargain you had from me when, with a Father's blessing, I gave you so good a daughter.

JACOB With lying and deceit you gave it! What good shall come of such a blessing to her or to me?

LABAN That concerns me, not you, Jacob. The deception – as you call it – was mine. But I did not *say* it was Rachel when I gave her to you. I only said 'this, my daughter' . . . And, Jacob, does it not sometimes happen that, in order to get the right thing done, a little deception is necessary?

CHORUS ONE What have you to say to that, Jacob?

CHORUS TWO Are you remembering, Jacob?

JACOB So! This is my punishment! The hand of my brother Esau is upon me. (*He breaks down and weeps.*)

LABAN Tut! tut! Jacob; be a man! Did you not enjoy yourself last night, before you knew? Very well then! just as one can deceive others, one can also deceive one's self – if one has a mind for it.

JACOB Am I never – never to have Rachel? Rachel, for whom I served faithfully, seven years?

LABAN If it be but a question of service, Jacob, you can serve me still.

CHORUS ONE More bargaining?

CHORUS TWO Who's going to win this time?

LABAN How long would you go on serving me, Jacob, were I to let you have Rachel also – now that you have married Leah?

JACOB (*hopefully*) You mean that I might have Rachel too?

LABAN Of course, I mean it. Why not? If you are willing, for her also, to serve a certain time, *without* wages, there is no reason why you should not have Rachel as well. How long would you be so willing?

JACOB For Rachel – I would serve you another seven years! – Aye, willingly!

LABAN Now that's very handsome of you, Jacob – very handsome. It shows a large, generous heart. I've always liked you, Jacob; you never make unnecessary difficulties – at least, you don't go on making them. Very well, then. You shall have Rachel. But we must be fair to Leah, Jacob. Give her your husbandry, for a month; and then – if you promise to serve me seven more years as faithfully as you have already done – you shall have Rachel without further waiting.

JACOB (*surprised*) Without further waiting, do you say? Then this time I will see to it that you do not again deceive me in like fashion, with one of those handmaids, maybe,

84

or by putting a sheep or a she-goat in my bed, and calling it 'Rachel' for the better keeping of your word.

LABAN Have no fear, Jacob, have no fear! This time it shall be Rachel. For I am a man of my word, when the Gods do not require that it shall be otherwise. And when the seven years are over, I will pay you good wages. Yes, you shall have your portion of the flocks and herds as though you were truly my own son. But, hark, I hear Leah weeping. Will you not go in to her now, Jacob, and comfort, and be kind to her? For surely she is not to blame – since she had to obey her Father.

JACOB No, I will not go in yet. I will see Rachel first; that she may hear the promise which you have made me. Leah, also, must hear it.

LABAN They shall hear it both together. After that there shall be no further misunderstandings. (*He goes to the door and claps his hands.* ZILPAH *enters.*) Zilpah, go and tell Billah to bring Rachel. (*She goes.*) And I will go and bring Leah to you myself.

(*On his way he stops to speak to the* TERAPHIM.)

Holy Ones, grateful thanks! All is now well; our little family trouble is over.

(*Exit* LABAN.)

CHORUS ONE Seven more years is heavy payment, Jacob.
CHORUS TWO Was ten per cent enough?

(JACOB *stands waiting. Enter* BILLAH *with* RACHEL, *and* LABAN *followed by* LEAH.)

LABAN My dear daughters; if you have had cause for tears, prepare to dry them now. Sorrow may endure for a night, but joy cometh in the morning ... Leah, your husband's countenance is no longer turned from you. He forgives you for having been an obedient daughter. Rachel, your little disappointment will soon be over. In a month from now you will marry Jacob.

> (LEAH *begins weeping.* JACOB, *leaving* LEAH, *turns to embrace* RACHEL.)

LABAN No, no, Jacob, Not yet! Go in, Rachel, go in! Jacob, here is Leah, your wife, waiting for you.

> (*And the patient* JACOB *accepts the situation with a quiet resignation which does him credit.*)

CHORUS ONE Patient Jacob you are learning your lesson well.

CHORUS TWO Learning to know Laban,

CHORUS ONE Some day you will learn to know yourself.

SCENE 2

CHORUS ONE Many years have passed, and Jacob is still serving Laban.

CHORUS TWO Leah has borne him children, Rachel none.

CHORUS ONE And he remembers the promise of the Lord God of his Fathers, that he should return one day to his own land in safety.

CHORUS TWO So now he is giving Laban notice.

CHORUS ONE But will Laban let him go?

> (*The Scene opens.*)

LABAN I don't want you to go, Jacob. I'd much rather you stayed. Nineteen years you've served me well – none better. What's come over you to make you so restless?

JACOB Is it not natural that a man should wish to return to his own land – before he dies?

LABAN What's the good? After all this time, your own

land will have forgotten you. Haven't the Gods of my house
been good enough to you? And haven't I been? And you are
getting good wages now, Jacob.

JACOB Am I, Uncle?

LABAN Well, aren't they?

JACOB They would be – if I could be more sure that,
having once raised them, you would not again lower them.
I don't want to drive a hard bargain with you, Uncle; but
it must be a fair one.

LABAN I don't want to drive a hard bargain with *you*,
Jacob; never have done. It wasn't treating you like a
stranger when I gave you my two daughters in marriage.
What more could I have done?

JACOB You might have done less, Uncle, I only wanted
one. You had seven years of service out of me for the one I
didn't want; and then seven more for the one I did – the one
which you first promised me.

LABAN Ah, well; that's over and done with, Jacob. I had
to get Leah married. And you've done well by her: She's
given you four sons of her own, and by Zilpah you have had
two more. And what has Rachel done? Nothing. If it was
sons you wanted – and you did want them – Leah has been
the better bargain. So what have you to complain of?

JACOB Nothing, Uncle. To complain now would be waste
of time. But you have taught me that wages had better be
fixed wages.

LABAN Fixed? After those fourteen years that earned
your wives for you, I've always paid you wages.

JACOB Yes; but you have since altered them several times
to your own liking – not up, but down.

LABAN Well, when it's been a bad year, you can't expect
the same.

JACOB There never has been a bad year since I've been
here; though some years have been better than others.
When they were better, you forgot to raise my wages; when

a less good year followed you remembered to lower them. That is why I am now asking that, in future, I shall always have a fixed share.

LABAN How big a share do you expect?

JACOB One-third of the whole year's increase, please, Uncle.

LABAN Impossible! Couldn't think of it!

JACOB You mean you would rather *not* think of it. Well, here is an alternative – which, being of a more speculative character – you may like better.

CHORUS ONE Look out, Laban!

CHORUS TWO Jacob is going to be your match this time.

JACOB You have now over five hundred head of sheep and goats, all white pure-breeds. You have also between fifty and sixty cross-breeds, speckled, spotted, or ringstraked. If, from now on, you will let *me* have the cross-breeds, I will take these as my wages.

LABAN Is that going to content you?

JACOB Yes, Uncle, provided, of course, that if among your pure-breeds any are born speckled, spotted or ringstraked they also shall be mine.

LABAN Ah ha! You are clever, Jacob, but you don't catch your old Uncle as easily as all that! Cross-breeding can be done in the dark – yes, in the dark! And with you in charge of them –

JACOB That you should think me capable of such a thing, shows how little you know me. After so many years of faithful service, is it likely that I would so deceive and cheat you?

CHORUS ONE That was beautifully said, Jacob.

LABAN I don't know, Jacob; I don't know. In my experience there are some who are quite capable of deceiving even their own Fathers.

CHORUS TWO That was a good shot, Laban.

JACOB (*not as conscience-striken as he ought to be*) Well, if you *have* any such doubt, you can make the doing of it impossible.

LABAN Aye? How?

JACOB Divide the two flocks – the pure-breeds from the cross-breeds. Put them into different pastures – as many miles apart as you choose, for safety. And every night let some of your own men keep watch over them; and if any of my rams or he-goats be found among your herds, or any of their wool upon their backs, I will pay forfeit; or, if any of your white ones be found among my herds, it shall be counted as stolen. There's a fair offer for you, Uncle. Take it, or leave it . . . Do I go – or shall I stay?

(JACOB *is now master of the situation:* LABAN *gives in.*)

LABAN You shall stay, Jacob. For surely, since you have been with me, in the work of your hands the Lord God of your Fathers has blessed me. I've thought – aye, more than once I've thought – that I would make him be one of *my* Gods also. But no, no: better not. It might make trouble with the others. Gods are jealous, you know, Jacob; they're jealous – they don't like each other – they don't get on well together. Now why can't they? I've thought sometimes that if there were only *one* God.

JACOB There *is* only one God.

LABAN Eh? What's that you say? Only one? And who's he, I'd like to know?

JACOB My God is the one true God.

LABAN Oh, don't talk nonsense, Jacob; don't talk nonsense! You've got such a belief in yourself that you think your God's the same as *you* are – no one like him! . . . Now, maybe, if you'd had more respect for *my* Gods, Rachel would have done her duty and given you children – not stayed barren all these years, making it look as if you hadn't been a true husband to her. You think of it, Jacob.

(*He goes over to the* TERAPHIM.)

I'm telling him, Holy Ones. I'm telling him. Maybe I should have told him before.

CHORUS ONE Is Laban right, Jacob?

CHORUS TWO Or is it because she worships false Gods that Rachel stays barren?

(*Enter* LEAH *and* RACHEL.)

CHORUS ONE Here is Rachel, with something to say, Jacob.

LEAH Tell him, Rachel.

RACHEL Jacob, will you please – will you please, go to Leah tonight?

JACOB (*coldly*) Why do you ask that, Rachel?

RACHEL Because – (*She stops, ashamed to go on.*)

JACOB It is not seemly for a wife to tell her husband to which of his wives he should go.

LEAH Is it seemly that a husband with two wives should show favour only to *one*?

LABAN My daughter is right, Jacob. You have not treated Leah fairly.

JACOB More fairly than I was treated when she was forced on me. Has she not had four sons of her own; and two by her handmaid? What more does she want?

LABAN Evidently she wants *more*, Jacob.

LEAH Has not a woman the right to have children, so long as she is willing to bear them? Since I bore the last, what chance have you given me of another?

JACOB (*angrily*) Go in, Leah! Your husband is not your man-servant. Go in!

LABAN (*smoothly*) Do as your husband tells you, my daughter. Your Father will speak for you.

(*Exit* LEAH.)

JACOB Rachel, why have you done this? . . . Answer me!

RACHEL The Gods are jealous, Jacob. Give me children!
I must have children! If I don't have one, I shall die.

JACOB (*angrily*) Am I a God that you ask this of me? Is it
I that have kept you from bearing children?

LABAN No, Jacob, no; it is the Gods of my house – as I
warned you. Now you see!

JACOB Rachel, have I not been a good husband to you?

RACHEL Yes, Jacob.

JACOB Have I not loved you well, and faithfully?

RACHEL Yes, Jacob.

JACOB Do you think that (*but for the promise I made to
Leah – not knowing*) I have ever wished for any but you?

RACHEL No, Jacob.

JACOB Then – what more can you ask of me?

RACHEL (*hysterically*) I must have children, Jacob! I
must! (*She runs across to the* TERAPHIM.) Ashera! Ashera!
Ashera!

JACOB Rachel, you are not to do that! Come away! I will
not have you praying to Gods that are not my God.

RACHEL But I must have a child, Jacob.

LABAN She must have a child, Jacob.

RACHEL If I leave off praying to Ashera, will you go to
Leah, tonight, as I promised her you should? . . . Will you,
Jacob?

JACOB Yes . . . I will go to Leah tonight! . . . I will go to
Leah.

> (*He stands downcast and humiliated: his two wives
> have beaten him.*)

LABAN We live and learn, Jacob. We live and learn.

CHORUS ONE Yes, Jacob, we live and learn. It is not for
nothing that Rachel still worships the Gods of her Father's
house.

CHORUS TWO And *fears* them.

Rachel's Dream

CHORUS ONE   Rachel is sleeping alone;
    Leah is sleeping with Jacob.
    A voice, from the Unseen, the Unknown,
    Tells Rachel to wake up.
CHORUS TWO   But Rachel wakes not, she sleeps;
    Through the dark night comes a beam;
    Into her sleep a dream creeps;
    And this is the dream.

(*Over the bed in which* RACHEL *lies sleeping the three*
TERAPHIM *stand motionless side by side in their*
wooden tabernacle; but when a glint of light crosses
the darkness and falls upon them, the jaws of one of
them drop open; out comes a voice, and presently two
other voices answer. BEOR *and* SHAMEM *have parrot-*
voices; ASHERA'S *voice is of a softer quality. It is*
BEOR *who speaks first.*)

BEOR   Ashera . . . Shamem . . . Wake up! . . . You awake,
Ashera? You awake, Shamem?

ASHERA   Yes. What is it?

SHAMEM   Eh? . . . What's the matter? What have you
woken me up for?

BEOR   We've got to have a talk – a talk.

SHAMEM   What about?

BEOR   About Jacob.

SHAMEM   What about him? What about him?

BEOR   Jacob's a bad man – wicked, won't worship us.
Doesn't believe in us; isn't afraid of us – he's got a God of
his own.

SHAMEM   What d'you want to do about it?

BEOR   Jacob's got to be told . . . got to be taught – taught
to behave better.

SHAMEM Who's to tell him?

BEOR Rachel . . . Rachel wants children; but Jacob . . . Ashera, you tell Shamem what Jacob did yesterday.

SHAMEM What did he do, Ashera?

ASHERA Rachel was praying to me, praying to have children. Jacob said: 'You're not to do that, Rachel! You're not to do that!'

BEOR There! What d'you think of that, Shamem? . . . What d'you think of that?

SHAMEM Well, what are you going to do about it?

BEOR Make Rachel tell him that if he doesn't treat us properly, she'll never have any, never . . . never . . . never.

SHAMEM Yes, Rachel, you tell Jacob *that*!

BEOR And tell him this too – that if ever you go away and desert the Gods of your Father's house, you will die . . . die . . . die.

ASHERA Rachel, do you hear that?

RACHEL Ashera!

(*In her sleep* RACHEL *stretches out her arms to* ASHERA. *Light falls on her.*)

CHORUS ONE Now into Rachel's dream
A ladder, like Jacob's, descends
With child-bearing Angels thereon;
And into her arms stretched out
In hope for a life to come,
Lo, a man-child is laid.

RACHEL Ashera! . . . Beautiful Ashera!

CHORUS TWO Nay, Rachel; not yet, not yet!
Not from false Gods comes the gift.
Two years more must thou wait,
Then shall Joseph be born:
Then – long looked-for, and last –
Benjamin bringing thee – Death.

93

SCENE 3

CHORUS ONE Two years have gone by, and Jacob is still serving Laban.

CHORUS TWO But their relations don't seem quite happy. Who's been getting the better of the bargain now?

(*The Scene opens.*)

LABAN It's no use pretending, Jacob! Last year thirty-five, this year eighty-five of my pure-breeds have borne cross-breeds – speckled, spotted, or ringstraked. How do you account for that?

JACOB I cannot, Uncle. I can only say – with all due humility and thankfulness – the Lord God of my Fathers has been good to me.

LABAN No God could have done all that, without a thief to help him.

JACOB Would any God accept help from a thief, Uncle?

LABAN I don't know, Jacob. Mine wouldn't. Yours might.

JACOB How do you think I helped him?

LABAN By putting your cross-breeds among my pure-breeds under cover of night. How else?

JACOB Then what were your own men doing?

LABAN You bribed them.

JACOB Have any of them told you so?

LABAN Bribed men don't tell tales against themselves.

JACOB Don't they? If you offered them a bigger bribe, they might even tell a lie for it. Yet that too I am willing to risk, if it will set your mind at rest . . . Yonder is Asa, your freeman – we will ask *him*. Asa!

ASA Yes, Master?

JACOB Come here. (ASA *enters.*) Asa, how long have you had charge by night of your Master's flocks?

ASA All this year, and last year.

94

JACOB With how much did I bribe you to let me bring my cross-breeds among them – either my rams or my he-goats?

ASA You never did bribe me.

JACOB Don't be afraid, Asa; you are quite free to tell your Master if I did so. And if you now tell him the truth, he will give you a bigger reward than any you got from me.

ASA But you never did, Master.

JACOB Then how do you account for so many of the pure-breeds bearing cross-breeds?

ASA Would you have me say true?

JACOB Surely.

ASA I say – and it's what all the others say too – that you are a wizard; that it's those rods, Master.

JACOB The rods which I put into the troughs to clear the water when it was muddy?

ASA Yes.

JACOB You are very simple, Asa; but you are honest. If that's all you have to tell us, you can go. (ASA *goes*.) Well? . . . Do you not think he has told the truth?

LABAN Yes, I do; for I think you *are* a wizard, Jacob.

JACOB People often think that of the fortunate ones, when they are less fortunate themselves.

LABAN You owned yourself, when you came, that you were a waterfinder.

JACOB Yes; and had I not found a fresh well for you during the drought two years ago, all your flocks and herds would have perished.

LABAN And when you did it, you used a divining-rod, which came to life in your hands.

JACOB Yes; but you did not call me a wizard then. You said then – that the Lord God of my Fathers had favoured you because of me.

LABAN If he ever did, he favours me no more. He has turned against me.

JACOB Whose fault is that, Uncle?

95

LABAN Yours! Had you done honour to *my* Gods, I would have done honour to *yours*. But you would not, so there was enmity between them. And it is because of that that your wife Rachel remains barren.

JACOB My God has been stronger than your Gods, Uncle; for Rachel is now with child.

LABAN (*maliciously*) Are you sure, Jacob, that that also will not be a cross-breed? Your God is good at cross-breeds.

CHORUS TWO That's a nasty one, Jacob.

LABAN Yes; you put a spell upon my flocks, to rob me of that which was mine; after all I've done for you, after all that you've had from me! I took you as my son. You came to me poor; now you are rich . . . I'm disappointed in you, Jacob. I never thought you'd treat your old Uncle as you have done. But you were a born deceiver, and by your deceit you have prospered – till now. But a day may come . . . a day may come, Jacob –

(*Exit* LABAN. JACOB *stands thinking.*)

JACOB So – the day *has* come . . . Yes, Uncle; so long as you got the better of *me*, you wanted me to stay. Now that I've got the better of *you* – at last – I'd better go.

CHORUS TWO Yes, Jacob, you'd better go.

CHORUS ONE Maybe you'd have gone sooner if you hadn't been so afraid of meeting Esau.

(*Enter* RACHEL.)

RACHEL Jacob, what's the matter with Father?

JACOB (*quietly*) Yes; what *is* the matter?

RACHEL He's angry. He was calling on the Gods to curse you. And when he saw me he laughed, and said, 'Well done, Mother of cross-breeds!' What did he mean, Jacob? He frightened me.

JACOB Have no fear, Rachel; my God is greater than his Gods. They cannot hurt me.

RACHEL But they may hurt *me*, Jacob! I'm not sure whether what I told you is true. I had a dream, that made me think so. But if the curse of my Father's Gods is on you before my child is born, I may die, Jacob, I may die!

JACOB You shall not die, Rachel. Some day – who knows? – you may have as many sons as Leah has had.

RACHEL It's too late for that now, Jacob. It was two years ago – my dream, and nothing came of it. And a few nights ago I dreamed it again; and this time they told me I *should* have a child – but only if –

JACOB *Who* told you?

RACHEL The Gods, Jacob.

JACOB Rachel, you are not to believe in those Gods, or have anything to do with them. I forbid you.

RACHEL I can't help it, Jacob. They are the Gods of my Father's house where I belong.

JACOB (*sternly*) Then from your Father's house I take you away, back to my own land, where the hand of the Evil Ones shall no longer be upon you . . . Say no more, Rachel. Go and tell Leah, Billah, and Zilpah that I want them – quickly!

(*Exit* RACHEL. JACOB *goes to the door and calls* ASA.)

CHORUS ONE Is that patient Jacob speaking?

CHORUS TWO No, the patience of patient Jacob is over. Jacob has become a man of action.

(*Enter* ASA.)

ASA You called, Master?

JACOB Asa, you were a child when I came here. Would you be sorry to see me go?

ASA Yes, Master.

JACOB Would any of the others be sorry?

ASA They'd all be. For your hand has not been heavy on us, as another's has been. We've always liked *you* the better.

JACOB If I were to go away, would you like to come with me?

ASA I would, Master.

JACOB Would any of the others?

ASA I think they *all* would. For there's not one of us that, at one time or another, has not been done out of his wages, or something else we'd a right to. We all hate him.

JACOB It is not right to hate anyone, Asa. But there is no reason why you should not like someone better than the man you must not hate. Well . . . I *am* going, Asa.

ASA When will it be, Master.

JACOB We start tonight.

ASA Leaving all your flocks and your herds behind you?

JACOB Not if I can take them with me. But for that I must have herdsmen. Tell any that are willing, that with me they will get better wages than with Laban.

ASA But how shall we get the flocks away, Master, without his knowing?

JACOB When you change their pastures for the night, you have but to drive them further. No one will see where you are taking them.

ASA Where are we taking them?

JACOB To the land I came from – Beersheba, which lies by the border of Edom.

ASA That's a long journey for herds to go, Master.

JACOB Yes; and for women and children also. For them we shall need three camels. You arrange that, Asa. Get Ebor, the Elamite, to hire them to me.

ASA Yes, Master.

JACOB Ah! In you Laban loses a good servant. Go, then; for you have much to do. We start tonight . . . And, Asa – not a word to Laban.

(*Exit* ASA.)

Yes, Uncle Laban; the day has come; I am quit of you at last.

CHORUS ONE Are you sure that you *are* – quit of Laban?
CHORUS TWO And of the Gods of his house, Jacob?

(*Enter* LEAH *and* RACHEL, *followed by* BILLAH *and* ZILPAH.)

LEAH Jacob! You're not to go! You're not to go! You *can't* go away with Rachel, and leave all the rest of us behind.

JACOB What has Rachel been telling you?

LEAH That you are taking her away with you – back to where you came from.

JACOB I *am* taking her; but I'm taking you too, Leah, *and* Billah *and* Zilpah; and the children. We are all going together.

RACHEL You didn't say so, Jacob.

JACOB I said only what concerned you, Rachel. I say now what concerns all. Get yourselves ready for the journey; but tell no one. We start tonight.

RACHEL Tonight!

LEAH But why, Jacob?

JACOB The God of my Fathers tells me that the day has come for my return. Because He has prospered me more than your Father's Gods have prospered him, Laban has become my enemy.

LEAH Your enemy?

JACOB Because I have now more flocks and herds than he has, he says that I have stolen them.

RACHEL But how did it come about, Jacob, that you have more than he has?

JACOB It was the Lord's showing, Rachel. I only did what He told me.

RACHEL How did He tell you?

JACOB He gave me knowledge, Rachel; and showed me how to use it. It was quite simple. When God made the beasts of the field, He made them so that, when they are with young, anything which they desire greatly leaves a mark on them; and when they bring forth, the mark is on their young also. Now there is nothing that sheep and cattle need more than water, or suffer more if they are kept without it. So, when the breeding season came, I took rods of green poplar and peeled them in streaks, so that they showed white and green; and laid them in all the drinking-troughs. And those which were with young I kept apart from the rest, till a great thirst was upon them. Then I let them come to the drinking-troughs, and there were the rods before their eyes, while they drank. So when they brought forth their young – because of the rods, they were all speckled, spotted, or ringstraked. And in all this I only did as the Lord showed me. So, if my flocks have increased more than your father Laban's flocks, it is God's doing, not mine; and he has no cause to be angry with me.

LEAH You have a wise God, Jacob.

RACHEL And his God has a wise servant.

JACOB Yes, Rachel; all the wisdom I have comes from Him. And he has promised never to leave me.

RACHEL And have you promised never to leave Him?

JACOB I promised that if He would bring me back safely to my own land, I would have no other Gods but Him.

RACHEL But, Jacob, aren't many Gods better than one God? Why not have *all* the Gods?

JACOB Because, Rachel, my God is a jealous God, and in the day when He fulfils His promise to me, jealously will I serve Him also; and Him only.

LEAH But, Jacob, why is Father not to know that we are going?

JACOB Because your Father's anger being hot against me, he may take from me you and all that I possess, and send me back to my own land naked as I came. Nay, so much has he become my enemy that even my life may be in danger. So choose now; are you mine, or are you his? Will you come with me, or will you stay?

RACHEL Why, of course, we will come, Jacob.

LEAH Yes, indeed; to you he sold us, and if you go, what portion or inheritance have we in our Father's house? We shall only be servants.

JACOB The Lord has given you understanding, Leah; you have chosen well. Make haste, then, all of you; for tonight we start on our journey. Many times has your father Laban got the better of me deceitfully. Now God is rewarding him as he deserves.

CHORUS ONE As *he* deserves, Jacob? And what about *you*?

(*Exit* JACOB.)

RACHEL Well, if he likes to think so; but *I* think it's Jacob. And *he'd* better not be too jealous for that God of his, as if *He* were the only one, till He's done all that He promised to do. Time enough, then . . . Billah and Zilpah, be off with you; you've lots to do, getting things ready to go. You too Leah, with all those children of yours, have more to do than I have. Though I've something to do too.

(*She gets out a large basket, and goes to the door with it.*)

LEAH What are you going to do, Rachel?

RACHEL Nothing *you* need know anything about. We've got a clever husband, Leah; but for all the children you've had by him, I'm a better match for him than you. When we go tonight, Jacob will be taking away with him more than he knows.

CHORUS ONE So you are not going to be quit of Laban yet, Jacob. Rachel is seeing to that.

CHORUS TWO Poor foolish Rachel.

ACT III

SCENE 1

CHORUS TWO Two days' journey from Padan-aram.
CHORUS ONE Two days free from the bondage of Laban.
CHORUS TWO Jacob has pitched his slow-moving camp.
CHORUS ONE By the waters of Jabbok.

(*The Scene opens.*)

(*A tent, widely open at the back, has been set up for the
women to rest in. The ground is strewn with baggage.
ZILPAH and BILLAH are podding lentils for the evening
meal. LEAH is nursing her youngest child. ASA enters
carrying a camel-saddle with side-bags, and a pile of
cushions.*)

ASA Here's the saddle, Mistress, and the cushions.

RACHEL (*anxiously*) You are sure that is from the camel
I rode on, Asa?

ASA Yes, Mistress.

RACHEL Be careful, then; there are things in it that might
break.

LEAH (*suspiciously*) Oh? Things that might break, are
there? . . . I don't want *my* saddle, Asa. You can leave it.

ASA But we are bringing them all in, Mistress. We
haven't to keep the camels saddled all night.

RACHEL All night? – all night, you say?

ASA Aye, and tomorrow night too, most likely; as it's here
we'll be staying.

(*Enter* JACOB.)

JACOB Asa, have drinking-water drawn from the brook
before you let the herds go down to it.

ASA Yes, Master.

(*Exit* ASA.)

RACHEL Why are we stopping *here*, Jacob?

JACOB Because we need water for the herds, Rachel; and here *is* water. Further on we may find none. Also, after a two days' journey, they need rest.

RACHEL But, Jacob, as they started before us, why cannot we go on, and they follow after?

JACOB Why are you in such a hurry to go on, Rachel?

RACHEL Because I'm afraid that my Father may be coming after us.

JACOB Why should he come after us?

LEAH (*slyly*) Tell us, Rachel.

RACHEL Well, you see, Jacob, we came away without saying goodbye to him. And if we are not coming back, he will never see us again.

JACOB Your Father would not come a two days' journey just to say goodbye to you, Rachel.

RACHEL No, Jacob; but as you and he quarrelled, he might be coming to make friends again.

JACOB That would be a reason not for going on, but for staying, Rachel. But I do not think your Father will want to be friends again with *me*.

RACHEL No, Jacob, nor do I. So he might be coming to take back those of his flocks which he said you stole from him.

JACOB He might, Rachel, but I don't think he will.

RACHEL (*nervously*) I want to go on, Jacob. I don't like this place; it frightens me!

LEAH (*sarcastically*) Surely the Gods of our Father's house will protect you, Rachel.

(*Enter* ASA.)

ASA Master, here's Laban; and the men of his house are with him.

CHORUS TWO That's a nasty surprise, Jacob.

RACHEL There, you see Jacob: I told you.

CHORUS ONE Yes, Jacob; Rachel told you. Why didn't you do as she told you?

JACOB Bring him here, Asa.

RACHEL Oh, I'm feeling so ill! I must lie down. Jacob, Jacob! . . . When I told you before, I wasn't quite sure; and Leah laughed at me. But I'm sure it's true now, Jacob.

LEAH Very sudden, Rachel.

(She throws herself down on the cushions, and starts writhing.)

RACHEL Oh! . . . Oh!

LEAH *(imitating her)* Oh! . . . Oh! Make enough noise over it; you'll believe it yourself presently. Howl louder; then, perhaps, it'll be twins.

RACHEL Leah, I hate you!

LEAH Yes; I've given you six good reasons for it – to your none.

(To all this JACOB *pays no attention: he stands at the entrance of the tent, looking out for* LABAN.*)*
(Enter LABAN *and* ASA.*)*

LABAN Well, Jacob; you didn't expect to see me, eh? – stole a march on me, and thought you'd get clean away, and have no trouble with your old Uncle? But you don't get rid of me as easily as all that . . . What did you do it for, Jacob?

JACOB Since my service no longer pleased you, it was better that I came away. What is your complaint?

LABAN Complaint? – more than one, Jacob. First, you carry away my daughters as though they were captives taken in war. Has a Father no right to know what has become of his own children? . . . Well, Leah; do you know your Father again, or have you forgotten him?

LEAH (*making dutiful obeisance*) Indeed no, I am glad to see you, Father.

LABAN And you, Rachel? What manners are these that Jacob has taught you? – not to rise up when your Father speaks to you?

RACHEL You must pardon me, my Lord; my time has come, and my pains are upon me.

LABAN So? At last, eh? It comes at a bad time, Rachel . . . Your doing, Jacob. My second complaint is this – that you have stolen my men from me – the best of them.

JACOB They were my men also.

LABAN How were they yours?

JACOB When they worked for me, I paid their wages.

LABAN Aye; some days, I let you have the use of them.

JACOB And, being free men, not bond slaves, had they not the right to choose which master they would serve?

LABAN And I to know nothing of it?

JACOB Had you known, you would not have spared me any; so my flocks would have remained with you, for lack of men to take charge of them.

LABAN Those flocks you tricked and stole from me.

JACOB Nothing that was yours have I stolen.

LABAN Nothing? Think again, Jacob; think again! After you'd left, I found that the Gods of my house were gone! If you did not steal them, who did? Oh! Your wives, your sons, your servants, your flocks – that should be *my* flocks – you may keep them all! But my Gods I will have back from you!

JACOB I have not taken your Gods. Why should I take them? They were never *my* Gods.

LABAN No, they were mine, Jacob. Where are they?

JACOB Why do you ask? Go where you will – search the whole camp – my goods and my chattels, my manservants and my maidservants – and whosoever it be that has taken them, this day shall that life be forfeit.

CHORUS ONE Take care what you are saying, Jacob!

LABAN I *will* search – till I find them.

JACOB Go with him, Asa; let him search till he be satisfied.

LABAN You must come too, Jacob. I'll not have you go finding a better hiding-place for them behind my back.

JACOB If you still doubt me, Uncle – here am I, and your two daughters. Begin here.

LABAN Ah, no, Jacob; my daughters would never have stolen their Father's Gods from him; nor would you have told *them* of the theft. I will seek elsewhere. Farewell, Rachel. It had been better for thee to have remained in thy Father's house. The Gods be good to thee, and grant thee thy desire.

RACHEL (*in the grip of her 'pains'*) Farewell – farewell, Father!

LABAN Farewell, my daughter. (*To* LEAH.) Take care of thy sister; be kind to her.

LEAH Farewell, Father.

LABAN Now, Jacob.

> (*Exit* LABAN *and* JACOB. RACHEL *sits up, watching* LABAN'S *departure; when he has quite gone she starts laughing.*)

CHORUS ONE So Laban has met his match at last.

CHORUS TWO Rachel and Jacob, between them, have beaten him.

LEAH How are the pains, Rachel? When you've quite done laughing, I've something to say to you.

RACHEL Well?

LEAH When are you going to tell Jacob?

RACHEL Tell him what?

LEAH About the 'breakables'.

RACHEL Jacob need never know.

LEAH He's bound to know. He won't let you keep them. If you don't tell him, *I* shall.

RACHEL Then why didn't you, just now?

LEAH I could not so shame him before our Father's face. You've no heart, Rachel.

RACHEL Oh, but you mustn't tell him, Leah! Don't, don't! I can't let Ashera go. Without Ashera I should die. She told me so, in a dream, didn't you, Ashera?

(*She starts opening the saddle-bag.*)

LEAH Oh, what a fool you are, Rachel! But a barren woman must always have something to pet and fondle and make believe with – to make up for what she's not got – and never will have. (*She reaches into the saddle-bag, and pulls out the* TERAPHIM *one by one.*)

RACHEL But Ashera has promised. Haven't you, Ashera? Oh! Ashera's broken! Her head's come off!

LEAH Put it on again. Then you will have done her a good turn and she'll be grateful.

RACHEL Oh! Ashera! darling Ashera!

CHORUS ONE Oh! these Gods and their makers!

CHORUS TWO What a poor blind lot they are!

RACHEL It's all right, Ashera; you weren't broken; you'd only come in two. And here are Beor and Shamem; for I was afraid that if I left them behind, and only took you, they would curse me for it, and I should die. So I've brought all three of you; and you are mine, and I am yours; and I worship you, and I believe in you, and I love you; And if you keep your promise to me, and give me what I asked, I will serve you faithfully, and have no other Gods but you.

(RACHEL *has set up the three* TERAPHIM, *and is kneeling before them in worship when* JACOB *enters.*)

JACOB Rachel!

(*He goes and knocks over the* TERAPHIM.)

RACHEL Jacob! You mustn't break them! They are Father's.

JACOB A late thought, Rachel. Oh, truly you are your Father's daughter! And it is your shame now that I have to bear.

LEAH I told you, Rachel.

JACOB Oh, Rachel, why have you done this to me?

RACHEL Jacob, I want Ashera.

(JACOB *goes over to the tent-door and calls*)

JACOB Asa! Quick, Asa!

(*He picks up the* TERAPHIM.)

RACHEL Jacob, I must have Ashera!

(ASA *comes running.*)

ASA Yes, Master?

JACOB (*giving him the images*) Go after Laban; take these back to him. (RACHEL *gives a squeal of despair.*) Tell him that I don't want them; that I've no use for them; that I didn't know I had them. How they came to be with me, say – I know not. And this, as my last word to him: 'May the Gods of your house watch over you, and reward you abundantly – as you deserve!' . . . Have you got that, Asa?

ASA Yes, Master.

JACOB Then now, after him quickly!

(*Exit* ASA. JACOB *goes to the tent-door.*)

CHORUS ONE To Laban, with Jacob's compliments, Asa.

CHORUS TWO Carry them carefully! They are Gods, remember!

JACOB Farewell, Uncle Laban! Rachel, sit up! Stop crying . . . if you don't stop crying I shall tell Leah to beat you. Listen, Rachel. Had I not found what you had done, and sent those false Gods back to Laban, ere this time to-morrow my life, and your life, and your sister's life, and the lives of all our children would have paid for it. For I made a vow to the God of my Fathers, that if He would bring me back in safety to my own land, I would put away from me all other Gods – I and my house with me. And here, though I knew it not, I was bringing death with me – death, Rachel, death – for you, and for all of us.

LEAH I told you what a fool you were, Rachel.

RACHEL But why shouldn't we be safe now, Jacob; if it is your own land we are going to?

JACOB Because, Rachel, there I shall meet my brother, Esau; and if he be my enemy, then only by my faith in the promise God made to me, and that I made to Him, shall our lives be spared to us. But we are not safe yet. Yesterday I sent a messenger, to tell him of my return . . . No answer has come.

RACHEL Then let us go back, Jacob! Let us go back.

JACOB I will not go back, Rachel. No! I will not go back now. For surely, this has God shown me, of the way He would have me go – that the anger of my brother Esau is better then the love of Laban.

CHORUS TWO So you've found that out, Jacob? You are getting on.

(*Enter* ASA.)

JACOB Well, what says Laban?

ASA He bade me say this, Master: 'Let him beware, in the day that he has promised himself, lest the God of a deceiver be not also, like himself, a deceiver.'

(ASA *goes.* JACOB *stands silent.* LEAH *and* RACHEL *look at him, waiting for him to speak.*)

JACOB Lest the God of a deceiver be not also, like himself, a deceiver . . . like himself . . . a deceiver.

(*He stands conscience-struck as the scene closes.*)

CHORUS ONE Jacob's afraid, and for good reason.
CHORUS TWO Aye! For now Laban has spoken truth.

SCENE 2

CHORUS ONE And now Jacob is alone with his fear.
CHORUS TWO And by the brook Jabbok he stands and prays.

(*The Scene opens*)

(*In the darkness is heard the sound of falling water.*)

JACOB Oh, God of my Fathers, let me not, because of my transgression, be deceived in the Promise which I had from Thee! Make me to know that Thou art faithful, and that Thy Word *was* true. Turn not away Thy face from Thy sorry servant! (*He starts, and stands listening.*) . . . What was that? Who – who comes here?

ASA (*from without*) Master!
JACOB Asa?

(ASA *enters.*)

ASA Here is good news, Master. The messenger has returned. Tomorrow your brother Esau comes to meet you with four hundred armed men.

JACOB *Armed* men, you say? Why does he come with armed men?

ASA I don't know, Master.
JACOB (*full of fear*) That means danger, Asa.

ASA Danger? Nay, but why?

JACOB If he meant well, would he come so armed – and so strong?

ASA Your *brother*, Master?

JACOB He comes not as my brother, but as my enemy. If his wrath be not turned from me, he may slay all.

CHORUS ONE There is yet time. Try a bargain, Jacob!

JACOB Listen, Asa. Tomorrow, rise early, before it is yet day; take with you one-tenth —

CHORUS ONE Only one-tenth, Jacob?

JACOB The best of all the herds – sheep, goats and cattle; and go forward till you meet Esau. And when you meet him, and he asks: 'Whose are these?' say: 'They are for my Lord Esau from Jacob his servant.'

CHORUS ONE Ten per cent? Is that enough, Jacob?

JACOB And, after you – have others to follow in like number; and let those which have charge of them, when asked, say also: 'These are for my Lord Esau from his servant Jacob.'

CHORUS ONE That's better, Jacob.

JACOB And after them shall follow a third; and those with them shall say likewise. And if his heart be not turned against me, then will he accept the gift I send him. But, if not, Asa —

CHORUS ONE Aye? What then?

JACOB Do this! Divide those which remain behind in two bands – the one from the other – men, women and children – and put a safe distance between them. Then, if he fall upon the one, the other may yet escape. Do this, Asa, so that some that are of my seed may live, and not die.

ASA If that be your fear, Master, will it not be better to go back?

JACOB How will it be better? Nay, for if I go back, then have I lost the Blessing and the Promise that He made me.

Oh, voice of my Fear, speak not again! Tell Him – I will *not* go back.

ASA Tell who, Master?

JACOB It was not to you I spoke then, Asa. Go now! Do as I have told you.

> (ASA *goes.* JACOB *stands silent for a while: hope seems to have left him.*)

So – to this end am I come!

CHORUS TWO Yes, Jacob.

JACOB (*startled*) What is that? Who called? . . . Who are you?

> (*NOTE: In the scene which follows* JACOB *stands against the rock upon which* CHORUS TWO *is seated. Light falls upon his face; all above remains in shadow. The hands of* CHORUS TWO *appear as if threatening to throttle him. He writhes in torment: presently they leave him free; and the wrestling is over.*)

CHORUS TWO *You* called. I am yourself, Jacob. The Voice you heard at Bethel you hear again.

JACOB The voice of my Fear?

CHORUS TWO The voice of your Fear.

JACOB I told you to begone.

CHORUS TWO Yes; but you are still afraid; so here I am. We are still two, Jacob.

JACOB What do you mean?

CHORUS TWO In every man there are two, Jacob: one is his weakness, the other his strength. Sometimes they meet, sometimes they part. Sometimes they wrestle together – to the death. How stands it with you and me – *now*, Jacob?

JACOB I know not. I no longer know, myself, what I am.

CHORUS TWO Know tonight, Jacob. Tomorrow may be too late.

JACOB How? How *can* I know?

CHORUS TWO Not while you are of two minds. Choose one. Which is it to be?

JACOB You torture me!

CHORUS TWO You torture yourself. (*There is a pause.*)

JACOB Oh! Where is the God of my Fathers, and the Promise He made me?

CHORUS TWO Not here, Jacob. You are alone.

JACOB Aye, surely alone! No help comes now.

CHORUS TWO None? Is not a friend speaking?

JACOB What does he say?

CHORUS TWO He only bids you be wise.

JACOB Speak!

CHORUS TWO All these years you have shown wisdom and prudence; and you have prospered. In Laban's service you were safe. Now you are in danger . . . Why have you come?

JACOB For the Promise that God made to me, and the Blessing it was to bring.

CHORUS TWO To *you*, Jacob?

JACOB Aye, surely! For to Abraham, and to Isaac, my Father, He gave it. And my Father gave it to me.

CHORUS TWO Did your Father know to whom he was giving it?

JACOB He knew – afterwards.

CHORUS TWO Will a blessing so given, hold good, think you?

JACOB It was mine! Esau had sold it to me.

CHORUS TWO Did he know what he was selling?

JACOB You asked me that at Bethel.

CHORUS TWO Yes; and you said he did not care. Yet you were afraid of him. You are still, Jacob.

JACOB Yes, I fear him still.

CHORUS TWO Why?

JACOB Because then I did him wrong.

CHORUS TWO That's better, Jacob. You are nearer the truth now.

JACOB What would you have me do?

CHORUS TWO Why not give back the Blessing which you took from him?

JACOB How can I do that?

CHORUS TWO Have the will, Jacob.

JACOB How can I undo God's doing? The Blessing was given me by God.

CHORUS TWO Only in a dream, Jacob.

JACOB That also came from God.

CHORUS TWO Are you so sure?

JACOB I *was* sure.

CHORUS TWO If you were, of what use was the bargain that you made?

JACOB I made no bargain.

CHORUS TWO You offered one. You said that if God would fulfil His promise, you would give to Him, of all that you had, one-tenth – always one-tenth. Are you sure that one-tenth was enough, Jacob?

JACOB Had He asked more, I would have given more.

CHORUS TWO No doubt. But He never answered. So the bargain was not made. Tomorrow you are sending to your brother Esau not one-tenth, but three-tenths of all your sheep and cattle. Are you sure that three-tenths will be enough – to satisfy him? And if not, why should the God of your Fathers be satisfied with only one-tenth?

JACOB He made His promise freely. He required nothing of me.

CHORUS TWO Why, then, did you make a bargain of it? That wasn't wise, Jacob . . . So today you were afraid, when you found that you had Laban's Gods still with you – afraid that the bargain had been broken.

JACOB When I found them, I sent them away.

CHORUS TWO Aye. But it was a late finding, Jacob.

JACOB Is God no better than man? Twenty years have I been faithful to Him. Shall He now be less faithful to me? Surely in God must be truth!

CHORUS TWO So only in truth can you serve Him.

JACOB How have I *not* served Him?

CHORUS TWO You are a coward, Jacob.

JACOB Because I fear death?

CHORUS TWO No; a man need be no coward who fears death. He only is a coward who fears truth.

JACOB What truth do I fear?

CHORUS TWO The truth about the man you are, Jacob.

JACOB Tell it me.

CHORUS TWO I cannot. You must find that for yourself . . . You think that I am the voice of your Fear; because conscience has made a coward of you. Cease to fear the Truth; and you will cease to fear me also.

JACOB Your voice has changed.

CHORUS TWO *Your* voice, Jacob. It is your own heart speaking now. And you hear it – for the first time. For when you deceived others, you deceived yourself also . . . How could a deceiver by deceit serve faithfully the God of Truth? And you were a deceiver, Jacob.

JACOB Yes.

CHORUS TWO You were not honest – to Laban.

JACOB No.

CHORUS TWO And you gave your dishonesty to God, saying that it was His doing, not yours.

JACOB Yes.

CHORUS TWO Therefore, also, has Rachel deceived *you* – as you deserved. But the bargain that you made with God was broken – not by Rachel, but by you, because you did not serve faithfully the God of Truth.

JACOB Alas! Then surely is He free from His Promise.

CHORUS TWO So you have come to the truth at last! And you also — are free.

JACOB How am I — free?

CHORUS TWO To return by the way you came. Tomorrow comes Esau, with his four hundred armed men; and your life, and the lives of those with you, will be in danger. It is still night; escape is easy. The way is clear. The forgiveness of Laban you can win more surely than the forgiveness of Esau.

JACOB Why are you tempting me?

CHORUS TWO Am I tempting you?

JACOB No! I will not go back to serve Laban. I will not go back.

CHORUS ONE Well said, Jacob — though the saying was hard for thee. But God is faithful and just, and has not taken His Promise from thee. For though Esau may slay thee, God's Blessing shall be upon thy sons, and on their sons after them; and the land which He gave to thy Fathers shall be theirs; and from thy seed shall come a nation . . . This night thou hast heard the voice of thine Accuser; and that of which he accused thee was true. But he has gone from thee, and thou hearest him no more. For now the truth is with thee, and thou knowest what manner of man thou art, and seest thyself as God sees thee; and hast judged thyself righteously . . . Therefore thy name shall no longer be called Jacob, but Israel; for as a prince thou hast striven with God, and thy strength has prevailed over thy weakness. You walk lame, Jacob; but you get there at last. Tomorrow thou shalt go forward and meet Esau.

JACOB This is no longer the voice I heard. It is no man's voice that speaks now . . . Tell me thy name?

CHORUS TWO Why dost thou seek my name? Is it not enough that thou hast heard my voice speaking to thee? Lo, now the day breaks, and the shadows flee away; the day of God's Promise has come; and on Israel His light shines.

(*Very slowly the darkness begins to break and there is a sound of birds.*)

JACOB Now have I seen God face to face; and my life has been spared to me. And though I fear death at his hand, I will go forward and meet Esau.

SCENE 3

CHORUS ONE Jacob has wrestled with God, and has found strength.

CHORUS TWO But Jacob still fears the coming of Esau.

(*The Scene opens.*)

(*It is morning; and in the camp at Jabbok* JACOB *is receiving* ASA'S *report of his meeting with* ESAU.)

JACOB And when you gave him my message, what did he say, Asa?

ASA Nothing, Master; only laughed.

JACOB Laughed, you say?

ASA Yes, Master.

JACOB And when they came with the second gift, what then?

ASA Only laughed.

JACOB And when the third came, did he still say nothing?

ASA Aye, he spoke then. 'How many more?' says he. And then: 'So it's the old Jacob, same as ever; hiding behind his own shadow – and still afraid of it.' And then: 'Tell my brother Jacob that when I come I shall have a surprise for him.'

JACOB (*uneasily*) So he did not accept the gifts?

ASA No, Master. He told me to take them back the way I'd brought them; because he was coming himself, he said; and the killing of them could better be done here. . . .

(*That word 'killing' increases* JACOB'S *fear of what* ESAU *intends to do.*)

JACOB Have you divided the two companies for safety, as I told you?

ASA No, Master, I've not had time; and he'll soon be here now.

JACOB Then go now and do it.

(*Exit* ASA.)
(*From outside comes a sound of sudden disturbance in the camp.* JACOB *stands listening.*)

Too late – too late now!

(*Enter* RACHEL, LEAH, BILLAH *and* ZILPAH.)

RACHEL Jacob! where have you been? Where have you been? Last night, where were you?

(RACHEL'S *shrill trepidation annoys* JACOB, *and he answers curtly*:)

JACOB Losing my way – and finding it, Rachel . . . Listen, all of you! . . . My brother Esau will soon be here, and four hundred armed men with him. Being my Father's first-born, he is lord and ruler of me, and all that is mine. We are but his servants, and must do his pleasure . . . Therefore, when he calls you into his presence, humble yourselves before him, and whatsoever he bids you do, do it – lest his face be turned against me this day, and he take from me all that I have.

RACHEL I don't think I shall like Esau, Jacob.

JACOB (*grimly*) Perhaps he won't like *you* – or perhaps he *will: for you are still fair*. Take off your jewels, and cover your face. Go back to your own tent, and wait.

RACHEL (*frightened*) Jacob! He mustn't see me! Hide me! Hide me!

JACOB Leah, take her away! (*They go; and as they go*
LEAH *is heard saying:*)

LEAH Your Gods won't protect you now, Rachel. Jacob
has sent them away.

(*Enter* ASA.)

ASA They are here, Master. We are surrounded by
armed men. My Lord Esau is seeking you.

JACOB How many are with him?

ASA He has come in alone, Master.

JACOB (*to himself*) Nay! Surely if he comes alone, he
means *not* to slay me!

(*He stands waiting.* ASA *goes to the door, and stands
aside for* ESAU *to enter.*)

ESAU Where is my brother, Jacob? Where are you,
Jacob?

(*As* ESAU *enters,* JACOB *bows himself almost to the
ground.*)

JACOB He is here, my lord.

ESAU Where?

JACOB Here, my lord, here.

ESAU Who is this fellow?

ASA My lord, he is your brother, Jacob.

(JACOB *is now kneeling. At a gesture from* ESAU,
ASA *goes out.*)

ESAU Get up, man! Get up! What are you crouching
like that for? (*He pulls him to his feet.*)

JACOB Oh, my lord, I feared lest your anger was still hot
against me.

ESAU My *anger*? ... You make me ashamed, Jacob!
Stand up, man! Stand up!

JACOB Oh, my lord!

ESAU 'My lord,' 'my lord!' Who d'you think you are talking to? Have you forgotten that we are brothers? What are you frightened about?

JACOB For the wrong I did you, when I took from you our Father's Blessing, and the Promise.

ESAU Oh, aye! You played me a trick then; you did, Jacob . . . But that was twenty years ago. Why didn't you come back?

JACOB I was afraid lest you might kill me.

ESAU Good Lord, man! If I'd meant to kill you, I should have come after you. I knew where you'd gone. What was to prevent?

JACOB I never thought of that.

ESAU Then clever Jacob was a fool . . . and is still. So that's why you never came back, eh? Oh, Jacob! Jacob! Did you never give a thought to how your Father and Mother were waiting for you? Come, come! That's finished; and we are brothers again.

(*He gives him a friendly shaking, and kisses him and now they look at each other face to face.*)

How you've aged, Jacob! What has done this to you? Fear of *me*?

JACOB Many years I have done hard service to a hard master, Brother.

ESAU So the Blessing has not come yet?

JACOB Maybe it *has* come now. But the price of it had to come first. Only at your hands can I receive it, Brother.

ESAU Well; it may have been worth the price to *you*; it wouldn't have been to *me*. You sold me something I wanted, for something I didn't want – riches, flocks, herds, land for a possession – no use to *me*! Though you got it by a trick, Jacob, it went to the right man. Oh, yes; I was angry enough at the way you got it – enough to give you a good hiding, maybe, if I'd caught you. But as for *killing* you – I may have said so, but I never meant it.

JACOB Your pardon, Brother!

ESAU My pardon? Pah! . . . So it was fear, was it – fear of *me* – kept you a bondsman to old Laban for twenty years – afraid to come back to your own people?

JACOB Is our Father yet alive, Esau?

ESAU Yes; and he sees better now than he did then. He'll know you from me *this* time, Jacob.

JACOB And our Mother?

ESAU She's dead, Jacob . . . Why didn't you come back when she sent for you?

JACOB She never sent for me!

ESAU Aye; three times she did, Jacob. And the only answer that came back was that you were doing well, and meant to stay.

JACOB Laban never told *me* of it! Not a word.

ESAU Why was that??

JACOB Because he had got a good bargain, and wished not to lose it. He was ever a deceiver; and he paid me – as I deserved.

ESAU So all that while the Blessing was kept waiting!

JACOB The Blessing that I stole from you.

ESAU And that I did not want. Don't trouble about it any more, Jacob.

JACOB And my Mother, that loved me, is dead! And my Father, who did not love me, lives! In this, also, I am paid as I deserved!

ESAU Nay! but he loves you *now*, Jacob. After you'd gone, he found out the worth you'd been to him. I could never serve him like you, Jacob. I didn't try. So all was left to the hired men – with no one to see after them. It's made a difference! Aye! he'll be glad to have you back. You'll be the favourite now.

JACOB And what sort of life is yours, Esau? What is it *you do*?

ESAU I do three good things, Jacob; and the more I have of them the better I'm pleased: I hunt, and I fight, and I marry. With four hundred armed men under me, I do service for the King of Edom.

JACOB In war?

ESAU Aye; war of a kind. Here, on the borders between Edom and Moab, travelling is dangerous – as you'd have found, Jacob, if I hadn't come to look for you. Travellers on their way to Edom need a strong arm to protect them from the bands of Moabites – and that's where *I* come in! 'Tis a good life, Jacob: the one God meant for me. So the shifting of the Blessing may have been His doing, not yours; and you're welcome to it.

JACOB You are very good to give it to me, Esau.

ESAU Why! before three days were over, Father knew it had gone to the right man. 'Jacob's been clever,' he said. 'He'll do well with it. You've got the hands, but he's got the head.' . . . One day I said – when I'd got tired of his praising you – 'There's one thing *I* can do that Jacob can't; I can bring you venison.' 'Oh, Jacob did that too,' says he. Mother was there listening. '*Jacob* didn't do it,' she said. '*I* did it.' 'And you ought to have been ashamed of yourself, Woman,' says Father – giving her all the blame for it, not you. Aye, Father forgave you the trick you played him; but he never forgave *her*. So she was always waiting for you to come back and give her the kind word. Aye! She'd a sad life of it. I tried to be kind to her; but I wasn't her Jacob. After the third messenger had returned, bringing no better hope for her, she never spoke your name again. It broke her heart, I think; for she died soon after.

JACOB It was Laban! It was Laban! Oh, God! Had I but known!

ESAU It's over and done, Jacob. Hold up your head! Be a man! Where are your wives. Am I not to see them?

JACOB They are here, Brother, waiting your pleasure.

(*He goes to the door and signals.*)

ESAU My pleasure? (*He gives a grunt of amusement.*) And how many children have you, Jacob?

JACOB By Leah, I have six sons. By Rachel none. By their two handmaids four.

ESAU Good Lord, Jacob! I've fifty and more. If you don't beget them quicker than that, I shall win the race and become a nation before ever you do!

JACOB (*nervous still*) Here they come, my lord.

ESAU Jacob, if you say 'my lord' again, I'll give you such a clout both sides of that clever head of yours that you'll be deaf for a fortnight.

(*Enter* RACHEL, LEAH, BILLAH *and* ZILPAH. *They advance bowing; after every three steps they pause and bow; each time, as they approach, the bow is deeper; finally they all kneel.*)

ESAU What! More fooling? Get up! Get up! Which here is Leah? And which is Rachel?

LEAH I am Leah, my Lord.

ESAU And I am Esau, Sister. So this is Rachel?

RACHEL Yes, Esau.

ESAU What have you covered your face for? Are you afraid to let me look at you?

RACHEL No, Esau. (*She unveils.*)

ESAU She is fair, Jacob. Among all my lot, I have none so fair . . . Don't be frightened, Jacob. Keep your Blessings. I've enough of my own.

(*From outside comes a sound of tumult, shouting, and the clash of arms. One of* ESAU'S *warriors comes running.*)

WARRIOR My lord! my lord! The Moabites are upon us.

(ESAU *gives a shout of joy*.)

ESAU Ah ha! That's good! Now – come and see me fight, Jacob! Come and see me fight!
> (ESAU *catches hold of* JACOB, *and runs out, dragging the unwilling* JACOB *after him*.)

SCENE 4

CHORUS ONE It is dark night; and once more Jacob stands alone by the brook Jabbok.

> (*Presently there will be moonlight: but now it is only dimly that we can see* JACOB.)

CHORUS ONE So – Esau has won his fight, and all is well.

CHORUS TWO Have you won yours, Jacob?

CHORUS ONE You are safe from Esau. Are you safe from – yourself?

CHORUS TWO Hark! Someone is coming.

CHORUS ONE And Jacob is not afraid.

> (*Enter* ASA.)

JACOB Asa? . . . Is all well?

ASA All is well, Master. The Moabites are beaten. Now we are safe for the rest of the way.

JACOB Aye, surely; safe for the rest of the way.

ASA Are you not coming back to the camp, Master?

JACOB Not yet . . . Good night, Asa.

ASA Good night, Master. (*He goes*.)

JACOB So, Thou hast fulfilled Thy Promise, and brought me back in safety to my own land. O Lord, who hast kept me alive this day, if Thou have still any charge against me – speak now!

CHORUS TWO Yes, Jacob?

JACOB That Voice again! My Accuser? Come back?

CHORUS TWO You did not expect me?

JACOB I thought that, last night, you had forgiven and blessed me – for good and all.

CHORUS TWO For good? Aye! You've had a good day, Jacob. You've been lucky – more lucky than you deserved. But – 'for good and *all*' – no; we shall never have done with each other, you and I. As long as we live we shall always be two, not one: Head and Heart never quite reconciled. But not so far apart now as we were twenty years ago – You are a strange man, Jacob; under your weakness lies strength. Today you did a brave thing; but you did it like a fawning slave – creeping and crawling to your own brother! You judged Esau by yourself: played your part to him as you thought he would have done to you, in like case. Esau is twice the man you are – the bigger, the stronger of body, the better of heart.

CHORUS ONE But you have this to the good, Jacob – you had faith in yourself, and in the life that God had given you. Twenty years ago, He came to you in a dream. It was your own dream that you dreamed; but had not God's Hand been on you, and His Will been in you, you would not have dreamed it. And the faith you had in your dream has brought you back to your own land – a wiser man than you were then, Jacob, when you stole your Father's Blessing.

JACOB Yes, Lord.

CHORUS ONE Why do you call me 'Lord'?

JACOB Because, surely, it is the Lord speaking to me now; and Him I hear – that I should have heard had I hearkened for Him in the days of my bondage.

CHORUS ONE You sound weary, Jacob.

JACOB Weary I am. But my Fear has gone from me: Esau and I are reconciled. The Blessing that I stole from him he has given me freely this day. It was waiting for that; and I might have had it twenty years ago, had I but known – had I but known!

CHORUS ONE Why are you weeping, Jacob?

JACOB Because my Mother's heart turned from me, when she sent for me, and I did not come. Nay! But that was Laban's doing – not mine.

CHORUS ONE Laban was good for you, Jacob.

JACOB Good? How from that deceiver has good ever come to *me*?

CHORUS ONE Because, from that deceiver, you have come to know yourself better . . . When you thank God for all He has done for you – thank Laban also . . . God be with you, Jacob. Lie down now, and rest. Good night, Jacob.

(JACOB *wraps his cloak about him, and lies down.*)

JACOB Good night, Lord.

CHORUS ONE Sleep well . . . and dream.

(*And as* JACOB *sleeps, again come the light and the sound, as they came at Bethel. Slowly the curtain closes.*)

CHORUS TWO This is the story of Jacob,
The man with the smooth face,
Who obeyed his Mother,
Cheated his Brother,
Deceived his Father,
Received a Blessing,
Dreamed a dream, the most famous in history,
Followed the dream and founded a race.

RAMOTH GILEAD

(Round about the entrance of the gate of Samaria a great crowd is gathered. In the centre of the gate upon a high dais are set two thrones. On the steps of the dais, AHAB, *King of Israel, stands waiting with his officers in attendance.* JEHOSHAPHAT, *King of Judah, enters preceded by his banner bearer, and followed by a train of Attendants.* AHAB *raises his hand in greeting; those about him do likewise. All the people shout.)*

PEOPLE Hail! Hail! Let the King live for ever!

*(*AHAB *descends from his throne and goes forward to meet* JEHOSHAPHAT.*)*

AHAB Let the King live! Welcome to Samaria, Brother. Thou comest to us in good time.

JEHOSHAPHAT Also with goodwill, Brother, at this our first coming to Samaria. We would that ere long we might also see thee in Jerusalem.

AHAB Wherefore not, Brother? For we be Kings of a kindred people, and being now at peace one with another, shall we not be friends also?

JEHOSHAPHAT Let the King say so, and it shall be.

AHAB Aye; and not friends only. Are not two stronger than one; and are not thy enemies my enemies? We be two kingdoms but one people. Israel was our father.

JEHOSHAPHAT Aye, surely; and Judah is now thy brother.

AHAB As I also am thine. Therefore have I sought thee; and this day would take counsel with thee of that which concerns both thee and me – thy people and my people.

JEHOSHAPHAT Let the King say on.

AHAB Hast thou considered Ramoth Gilead – Brother?

JEHOSHAPHAT How would'st thou have me consider it? Wherefore dost thou ask me this?

AHAB Because once it was Israel's – yours and mine; but now, the King of Syria holds it.

JEHOSHAPHAT The King of Syria is strong, Brother, in men and chariots.

AHAB He is not stronger than we should be, were we both together, of one mind, and of one purpose.

JEHOSHAPHAT To what end?

AHAB Ramoth Gilead lies near at hand. Syria holds it. But not at Ramoth Gilead lies the strength of the King of Syria, his horsemen, or his chariots. They be far away, we are near. Is not Ramoth Gilead ours, Brother? Why are we still? Who shall prevent that straightway we take it not out of the hand of the King of Syria?

JEHOSHAPHAT Was it for this that thou hast called me hither, to have counsel with thee?

AHAB Aye. What say you? . . . Now let the King speak!

JEHOSHAPHAT (*doubtfully*) 'Tis a large matter.

AHAB Even so, matter for two – not one. Therefore have I sent for thee.

JEHOSHAPHAT Surely, Brother, for thee or for me, too large a matter, maybe.

AHAB Aye, singly; but for both together, a sure reward – yea, a city to be saved which once was Israel's, and shall be Israel's again, if thou and I be of one mind in this matter. Shall not Judah and Israel henceforth be as one people? Do we not share the Land which was promised to our Fathers to be ours for ever? And shall the King of Syria take from us that which is ours?

(AHAB *leads* JEHOSHAPHAT *up to his throne.*)

Say, then – wilt thou go up with me to battle to Ramoth Gilead? . . . Let the King speak.

JEHOSHAPHAT The King speaks, Brother. I will go up with thee to battle: and Ramoth Gilead shall be ours. I am as thou art; my people as thy people, my horses as thy horses.

AHAB Well has the King spoken. So now let it be told in the ears of this people, which are now thy people.

JEHOSHAPHAT Stay awhile. Inquire first of the Lord, I pray thee; for without the Word of the Lord, we shall do nothing.

AHAB We *will* inquire . . . Call hither the prophets, and let them stand before us.

OFFICER Hear all! The King speaks. Call hither the prophets.

JEHOSHAPHAT How many of the prophets are there here among you?

AHAB Throughout the land, all told, about four hundred.

JEHOSHAPHAT Of what Gods are they the prophets?

AHAB Of *all* the Gods, Brother. Aye, even of the Gods of Syria we have *some* prophets here among us.

JEHOSHAPHAT How come *they* here?

AHAB To the house which we have built for their Gods, Brother. Build a house for a God, and he will come and dwell in it. Then will his prophets come also, and will prophesy good concerning you. Do this, Brother, and it shall be well with you.

JEHOSHAPHAT I worship but one God, Brother, even Jehovah, the God of Israel.

AHAB It is not enough, Brother. Had He kept us safe from all our enemies, and our cities from the hands of the King of Syria, I also would have worshipped Him only. But when there be so many Gods, and each one a God of battles, we must get help from all we can.

JEHOSHAPHAT My help comes from the Lord Jehovah. These be your prophets; but I would that there were here also among them a prophet of the Lord.

AHAB Surely there is safety in numbers. If, among so many, all speak with one voice, shall not that satisfy thee? Nay, wait, and hear. Yonder they come.

(*The* PROPHETS *enter, their processional order some-what broken by rivalry as to who shall be leader.* ZEDEKAIAH, *using his 'horns of iron' with effect, secures first place, and keeps it.*)

PROPHETS Hail, Hail, Hail, King of Israel! Hail, King of Judah!

AHAB Ye prophets of the Gods which dwell in this land, the mighty and the many – of Baal, Berith, Baalim, Peor, Perazim, Sephon, Zebub and of Ashtaroth, for each of whom we have built houses and set up altars and planted groves, making therein sacrifices daily, prophesy unto me now; and let the word that ye speak be not as the voice of men, but the voice of Gods. Shall I go up against Ramoth Gilead to battle, or shall I forbear?

PROPHETS Go up! go up! for the Lord shall deliver it into the hand of the King.

AHAB Is there any prophet here among you whose word is contrary? Says any prophet, Do not go up – forbear?

PROPHETS None, O King. There is not one.

AHAB Ye are all of one voice?

PROPHETS It is not our voice, great King, but the voice of the Gods that thou hearest. Go, prosper, and prevail; and lo, Syria shall fly before thee as a leaf before the wind, and fall as dust under the wheels of thy chariots.

AHAB Thou hast heard, Brother. Art thou not yet satisfied?

JEHOSHAPHAT I would be more satisfied were there here besides a prophet of the Lord Jehovah, that we might inquire of Him also. Is there none that can be found?

AHAB There is yet one man, Micaiah, the son of Imlah, by whom we may inquire; but I hate him, for he does not prophesy good concerning me, but evil.

JEHOSHAPHAT Oh, let not the King say so. For if he also speak with the same voice, then indeed shall we know surely

that the God of our Fathers is with us and not against us . . .
Let the King's word for this be spoken.

AHAB Captain of the Guard. Bring hither Micaiah, the
son of Imlah.

CAPTAIN He is in other keeping, my Lord, not mine.

AHAB Go, then, to Ammon the Governor of the city, and
bid him release into thy hand Micaiah from his prison
wherein he now lies. Quickly.

(*The* CAPTAIN *goes.*)

Now if the prophets have more to tell, let them speak. By
what way, and wherewith, shall the Gods give us victory?

ZEDEKAIAH Thus, O King. Behold, here be two horns of
iron, sharp and strong. Bind these to the yoke of thy chariot
when thou goest into battle. And thus saith the Lord: 'With
these shalt thou push the Syrians until thou have consumed
them.' Take them, O King! For they shall deliver into thy
hand the King of Syria.

AHAB Thou sayest well. Say ye so, all?

PROPHETS All, O King! Go up and prosper! Ramoth
Gilead shall be ours. The Lord shall deliver it into the
hand of the King.

AHAB See yonder; here comes Micaiah.

JEHOSHAPHAT In chains!

(*Enter* MICAIAH *chained, and accompanied by Guards.*)

AHAB Aye, surely; for he is my enemy.

JEHOSHAPHAT While he prophesies, shall he not be loosed
of his chains?

AHAB Wherefore?

JEHOSHAPHAT Should not a prophet be free to speak the
Word of the Lord, while he speaks it?

AHAB Let the King's will be done. Take his chains from
him, and let him stand free – till he have spoken . . . And
let it so be, Brother, that should he now speak evil concern-

ing me, and not good, as all the other prophets have spoken, then it will not be the word of the Lord, but the word of Micaiah that thou hearest.

(*Meanwhile* MICAIAH'S *chains are being taken from him.*)

CAPTAIN Hearken, Micaiah, here is counsel for thee. All the prophets have said well, and declared good for the King, with one voice. Let thy word be as their word, and thou wilt be free.

MICAIAH As the Lord liveth, what the Lord saith unto me, that will I speak. Or must I speak only that which the King wishes me to speak?

CAPTAIN Speak so, Micaiah, and be wise.

AHAB Bring him hither! Let him come near; but not too near, I like not the smell of him.

(MICAIAH *is brought forward, and halted at a safe distance.*)

Micaiah, shall we go up against Ramoth Gilead to battle, or shall we forbear?

MICAIAH (*ironically*) Go and prosper, for the Lord shall deliver it into the hand of the King. (*Applause.*)

AHAB So! This time, Micaiah, thy voice is as the rest. Thou hast said well.

JEHOSHAPHAT I think not so; for he spake it not by the Word of the Lord – not truly, Brother. Bid him speak again, as the Lord bids him speak.

AHAB Micaiah, how many times shall I adjure thee that thou tell me nothing but that which is true in the name of the Lord?

MICAIAH Have I not spoken as all these thy prophets have spoken? And spake they not also by the Word of the Lord?

JEHOSHAPHAT Is their lord *thy* Lord, Micaiah?

MICAIAH Nay, O King; for surely had he been, I had not come here this day in bonds, and a prisoner.

JEHOSHAPHAT Speak, then, I pray thee, the Word of the Lord only – thy Lord and my Lord, Micaiah.

MICAIAH Hear, then, ye Kings, the Word of the Lord. I saw all Israel scattered upon the hills, as sheep that have not a shepherd, and the Lord said: 'These have no master: let them return every man to his house in peace.'

(*Angry murmurs have begun among the crowd.*)

JEHOSHAPHAT In peace?

AHAB Did I not tell thee that he would prophesy no good concerning me, but evil?

JEHOSHAPHAT Peace, thou sayest? Not battle?

MICAIAH Hear *thou*, therefore, O Ahab, the Word of the Lord. I saw the Lord sitting on his throne, and all the host of Heaven standing by him on his right hand and on his left. And the Lord said: 'Who shall deceive and persuade Ahab that he may go up and fall at Ramoth Gilead?' And one said on this manner, and another said on that manner. And there came forth a spirit, and stood before the Lord, and said: 'I will persuade him.' And the Lord said unto him 'Wherewith?' And he said: 'I will go forth, and I will be a lying spirit in the mouth of all his prophets.' And he said: 'Thou shalt persuade him, and prevail also. Go forth and do so.' (*Murmurs from the crowd.*) Now therefore, behold, the Lord hath put a lying spirit in the mouth of all these thy prophets; and the Lord hath spoken evil concerning thee.

(*The murmurs grow louder.*)

ZEDEKAIAH Now, shalt thou hear the word of the Lord, by the mouth of Zedekaiah! (*He strikes him.*) Which way went the spirit of the Lord from me to speak unto thee?

MICAIAH Behold, thou shalt see in that day when thou shalt run into an inner chamber to hide thyself.

(ZEDEKAIAH'S *countenance changes to a look of fear.*)

AHAB We have heard enough. No more! The prophets have spoken; Ramoth Gilead shall be ours. Take Micaiah, and carry him back to Ammon, the Governor, and say: 'Thus saith the King. Put this fellow in the prison, and feed him with bread of affliction, and with water of affliction, until I come – in peace. (*Applause.*)

MICAIAH If thou return at all in peace, the Lord hath not spoken by me. Hearken, O people, every one of you!

(*With cries of rage, the* PROPHETS *and the people rush upon* MICAIAH. *The Guard carry him back to prison.*)

ALL Kill him! Kill him! Let him not live!

(AHAB'S ARMOUR-BEARER *brings* AHAB *his helmet, which he puts on in place of his crown.* JEHOSHAPHAT *does the same. They descend from their thrones. The people cheer.*)

CURTAIN

(*Descriptive music: the sounds of fighting and chariot-wheels, the trampling of horses, the shoutings of men, and the twanging of bow-strings. Suddenly a cry, and a sound of wailing, then of flight and pursuit. It dies away into the distance. Dead silence. The curtain rises, and to slow-measured tread, the body of King* AHAB *is borne across the stage, accompanied by a* CHORUS *of* SINGERS.)

LEADER The battle is over and done,
      The King has fallen in the fight.
CHORUS   (Ahab is slain! is slain!)

LEADER   Darkness lies over the face of the sun,
          Now for Israel comes night,
CHORUS   (And morning never again.)
LEADER   A man at a venture drew
          His bow, and the arrow sped.
CHORUS   (O prophets, ye spake in vain!)
LEADER   Through the press of battle it flew,
          It struck, and the King lies dead.
CHORUS   (Ahab, our King, is slain!)
LEADER   They bore him back to the city,
          His life ran out in a flood.
CHORUS   (His blood ran down like rain.)
LEADER   He died; the Gods had no pity.
          Dogs came, and lapped his blood.
CHORUS   (Ahab, our King, is slain!)
LEADER   This, the word thou did'st spurn,
          MICAIAH spake unto thee:
CHORUS   (He spake, but he spake in vain!)
LEADER   'If in peace thou ever return
          The Lord hath not spoken by me.'
CHORUS   (Ahab, our King, is slain!)

THE BURDEN OF NINEVEH

(JONAH *is busy packing for the journey which he has devised for himself. Today he is starting for Joppa where he intends to take ship to Tarshish. His friend* SHEMMEL, *a brother-prophet, small, elderly and of mean appearance, sits watching him. As he moves to and fro* SHEMMEL'S *eye follows him.*)

JONAH Don't look at me like that, Shemmel!

(SHEMMEL *wags his head sarcastically.*)

You've no right to look at me like that!

SHEMMEL I look at you as I like, Jonah . . . and at what I don't like.

JONAH And what's that?

SHEMMEL *You.*

JONAH And what is it about me that you don't like?

SHEMMEL Your being such a coward.

JONAH Why am I a coward?

SHEMMEL God knows *why*. I only know that you *are*.

JONAH Because I won't go to Nineveh? What does Nineveh matter to me, or to you? The people of Nineveh are not God's chosen people; and they have prophets of their own – plenty of them. Why should I go and prophesy to Nineveh?

SHEMMEL Prophecy is not a matter of choice, Jonah. If the Word of the Lord comes to you, you must speak it.

JONAH How do I know that His Word *has* come to me?

SHEMMEL You may not know *how* – but you know it *has* come, Jonah . . . Don't you?

(JONAH *does not answer. He goes on with his packing.*)

You are taking a lot of things with you . . . Going for long? Where *are* you going?

141

JONAH Why do you want to know?

SHEMMEL Isn't it natural? After we've been together all these years, like brothers – though I so much the elder. Are you afraid I shall tell God where you are running off to? No need; He'll find that out for Himself – if He wants to. Aye, He'll have His hook in your nose, and you back – a fish to his net, when you are least expecting it, Jonah.

JONAH What's that? Why did you call me – a fish?

SHEMMEL Because you are such a queer one, Jonah – to take to the water, where you don't belong, and have never been yet. Ah, you thought I didn't know . . . So you're going down to Joppa – and from there to Tarshish, eh? Yes! Tarshish is a long way, isn't it? – takes you further from Nineveh; so you think Tarshish is the safer place for you. But you'll hear the cry of Nineveh even in Tarshish, Jonah. For a man may leave his footprints behind – choosing hard ground so they shan't follow him; but what he knows goes with him, because knowledge is of God. And the cry of Nineveh has come to you, because the wickedness of the people of Nineveh has waxen great: and there is no prophet of the Lord in Nineveh to speak to them – the Word of the Lord . . . That is why the Lord's Word has come to *you*.

JONAH What good is the Word of the Lord to a people that will not hear? And why should they hear *me*? What good did it do to Ahab – or to Micaiah either, when he prophesied before Ahab, and all the other prophets prophesied falsely? He was brought out of prison for it, and sent back to prison for it. And when what he foretold came true, they said that it was *he* who had put a curse upon Ahab; and for that they slew him. He never came forth alive. Why should I go to Nineveh to be slain?

SHEMMEL The word of Micaiah was not slain. The Lord spake by his mouth; and the record of it stands to this day, and shall stand – for ever. It takes long for man to learn God's ways; but he *will* learn them some day.

JONAH I think God has a hard heart, Shemmel; for hard are His ways to them that serve Him. He doesn't treat His prophets as they should be treated. Who *wants* to be a prophet?

SHEMMEL When the Word of the Lord comes to you, it's no question of wanting, then. It takes hold of you – won't let you go. You become a different man . . . You are not your own any more. Five years ago, when you told Israel (so proud as they were then of having beaten Syria three times) that three times wasn't enough, and that Syria would beat them yet – they were so angry that some were wishing to kill you. But you were not afraid of them: you were the true prophet then. And you didn't get that from yourself.

JONAH No; I got that from our Lord and Father Elisha just before he died. 'Twas *his* prophecy, not mine. That's how I came by it – just took it from *him*. And being his, I was sure of it.

SHEMMEL So you weren't afraid?

JONAH And now you are wanting me to take this from *you*; but *you* are not *Elisha*. Why don't you go to Nineveh yourself?

SHEMMEL You know why, Jonah. I haven't the voice for it – nor the speech. And 'twas to *you* the Word came.

JONAH It came, but it went. For, had it come truly to me, I should not now be afraid.

SHEMMEL Ah? So you've a doubt? . . . But if it is only a doubt, why are you going away? Why not wait, and see – whether His Word will not come to you – more plainly, Jonah?

JONAH If it should come to me when I am further away, I should know better then than I know now, Shemmel.

SHEMMEL I think your doubt is not so great as your fear, Jonah. But if the Lord *has* called you, you'll never get away from His voice, however far you may go.

JONAH (*as he ties up his bundle*) I'm going now, Shemmel. You haven't been kind to me.

SHEMMEL Kind? Maybe I should have been more 'kind' as you call it, had I cared for you less . . . Here's a last word for you, Jonah. You can help being a coward; but you can't help being a prophet. Remember Balaam. He didn't want to do what the Lord told him; but he had to. And 'twas an ass taught him. This day my voice has been to you as the voice of Balaam's ass was to him. But you haven't heard me so well . . . The Lord be with you, Jonah, and bring you back a wiser man than you went. I think He will. Yes; I think He will.

(*He laughs softly.*)

JONAH What are you laughing for, now?

SHEMMEL You'll be very sea-sick, Jonah – very sea-sick. The Lord bless it to you!

(JONAH *gives an angry grunt, and, without a word of farewell, shoulders his pack, and goes.* SHEMMEL *listens to his departing footsteps, and sighs deeply.*)

Aye! aye! My poor Jonah! I'm sorry for thee.

SCENE 2

(*Three months have gone by.* SHEMMEL *the prophet sits at his workman's bench plying his trade. He is a metal-worker; and the quick beating of his hammer prevents his hearing approaching footsteps.* JONAH *enters, looking, as* SHEMMEL *foretold that he would, a wiser man than when he went.* SHEMMEL *is glad to see him: but is not going to show it, till he knows more of what has happened.*)

SHEMMEL Ah! So you've come back, Jonah.

JONAH (*speaking slowly*) Yes: I've come back.

SHEMMEL Is it from Tarshish that you've come?

JONAH No.

SHEMMEL Did you not go to Tarshish?

JONAH I did not *get* to Tarshish.

SHEMMEL But you said that the ship you were to sail on was going to Tarshish.

JONAH Yes; it *was* going to Tarshish.

SHEMMEL Didn't it get to Tarshish?

JONAH I don't know. I wasn't on it.

SHEMMEL But you *were* on it. They told me at Joppa that they'd seen you go.

JONAH What took you to Joppa, Shemmel?

SHEMMEL I went, hoping to get news of you, Jonah.

JONAH That was kind of you.

SHEMMEL No; it wasn't kind. I just couldn't rest. I wasn't easy in my mind about you; I was troubled, Jonah . . . I'd hoped to find that you hadn't gone.

JONAH And you found that I *had* gone.

SHEMMEL Yes. But now you say that you didn't go – or didn't get there. What stopped you? Was the ship wrecked?

JONAH No: at least, I hope not. It may have been; but I wasn't on it.

SHEMMEL Then where on earth were you?

JONAH On *earth* – nowhere. I was in my grave, Shemmel, swallowed up in it, alive. Aye, I should know now what it's like to be a fish. For three days I was in it.

SHEMMEL What? A fish?

JONAH No; the sea – *my grave*, if God hadn't saved me.

SHEMMEL Well, if He did that, He must have had a reason for it, and a good reason.

JONAH I doubt not that He had, Shemmel. I doubt not *now*.

SHEMMEL (*with understanding*) Ah! So God has been good to you?

JONAH He has, Shemmel.

SHEMMEL Surely, I'd the hope of it; for, when you came in, I saw the look of the prophet in your eyes: all the fear and the doubt were gone . . . Where are you for now, Jonah?

JONAH Nineveh.

SHEMMEL When? How soon?

JONAH I'm going now.

SHEMMEL Have you not time to tell me before you go what happened, Jonah?

JONAH Aye; you are the only one I would tell. You have the right, Shemmel. Listen then, and you shall hear. As they told you at Joppa, I took ship the next day after we parted, and sailed for Tarshish. And it was with me even as you said, Shemmel – I was very sea-sick; body and soul I could get no comfort; the life went out of me, and my spirit was brought low. And on the third day the Lord sent forth a strong wind, and there rose a great storm – so great that the ship was like to be broken. And on the second day, seeing that the storm did not abate, the men of the ship cast forth their bales to lighten it, and fear came on them, and they cried aloud, each man to his god that he would save them. And when they saw that I did not pray (for I feared to pray lest the Lord might hear me) they came and said to me: 'Why do *you* not pray to *your* God also, that he may save you and us together?' And I said: 'Except it be to do His Will no prayer can I make that my God will hear, or that He will answer.' Then they said: 'There is evil in our midst. Let us cast lots that we may know for what cause this evil is come upon us.' So they cast lots, and the lot fell on me.

SHEMMEL (*speaking softly*) Aye, surely, surely. 'Twas the Lord spoke then.

JONAH And they said to me: 'Who art thou? and what hast

thou done to bring destruction upon us for that of which we are guiltless?' And I said: 'I am a Hebrew, and one also that is a prophet. And I have fled from the presence of the Lord because I would not hear His voice to do His Will.' Then were they full of fear; and they said: 'What shall we do to thee that His wrath may be turned from us?' Then saw I the way straight before me, and the Lord's will made plain; for I said to myself – 'Now surely, if I am to perish, then has the Lord *not* called me; but if He save me, then He *has* called me to go and prophesy to Nineveh'. So I said: 'Take me, and cast me forth into the sea; so shall ye be rid of the evil which I have brought on you.' But they would not, being afraid, having heard me say that I was a prophet. So they rowed on; but the rowing was hard, for the sea beat tempestuously, and the wind was against them. And when the ship seemed about to sink, I said again: 'Take me, and cast me forth, and save yourselves from the wrath of God; for against you He has nothing.' So they took, and made ready to cast me forth into the sea. But because they wished not my death, they made a crossbeam of wood, and bound me to it, and therewith they cast me from the ship; and it passed on, and I saw it no more. And the raging of the sea was round me, and the roaring of its waves went over me. But the beam bore me up through the midst of it; and the Hand of the Lord held me so that I did not die. Three days it bore me; three days I was without food or water, yet my life stayed in me, and my strength failed not. The waters compassed me about even to my soul; the depth closed me round about, its weeds were wrapped about my head; the roots of the mountains lay under me, the bars of the earth were drawn against me. I saw no land – yet was my life saved to me. Then I prayed, and said: 'This salvation is of the Lord. Speak, Lord, for thy servant heareth.' And out of the belly of Hell He heard my prayer; and on the third day the storm ceased and the sea grew calm, and its waters drew away from under me, so that my feet touched land; and I lived and gave thanks to the Lord, who is my strength and my salvation – to do His Will.

SHEMMEL Ah! now surely it is the voice of the prophet I hear; for you don't speak like that when it's only yourself, Jonah.

JONAH I speak only the truth, Shemmel.

SHEMMEL Aye; but 'tis the way you speak it! God has given you a gift that He has not given to me. There be two kinds of prophets – both alike called of God, but their service is different. Some He has called to be preachers, others to be counsellors. I am no preacher; I can only give counsel.

JONAH You gave good counsel to me, Shemmel, when I would not hear you. You were right then, and I was wrong. Who knows, but that some day, I may need your counsel again, Shemmel – when the need of the preacher is over. Well, be that as maybe! 'Tis time now that I was going . . . Wish me well, Shemmel.

SHEMMEL I'm coming with you, Jonah.

JONAH Nay, but why should *you* come? Are *you* called of the Lord to give counsel to Nineveh?

SHEMMEL No; yet has He put it in my heart that I should go with you. For this is a great and a hard thing that He has given you to do – to speak to a people that know not Him, and pronounce His judgment upon them . . . You are not afraid, Jonah?

JONAH No, I am not afraid.

(SHEMMEL *has laid down his work, and is now making preparation to go.*)

SHEMMEL God grant that – after they have heard you – the fear may be on *them* – so that – if it be His Will – they may repent of their wickedness.

JONAH They should have repented before, Shemmel.

SHEMMEL (*after a pause*) Do you know what you are going to say, Jonah?

JONAH Nay, I know not. But whatsoever the Lord bids me speak – that shall I speak. The people of Nineveh shall hear the Word of the Lord – whether it be of life or of death.

SHEMMEL Life or death; aye, surely – life or death.

JONAH Come then, Shemmel; make haste and let us go.

(SHEMMEL *is ready; they go out together.*)

SCENE 3

(JONAH *has come to Nineveh. He stands upon a wall in the centre of the city, and below him is a great crowd, moving and murmuring tempestuously; at his feet sits* SHEMMEL. *Through the tumult of voices raised against him he utters his word of prophecy.*)

JONAH And this is the Word of the Lord which He hath sent me to speak in the ears of this people. Now is His judgment upon you: the days of Nineveh are numbered, and her glory is ended.

(*The tumult increases: his voice is drowned by cries of rage. 'Throw him down! Slay him! Let him not live! Stone him! Stone him!' Missiles are thrown;* SHEMMEL, *on whom the fire of prophecy has not descended, does his best to dodge them; but* JONAH *is full of it, and remains unmoved: even when he is hit he seems unaware of it.*)

Aye! slay me! slay me, if you will; but first hear me! For this is not *my* word that I speak unto you, nor is it I that have judged you for the evil that ye have done; or measured the weight of your transgressions. (*Loud uproar.*) But He, the most High, who dwelleth above the Heavens, and holdeth the earth in the hollow of His hand, in whose eyes ye are but as grass, and your Nation but a little thing, He it is who cometh to you in judgment, and whose Word I declare unto you. (*Loud murmurs.*) Nay, who am I that ye should take heed of me, or hearken unto my word? For I come of a small Nation, but Nineveh is a great one, high and mighty, and full of riches, and feared by the Nations which are round about her. And her rule reacheth from between the two rivers even to the sea. Yet saith the Lord: her life is but a breath, and her praise a sound that shall be heard no more; because she hath done wickedly, and hath not put away evil from the midst of her. (*Prolonged uproar.*) Nay, hearken, open your deaf ears, ye men of Nineveh; and if ye believe me not after I have spoken, I will come down to you to my death. Yea, I will give myself up into your hands to be slain. But hear ye first the Word which the Lord hath given me to speak, that ye may know and believe after I am dead, that the Word which I spake unto you *was* true. (*The uproar diminishes.*)

SHEMMEL (*as the voices begin to die down*) Look, Jonah, look! Now are they willing to hear you. The power of the Lord is upon them.

JONAH When the Word first came to me, I was greatly afraid, and my heart died within me. And because I feared to do His Will and to speak His Word, I fled from the presence of the Lord, so that I might not hear His voice speaking to me. And I went forth from my own land and the people among whom I dwelt, and I took ship to a country that was afar off, even to the ends of the earth, so that there He might not find me to make me obey His Word . . . But the anger of the Lord came after me, and the power of His wrath fell upon me; for He sent out a great wind into the sea; and the wind and the sea became a tempest, and smote upon the ship wherein I lay, so that it began to sink. Then the Lord made known His Will to those that were in the ship; and they took me, and cast me forth into the deep. And there was none that could save me, but God only.

SHEMMEL See! They are hearing you now, Jonah. They are *wanting* to hear.

JONAH Hearken now, O people of Nineveh, how the Lord spared my life, and did not destroy me in His wrath, but brought me back alive to do His Will, and to speak unto Nineveh of that which shall be done to her, when the hour of her end cometh. For lo, the Lord prepared a great Fish; out of the deep He called it, and it came. And the Fish opened its mouth, and swallowed me. (*Exclamations of wonder from the crowd.*) And I was in the belly of the Fish three days and three nights, I went down to the bottom of the sea, to the roots of the mountains, where the foundations of the world are laid; the deep waters were over me, the seas covered me; yet I died not. (*A murmur of wonder rises from the crowd.*)

SHEMMEL That's done it, Jonah, that's done it!

JONAH Now therefore hear, O people of Nineveh, the Word of the Lord, spoken by Jonah the prophet! Because of her wickedness that is come up before me, in forty days Nineveh shall be overthrown; her towers shall fall, her walls shall be broken; she shall become a prey to the spoiler, her king and her people shall perish together. Because she repented not of her wickedness, and would not put away the evil that was in the midst of her, therefore shall Nineveh become a name, and her place shall know her no more. I the Lord have spoken it.

(*As* JONAH *ceases to speak, there rises from the crowd below a prolonged cry of fear and lamentation: it goes on, rising and falling; the words are indistinguishable. Presently there comes a confused sound as of the movement of a great multitude; and the mingled sound of feet and voices dies slowly away.*)

JONAH Well? What d'you think of that, Shemmel? Did I speak the Word of the Lord as it should be spoken?

SHEMMEL You did, Jonah. Aye, you were wonderful . . . but – have you no grief?

JONAH Why should I have grief – speaking the word of the Lord?

SHEMMEL The doom of a city; the doom of a city and its people! Surely when the Lord's anger has turned Him from mercy, terrible it is to be a prophet.

JONAH Aye, terrible. For was not my life in danger, and thine also? But now we can go forth in safety, and no man shall harm us.

SHEMMEL Where are they going, Jonah?

JONAH To their temples, to pray – that their gods may save them. But if the Lord hath spoken by *me*, *He* shall not hear them.

SHEMMEL What is that sound I hear?

JONAH Nineveh – weeping. Come, Shemmel.

SCENE 4

(JONAH *has left the city, and on the east side of it, beyond the river, has made for himself a booth under the shade of a gourd-palm, and there has remained in solitude, while* SHEMMEL *goes to and fro daily, bringing food and news from the city. Nothing has yet happened that* JONAH *expected to happen; but two of the forty days are still to run; so there is yet time (though it is growing short) for the fulfilment of the prophecy. But the strain of waiting is telling upon* JONAH; *he is moody, and anxious, though he does not own it; and there are times when* SHEMMEL *finds him difficult. The heat of the day is over, night is begin-*

ning to fall, JONAH *stands looking at the towers of Nineveh which are still standing:* SHEMMEL *sits watching him.*

SHEMMEL Why are we still here, Jonah?

JONAH Would you have us go before I have seen fulfilment of the Lord's Word which He spake by me against Nineveh?

SHEMMEL He will do that in His own time and His own way, Jonah. He does not need your help.

JONAH If Nineveh be not destroyed within forty days, then was I a false prophet.

SHEMMEL Nay, did you not speak as the Lord bade you speak?

JONAH When I spoke, I had no doubt of it.

SHEMMEL And did you say anything that He did not *tell* you to say?

JONAH Why do you ask that, Shemmel?

SHEMMEL What made you say 'forty days'?

JONAH I spoke as the Word came to me.

SHEMMEL Maybe. But when the Lord says 'days', sometimes it has meant years – even thousands of years; for has not the Psalmist said 'A thousand years in Thy sight are but as yesterday'? So may not those forty days have meant years, Jonah?

JONAH Had I said 'forty years', Shemmel, how much would they have believed – or cared? Would it have put fear in their hearts, as it has done? Would they have repented in sackcloth and ashes as you tell me they are now doing – had I only said 'in forty years'?

SHEMMEL Nay, then, I think that you were right, Jonah. If that word has brought repentance, surely it was the Lord's.

JONAH Repentance! Aye! Let them repent; but their repentance comes too late, if the word that I spake *was true.* (*A sudden fear seizes him.*) If not – what is truth?

SHEMMEL Surely truth is that which brings men nearer to God – that only is truth as we can know it . . . You said another thing, Jonah, which, though it had truth in it, was – as one *might* say – not true.

JONAH What was that?

SHEMMEL About the great Fish which swallowed you, and held you in his belly three days and three nights.

JONAH Yes. And did you not see, Shemmel, how it was that, and that only, which made them believe I was truly a prophet of the Lord? When I spake to them but truth, they were angry and would not hear me. But when I told them of a great marvel, such as had never been heard of before – nor ever will be again – then they hearkened, then they believed, then they were afraid. 'Twas that which did it, Shemmel; the Fish that swallowed me, swallowed them also.

SHEMMEL Yes, Jonah; you made a great story of it. It was wonderful. But why had you not told me the same?

JONAH You? Because you believed in God, Shemmel, and know His ways. There was no need to tell you that story. But a people which know not God, being without understanding, must seek always for signs and wonders, and without them they will not believe. And though with God, I doubt not, all things *are* possible, yet He does not do all that we say He does. Is it not strange, Shemmel, that to make men believe the truth, we prophets have to tell lies?

SHEMMEL Not lies, Jonah; there are ways and ways. You do not tell the truth to a child as you do to a wise man; for he would not understand it. Even so has God spoken in parables by the prophets of old. But the parables were true parables. So may it not also be, Jonah, that God has spoken by you in parables? For now has a great thing happened: Nineveh has repented of her wickedness.

JONAH Repented, you say? Only because now Nineveh is afraid. What worth is there in that? And should God's judgment fall not upon her, she would but return again after a while to her wickedness.

SHEMMEL Even so has Israel done – aye, many times, Jonah. Yet has God pardoned her.

JONAH Because Israel is God's chosen people. He has none other.

SHEMMEL Why, then, did He send thee to Nineveh?

JONAH (*astonished*) Dost thou think that He will *save* Nineveh?

SHEMMEL I know not, Jonah. But the forty days are nearly ended. How, in two days from now, think you, shall the Lord's Word be brought to pass – if truly it *be* His Word?

JONAH Had I as little faith as that, Shemmel, I should be no prophet. Has not the Lord power to send, in one day, flood and fire and earthquake, and destroy Nineveh utterly?

SHEMMEL Aye; by signs and wonders, I doubt not He can – if it be His Will.

JONAH Also is not the King of Babylon with his army even now coming against her?

SHEMMEL No, no, Jonah. Did you not know? When Nineveh repented, then also fear came on her lest her warfare and the strength whereof she boasted might fail and bring on her the destruction that you foretold. So she sent and made peace with the King of Babylon on the terms that he required of her; and he with his army has now returned to his own land. And that also, Jonah, is because of the Word of the Lord which you spake unto them. It has brought peace. Is not that a good thing? Nay, is it nothing, Jonah?

JONAH (*much disturbed*) It is worse than nothing! If the Lord's Word, spoken by me, be not fulfilled against Nineveh then am I no prophet. Surely this is why I fled from before the face of the Lord, because I feared that He would not keep His Word. And of what I did, and why, will the truth never be told, or my name ever remembered, save as that false prophet, who spoke as God bade him speak; but whose word did not come true?

SHEMMEL But yet brought wonder to pass. Nay, have no fear, Jonah; the story of you and the whale men will always remember.

JONAH (*angrily*) I did not *say* it was a whale.

SHEMMEL No; but they will.

JONAH Why?

SHEMMEL Because a whale is the only thing they know big enough.

JONAH Big enough for what?

SHEMMEL For them to swallow, Jonah, to make what you said to be true.

JONAH Aye! There's the bitterness of it! The lie that I had to tell – that God bade me tell – so that the truth might be believed!

SHEMMEL It was no lie, Jonah. The great Fish that swallowed *you* was the power of God and His righteousness, and His great mercy and loving-kindness to a people that knew not Him, and a Nation that would not come unto Him. Aye, maybe, as you say, Nineveh will return to her sins, and again do wickedly. And a day will come, and Nineveh will perish from the face of the earth and be only a name. But the story of Nineveh will be told for ever – so that God's mercy to sinners may be known among men.

JONAH You speak, Shemmel, as though prophecy were made to be broken. And you have made me also to doubt whether God *will* be true to His Word. But if, when the days are ended, Nineveh be not overthrown, then I beseech the Lord to take my life from me – for it is better for me to die than to live. Go; leave me, Shemmel! and come not back till I call thee; for my soul is full of bitterness. And there is none that can comfort me if God have laid on me this reproach, making my word vain.

SCENE 5

(The same as Scene 4; but the booth is no longer there; the gourd-palm lies withered and brokem.)

SHEMMEL Jonah, I have come back to thee.

JONAH Why? I had not called you.

SHEMMEL It is now two days, Jonah.

JONAH What of it? Save only that Nineveh still stands, because God has mocked at me in making me speak His Word.

SHEMMEL Jonah, if it was the Lord's will to spare Nineveh, dost thou well to be angry?

JONAH I do well to be angry.

SHEMMEL I am troubled for thee, Jonah.

JONAH My trouble is my own, Shemmel, you cannot share it — or mend it. For the God I served has set His face against me, to show me that He holds me as nought. So be it . . . let that which is nought – die. Wherefore should it cumber the ground?

SHEMMEL Surely, Jonah, some sickness is upon you. Why are you lying here without shelter?

JONAH Because the shelter that I made for myself has been taken from me. Aye! The God who spared Nineveh spared not to slay the gourd which sheltered me.

SHEMMEL What do you mean, Jonah? What happened?

JONAH On the day, and at the hour, when Nineveh should have perished, there came a blight upon the gourd, so that all its leaves withered; and after the blight came a strong wind, and tore it, and broke it – the only thing in the land that had been kind to me – making it useless! Then came the sun and smote me, and spake to me the Word of the Lord, 'Behold, thou art nothing!' That is what has come to me from God, after all that I did for Him.

SHEMMEL Jonah, Jonah, let me speak to thee.

JONAH I have heard enough of thy speaking, Shemmel. Where is the mercy of God that you are so loud about? Was there mercy in that which He did, either for the gourd – or for *me*? He keeps His mercy for Nineveh!

SHEMMEL Jonah – I have counsel for thee.

JONAH I have counsel enough of myself. I need no other.

SHEMMEL The more, therefore, it waits for thee. For I think this counsel which I have for thee is of God. Be patient, therefore, and hear me.

JONAH (*after a pause*) Speak, then . . . Aye, speak.

SHEMMEL Jonah, God is good, and full of wisdom; and when we understand Him not, the fault is not His but ours, because we are less good than He, and less wise. Yet does He speak to us according to our understanding. So, in this that He has done to the gourd, has not God spoken to thee in a parable? All things are of God. He sends forth the strong wind, and makes the sun to shine, and the gourd to grow. But these, that are His creatures, know not whether what they do is good or evil; for they know not of themselves what they are. But God knows. So also is man His creature – knowing little. Now because the gourd had given you comfort and shelter, therefore in your eyes it seemed good, and the wind and the sun evil. And you are angry because God has not spared the gourd but has spared Nineveh; and it had pleased you better had He destroyed Nineveh, and saved the gourd . . . Listen, Jonah. When the Lord first called you, you turned away and would not hear; because it was not in your heart to do His Will. And He was angry with you; but He forgave you. And now, Jonah, it is the other way about; you are angry because it is not in the Lord's heart to do *your* will. You wish Nineveh to be destroyed; He wishes to save it.

JONAH Why, then, did He send me to preach against Nineveh?

SHEMMEL Your preaching has done a great thing, Jonah.

Nineveh has repented . . . I am no preacher, only a counsellor. But hear now from me the Word of the Lord, which I speak unto thee: 'Thou hast had pity on the gourd, for which thou hast not laboured, neither madest it grow, which came up in a night, and perished in a night. And should not I spare Nineveh, that great city, wherein are more than six-score thousand persons that cannot discern between their right hand and their left; and also much cattle?' (*There is a long pause.*)

JONAH You are a greater prophet than I, Shemmel, for in you is more understanding of God, and of His ways.

SHEMMEL I am no prophet, Jonah; only a reader.

JONAH A reader?

SHEMMEL Of men's hearts, Jonah. And yours has been one of them. Maybe, some day, also a writer. Then will this story of Jonah be written for man's learning. But *my* name will not be known, nor by any shall I be remembered. What matter?

SAMUEL THE KINGMAKER

PREFACE

BLAKE'S discovery of the raw material for prophetic utterance holds good for true prophets and false prophets alike; they all speak for the God that is in them. The true prophet, true to Type, speaks for the God of Truth; the false prophet, equally true to type, speaks for the God of lies – his own God: in other words, for himself. For ever since the world began man has been a consistent maker of Gods – in his own image.

And so, because Samuel made God in his own image, his indignation against the Children of Israel for asking for a King, and later against Saul for his determination to be a King and not a mere puppet, was very genuine. But that did not make him a true prophet of the Lord; Samuel was only true to himself.

Yet he began well; and even when he did less well, he played a very important part in the history of Israel, for it was his vengeful dividing of Israel against Saul which, seven years after Saul's death, gave first to David and then Solomon the kingship of a united people; and to that people two Kings of exceptional quality. So, if the result justified the means, Samuel was justified; and according to the Bible narrative all that he did was done in obedience to the Word of the Lord.

Are those who call themselves Christians bound to believe it? Does not the moral obligation lie very much in the other direction?

The writers of the historical books of the Old Testament cannot be regarded as impartial historians. They had an axe to grind, and they ground it very industriously; and probably, for the most part, in all good faith that everything they set on record was true. For they were writing the story of 'the Chosen People' of a very tribal Deity, whose care was for them only; for other nations he Had no bowels of compassion, and their extermination was, for the Children of Israel, not merely an approved policy, it was a divine command.

It was only natural, therefore, in an age when miracle and material intervention were regarded without question as God's chosen means for making His ways known unto men, and His saving health unto one nation in particular, that signs and wonders should be the running accompaniment of that nation's history. A God who did not intervene materially would hardly have been a God worth having; even belief in him would have been difficult. And so, when history came to be written, the wonders had not to be invented by the historians; sacred tradition abundantly supplied the material: any event unexpected or catastrophical in character had already received an interventional interpretation; and the greater the wonder (God's power being thereby more fully manifested) the more likely it was to be true.

Under such circumstances one could hardly expect history to be written otherwise. Is there, indeed, any history of an ancient people which is not plentifully larded with miracle? Is there, then, any reason why we should regard the miraculous accretions of Hebraic history as having more truth in them than these others?

But here is the extraordinary fact, that, even today, when scholarship has proved beyond doubt the inaccuracy of certain passages in Old Testament history, its miraculous element is still regarded by so many as having a special sanctity; to doubt the accuracy of its numerals, its chronology or its natural history is permissible – to doubt the truth of its miracles is impious. That feature which, in the ancient history of all other nations we sensibly discard as unworthy of credence, is the very one which – when we come to Bible history – people of misguided piety still try to impose on us.

Take, for instance, that most stupendous of all Old Testament miracles – Joshua's command to the sun and the moon to stand still while he finished his defeat of the Amorites; because that quotation from a war-poem is followed up by the affirmation, 'And there was no day like that before it or after it, that the Lord hearkened unto the voice of a man', for many, who are otherwise intelligent, it becomes a matter of faith – the story has got to be believed; and those who refuse to believe it are charged with lack of reverence for the Word of God.

Yet surely the real lack of reverence lies in ascribing such fussy intervention to small ends to the sort of God whom Christians can now worship. We have only to look at the details of that story to see how superfluous was the miracle – an instance of the incurable megalomania with which Hebrew historians enlarged their victories in battle to incredible proportions, by adding to them incredible features. For before ever Joshua gave command to the sun, the Amorites were already utterly smitten – by the Israelites, 'with great slaughter', in the first place, and then with greater slaughter by the Lord himself, by means of a lesser miracle – a storm of hailstones; 'and there were more which died of the hailstones than those whom the children of Israel slew with the sword'. It is after that utter discomfiture of the enemy, that the solar system has to be disturbed to give it a finer finish; actually, of course, it was not the sun which had to stop, but the rotation of the earth: a terrestrial detail of which the writer of the story was quite unaware.

Now how does all this concern the critical commentary on the life and character of 'Samuel the Kingmaker', which here follows? It concerns it for two reasons: Samuel was the reputed author of the Book of Joshua and the Book of Judges – of those portions of them, at least, which were not the product of a later generation; for, like the Book of

Samuel and some of the other historical Books of the Old Testament, they are now known to be compilations from various sources of different dates, in which certain lost Books are referred to, and sometimes quoted: the 'Book of the Wars of Jehovah' (Numbers XXI, 14.) is one; the Book of Jasher, which vouched for Joshua's miracle of the sun, is another. The title of the former Book, indicates well enough what was already known – that Jehovah was indeed a God of Battles, that he won them mainly by miracle, and that there were very few battles in which he did not intervene against the enemies of Israel, either by 'vexing them' in unspecified ways, or thundering at them out of Heaven, or sending upon them darkness or earthquake; and when these larger measures of intervention were not employed he still required preliminary sacrifice, fixed the propitious date, and laid down the conditions for the saving or the destruction of the spoil, and the extermination of whole populations, men, women and children. For these smaller interventions the mouth of a prophet speaking 'the word of the Lord' was the approved medium; and the prophet's word for it, that it was the Word of the Lord, was accepted without question. And that is where Samuel comes in; and in the play which I have written upon that theme, Samuel's credentials are, both for moral and historical reasons, seriously questioned: was he really speaking 'the Word of the Lord', or only the word of Samuel? And if one has good reasons for more than doubting the truth of Joshua's miracle of the sun, may one not have equally good reasons for doubting whether Samuel's 'Word of the Lord' came from the source to which he ascribed it, and whether he was not in fact playing for his own hand, and attributing to a jealous God his own jealousy at being required to give place to another in the ruling of Israel?

Surely for a true reading of Old Testament history, one must be just as free to question the authenticity of its miracles, or the credentials claimed by its prophets, as one is free to question the correctness of its numerals and its chronology.

And that is my second concern. The chronology of that part of the Book of Samuel where it deals with the relations of Saul and Samuel, and later of Saul and David, is not only puzzling, it is sometimes contradictory; the reason being that it is composed of extracts drawn from different sources, and these extracts (not always arranged in proper sequence) give the story, with variations in time and circumstance, which are difficult if not impossible to reconcile. One instance is the double account, under very different circumstances, of the spirit of prophecy coming upon Saul, from which arose the saying 'Is Saul also among the prophets?' In the earlier version Saul, fresh from his anointing as King, meets a company of the prophets, and fulfilling the word of Samuel is, by the power of the Spirit, 'turned into another man', and prophesies with them. In the later version it comes rather as an affliction, falling like a contagious disease not only upon Saul, but upon the three sets of messengers who had preceded him with orders to drag David away from the protection of Samuel. It is a similar story (of a wonder three times repeated) to that of the three companies of fifty with their captains sent by Ahaziah (2 Kings I, 1-9) to capture Elijah on Mount Horeb; and each company in turn is gobbled up by fire, until, of his own free will, the prophet goes to the king. Those who are able to believe that story will have no difficulty in believing the other, and may even prefer it to the earlier and simpler one, in which the spirit of prophecy fell upon Saul not derisively (as in this case) but as a confirmation of his kingship.

An instance, where it is still more impossible to accept both accounts as true, is the story of David's two comings to Saul. Of the first (1 Samuel XVI, 17-18) we are told that David was sent for by Saul, as a skilful player upon the harp, to cure him of the evil spirit from the Lord which troubled him; and according to this account Saul knew who David's father was, had sent messengers to him, and had received presents from him; after which David became Saul's musician and armour-bearer, and 'Saul loved him greatly'. But on the second occasion where David comes to Saul as the would-be giant-killer, Saul does not know him, or who his father is, or anything about him; and David says nothing to remind him. In the earlier account, though still a keeper of sheep, David is described as 'a mighty valiant man, a man of war, and prudent in speech'; in the second he is still 'a stripling' and is treated by his brother as a naughty boy for leaving his father's sheep in order to see something of the war; all of which makes nonsense of the suggested explanation by certain commentators that 'the stripling' had so outgrown the youthful looks of 'the mighty valiant man, the man of war', that Saul failed to recognize him. The two accounts are utterly inconsistent; and the chronicler (in piecing his material together) has let them stand side by side, apparently without perceiving how the one contradicts the other.

I give this instance of the unreliability of the text as it has come down to us, because, though it has no immediate application to Samuel himself, it serves to show quite definitely that the Book which is named after him is not a consecutive narrative – that its events do not always fall in their right order, and are sometimes told twice over with variations which are impossible to reconcile. And lest it should be thought that I claim to have made these discoveries all by myself, let me add, in scriptural phrase, 'are they not written in the Book of the *Encyclopaedia Britannica*' – and elsewhere, by Biblical scholars whose right to speak with authority only the Fundamentalists will deny.

But though modern scholarship has freed those who have a mind to be freed from the superstition of the verbal inspiration of Scripture, I would remind my readers that a play-writer does not claim to be a historian. He takes an historical character, or a series of historical events, and out of the material with which history or legend provides him, endeavours to construct a dramatic figure which shall be consistent throughout. He may take an unduly favourable, or unfavourable view of the man and of his motives; but whatever liberty he takes with history, his main duty as a dramatist is to make his chosen character consistent; it is only of secondary importance that his reading should have behind it the support of history.

Nevertheless I do wish my reading of the character of Samuel to have the backing of probability, even though many of the incidents – including the frequent appearance of the Witch of Endor – are my own invention. And that probability I cannot find in a narrative which is so largely devoted to the whitewashing of Samuel under cover of the repeated statement that 'the word of the Lord came to him', whenever Samuel was bent upon having things his own way. My play is written to demonstrate that on those occasions Samuel's God was Samuel himself. And in order to run Samuel down to earth (where he properly belongs), I have made the Witch of Endor my stalking-horse.

Samuel was the first, and only character in Old Testament history, who combined in his own person the functions of prophet, priest, judge and ruler of Israel. How he came by them all, whether, as the chosen of the people, or 'by the word of the Lord', we are not told; but as no other is mentioned as holding authority after Eli, it seems probable that, before Eli's death, his reputation was already made, so that he stept naturally into Eli's shoes, and presently, as the accepted prophet of the Lord, became Judge also.

As a prophet he began early and started well. In the Bible story it was an audible Voice which spoke to him, denouncing the misconduct of Eli's sons, and Eli's failure to restrain them. It was the only time when we are told that the Voice was audible, though afterwards it spoke to him with great frequency; and I make no apology for applying Blake's interpretation of prophecy to that incident, when I make Samuel say to his son Abiah, 'I heard no voice – only in my own heart 'twas the Lord speaking; and *my* wrath against Eli and his sons was *His* wrath'. For that surely is how and why the prophets have spoken all down the ages; and are we to be headed off from that wholesome truth by a convention of Old Testament phraseology?

The Bible narrative makes it somewhat doubtful whether Samuel did in fact exercise effective judgeship over all Israel; for at that time the Tribes were very loosely connected, and the circuit within which we are told that Samuel judged Israel was within only a few miles of his own home at Ramah; and even when coming from so short a distance as Gibeah of Benjamin in search for his father's asses, Saul was quite unaware that Samuel was the prophet who lived there.

Another matter in doubt is whether Samuel gave the Israelites as full a deliverance from the surrounding nations as he claimed to have done; for though we are told that 'the Philistines were subdued, and came no more into the coasts of Israel all the days of Samuel', we find that one of their causes for national discontent, when Israel came asking for a King to rid them of their enemies, was that garrisons of Philistines had made strongholds of some of their cities, and to drive out these garrisons was one of the first things which Saul had to do. At any rate Samuel's policy had been a policy of live-and-let-live; he had made peace with the Amorites, and in no case had he set himself the task of exterminating the enemy to the last man, woman, and child, which he imposed upon Saul as a divine command when Saul made war upon Amalek.

The Book of Samuel gives two different versions of the

Israelites' request for a King to rule over them. In the one (1 Samuel VIII, 1-9) the main reason was not Samuel's failure to withstand the inroads of the Philistines and the Ammonites, but the misgovernment of his two sons, whom, in his old age, he had appointed to be judges, and whose misdoings he did not restrain. It was a similar charge to that which Samuel, 'speaking the word of the Lord', had made against Eli. But now it is no longer against the neglectful ruler that the wrath of the Lord is to be kindled, but against those who make complaint. And so 'because the thing displeased Samuel', the God of Samuel begins speaking the word of Samuel; and in the person of Samuel it is the Lord Himself whom they have rejected that He should not reign over them.

In the other version (1 Samuel XII, 1-13), Samuel, in his valedictory address, states quite definitely that it was Saul's defeat of Nahash the Ammonite, which caused the Children of Israel to ask for a King, and that Saul was the people's choice because of it. And in that version so little is the misgovernment of Samuel's sons the cause of discontent, that he actually names them among the benefits which his long and blameless judgeship has conferred upon Israel.

But though the reasons differ, the condemnation remains the same; and in asking for a King in the place of Judges the people have done very wickedly. And yet we find in the Book of Deuteronomy (Deut. XVII, 14-15) that the substitution of Kings for Judges, when the Children of Israel had entered into possession of the land, was not only provided for, it was approved. Possibly Samuel had not the advantage of having read the Book of Deuteronomy, because it was not compiled, in its present form, till after his day; but for those who have, the sanction conferred on Kingship in Deuteronomy, entirely disposes of Samuel's condemnation of it. His objection was merely personal.

The two versions I have quoted make it difficult to decide

how Samuel's anointing of Saul to be King came about. The one thing that is quite certain, if we accept the second version, is that Saul was not unknown to Samuel, he was already the people's choice; and Samuel's problem was to make the people's choice seem secondary, and to impress upon Saul that the decision of the matter rested not with the people, but with the Lord Himself by the mouth of his prophet. Samuel's only hope, of retaining the power which he so grudged to give up was to make Saul recognize that his authority was only a delegated authority, and that all the initiative of kingship was to remain with Samuel.

And so, in the generally accepted story, 'the Word of the Lord' gets busily to work, and prophetic vision becomes the *modus vivendi* for impressing upon Saul that Samuel is still to be the virtual ruler of Israel. So Samuel hears from the Lord of a young man, quite unknown to him, who has lost his father's asses, and has gone in search of them, and as (by some chance, or device) the asses have found their way into Samuel's safe-keeping, presently the young man turns up, and is duly impressed at finding that he and his asses have been brought to Samuel by divine intervention.

If Saul had already done a notable deed in the routing of the Ammonites, so that he had become 'the desire of Israel' (1 Samuel IX, 20) the finding of the lost asses was a curiously superfluous device for the Lord to employ for bringing Saul to the notice of Samuel; only if it was Samuel's device does it become understandable; and it is on that ground that I have adhered to a story which may only be legend. Samuel's motive is plain: compelled to yield to the popular demand, he starts training Saul to accept a subservient kingship, and sends him home to await further orders: 'seven days shalt thou tarry till I come to thee and shew thee what thou shalt do'. And then, though he has already anointed Saul to be King, he calls the people together, and to make it quite clear that Saul is not the people's choice but the Lord's, he causes lots to be cast, and the lot falls first on the tribe of Benjamin, then on the house of Kish, and finally on Saul. Why Saul, already the anointed of the Lord, hid himself from the honour that had thus fallen upon him, and had to be routed out, is not explained. Was it that he had begun honestly to doubt whether he was, indeed, the chosen of the Lord, or only of Samuel?

But though Saul has now been publicly made King, the government is still with Samuel; he draws up the laws for the ruling of the kingdom, writes them in a book, and sends Saul and the people back to their homes; king and people are to wait for the prophet's word of command.

And according to the Bible narrative (though here the sequence is doubtful) it is only after this that we get what, in Samuel's valedictory address, is given as the initial reason of the people's demand for a King – Saul's summoning of the Tribes to the defeat of the Ammonites. Without any bidding from Samuel he takes the initiative, and in doing so lays down a new policy – namely that when one Tribe is attacked all the other Tribes shall come to its assistance. Their failure to do so in the past has kept Israel in a state of subjection. Saul will have no more of it; he unites the Tribes for battle, and is brilliantly successful. If this is allowed to go on, Saul will become dangerous to Samuel.

Now if this is indeed the true sequence of events, though the Kingdom has now been established, the laws written, and the people sent back to their homes, there has been as yet no sign of God's wrath against Israel: indeed very much the other way – the Lord has told Samuel that He has heard the cry of his people, and has chosen Saul to be their captain, 'that he may save them out of the hand of the Philistines', Saul has been kissed and anointed, sent on his way with blessing: the spirit of the Lord has come upon him, and the gift of prophecy – making a new man of him. Only as an afterthought does the Lord's wrath descend upon Israel for having asked for a King in accordance with what was laid down for them in the Book of Deuteronomy. There are, in fact, two stories, which with all their contradictions have been roughly, and somewhat inconsecutively joined together; and through these inconsistencies one has to find one's way without any certainty as to which was the truer story. But in the sequel there is no doubt whatever that Samuel is bent on keeping up his prestige as prophet, and retaining as much power as he possibly can: and for that he uses the technique of his day – the technique of divine intervention. And so, when a devastating storm of thunder and rain falls upon the harvest, it is the wrath of the Lord declaring itself (somewhat belatedly) for the wickedness of Israel in asking for a King. And because Saul turns out not to be the sort of King that Samuel would like him to be, henceforth there is conflict between them, and Samuel does all he can to undo Saul's work for the establishing of his kingdom over a united people.

In his attempt to dissuade the Children of Israel from desiring a King, Samuel had, quite untruthfully, told them (1 Samuel VIII, 11-18) the sort of King that Saul was going to be. There is not a shadow of a suggestion that Saul ever was that sort of King, or that the people ever asked to be delivered from him. On the contrary, after his death we are told that he was 'lovely and pleasant' in his life, and the daughters of Israel are adjured to weep for him because of all the benefit which they had received at his hands.

Saul's offence, for Samuel, was that he was too successful, and did not wait sufficiently upon Samuel's word of command. When, on his own initiative, he had gathered the people together for the rescue of Jabesh-Gilead from the Ammonites, Samuel had not been consulted, or called on to offer sacrifice or give his blessing to the enterprise. It was too signal a deliverance to be censured after the event, but – it was not to happen again! And so, from then on, Samuel

begins to impose conditions, making Saul's task more difficult – sometimes impossible. On one occasion he fixes a day,
breaks his word, waits till the people are scattered before an
enemy arrayed for battle; and when forced by that circumstance, Saul offers the sacrifice himself – for that single
assumption of the priestly office, he is denounced by Samuel
and the Kingdom is to be taken from him and given to another.[1] And presently, behind Saul's back, Samuel begins
to devise how to divide the Kingdom against him, and
supplant him with a man more to his own liking.

And in all these underhand doings 'the Word of the Lord'
is the accompaniment. It is the Word of the Lord which
forbids any taking of the spoil after the defeat of Amalek,
though on many previous occasions (as recorded in Numbers
and Deuteronomy, and the Book of Joshua) spoil *was* taken
as a matter of course as the reward of victory. It is the Lord
who tells Samuel to go and anoint David (another case of an
unknown person whom he had never heard of); it is the
Lord who instructs him to tell lies, should Saul hear about
it; always, in his malicious devices against Saul, the Lord
is his guide; and when David, the beloved of Saul, becomes
his accomplice in treachery, they divide the Kingdom against
him; David seeks alliance with Achish, King of Gath, an
enemy of Israel, Samuel dies, and Saul goes to meet defeat
and death at the hand of the Philistines on Mount Gilboa.

On all these matters the action of my play follows the
Bible narrative fairly closely, though in the commentary
of the characters I give a very different reading of the mind
and motives of Samuel, the Kingmaker, to the one which is
generally accepted. But in one scene where the chronicler's
whitewash has been laid on too thick to be tolerated, I have
devised that Samuel himself, shall for discerning readers,
remove the whitewash, by making him dictate, for the

---

[1] Yet, on a later occasion, when David took upon himself the priestly
office and offered sacrifice (2 Samuel VI, 17-18) he was *not* judged for it.

admiration of posterity, how deeply he mourned that the Lord should have repented for having made Saul King over Israel. If Samuel wrote the history of the Judges he may also have written some of his own; if he did, it would account for much. And so I have taken dramatic licence to account for a declaration of Samuel's personal benevolence towards Saul which the rest of the story makes quite incredible.

I suppose that some, perhaps many, of my readers hold views which do not allow Samuel's credentials to be questioned: for them – belief in the verbal inspiration of the Scriptures stands between him and any freer reading of a traditionally revered character. But as I believe that a good deal of Old Testament history has, from its too literal acceptance lain as a dead weight, not only on the intelligence of its readers, but on Christianity itself, I have had a very real concern in the writing of this play. For I believe that 'the Word of the Lord', which came so frequently to Samuel, was not the word of a God who has any right to our respect, but only the word of a prophet jealous in his own interests, greedy of power, vengeful, double-dealing and deceitful. Possibly the one he most deceived was himself – so sincerely deceived that, when he spoke 'the Word of the Lord' he did not know that he was only speaking the word of Samuel.

(JASHER, *an old man, sits looking quietly back into the past. There is a long pause before he speaks.*)

JASHER I am Jasher, the writer of history, faithful servant to my Lord Samuel. What he bade me write, I wrote for him in his two books, the Book of Joshua, and the Book of Judges. What he did not bid me to write, I wrote in my own book – the Book of Jasher. But after that he was dead, my own book was taken from me; they took it and burned it, because there was truth in it that was not to be told. Nevertheless, in his Book my name is recorded for posterity to remember: with the words which he bade me write in it – and which, maybe, were not true.

I served Samuel, and feared him. But I loved Saul. Was it not written in the Book of Jasher?

(*Slowly the curtain closes.*)

ACT I

SCENE 1

(SAMUEL *sits in his house at Ramah; before him stands* JASHER, *his amanuensis, and trusted servant.* JASHER *has told the old man something which has not pleased him.*)

SAMUEL The elders of Israel coming, you say? I did not say that they might come.

JASHER No, Holiness. I think that is why.

SAMUEL (*suspiciously*) What do you mean – 'that is why'?

JASHER Because, Holiness, to the messengers they sent, you gave no answer . . . They have waited, Holiness.

SAMUEL They should have waited longer.

JASHER No doubt, Holiness. But now they have sent to say that the matter is urgent.

SAMUEL And what that matter may be, they still do not tell me.

JASHER Did Holiness need telling?

SAMUEL Eh? Why do you ask that, Jasher?

JASHER Surely the Prophet of the Lord, the High Priest, and Lord Judge of Israel, knows – everything.

SAMUEL Not everything, Jasher. Sometimes I hear the Word of the Lord speaking to me. Sometimes it is only rumour that I hear . . . I do not know the Lord's Will until He has spoken to me . . . Tell me, Jasher, why are they coming?

JASHER With all submission, Holiness, I would rather leave the saying of it to them.

SAMUEL Ah! So they are coming to complain, are they?

JASHER Not exactly to complain, Holiness.

SAMUEL Oh, yes: But they are! I know, I know! Those sons of mine have been making trouble for me again. It's the old story: behind my back they are doing as Eli's sons did when *he* grew old. And it'll be the curse of Eli they'll bring on me, if I let it go on. I must see them; where are they?

JASHER My lord Abiah is here, Holiness; but my lord Joel is giving judgment at Mizpah and does not return till tomorrow.

SAMUEL Judgment! What sort of judgment will that be? Now that I am old, my sons walk no longer in *my* way, nor give heed to my counsel. What they do, I know not.

JASHER That is what the elders say, Holiness.

SAMUEL Are *coming* to say, you mean?

JASHER Yes, Holiness: I think so.

SAMUEL You don't think – you *know*. Come, out with it,

178

man! Speak! (JASHER *hesitates.*) Nay, is it not better that I should know, so as to have my answer ready for them?

JASHER They are coming to make request, Holiness.

SAMUEL Aye? For what?

JASHER That they may have a King.

SAMUEL A King! So! Aye, surely they are a rebellious people! Forty-two years have I served them faithfully and well, speaking to them the Word of the Lord, giving them just judgment, and peace from all their enemies. But now it is a King they want! And I might have made myself their King, had I so chosen – what was to prevent? Nay, in all but in name, I was, and still am . . . And they come wanting a King! . . . Well, the Lord shall hear of it. Yes! He shall hear of it! And it's not going to please *Him*, any more than it pleases *me* – not if I know it! Not while I am still Judge of Israel . . . It's not going to be so easy for them as they think. (*He rises from his seat.*) When they come, I shall be gone . . . They should have waited.

JASHER (*diffidently*) But, Holiness . . .

SAMUEL Yes; well? Do you expect *me* to wait for *them*?

JASHER Holiness, they are here now.

SAMUEL So you also have deceived me, Jasher. Why did you not warn me?

JASHER I did not know they would be here so soon. Their messenger has but just come.

SAMUEL Well, we will see them . . . Let them come in.

(JASHER *goes.* SAMUEL *claps his hands three times.* Two LEVITES *enter.*)

Bring me my vestments.

(*The* LEVITES *go up two steps through curtains at the side: they come out again carrying the High Priest's head-dress and vestments. They array* SAMUEL: *then they open the curtains.* SAMUEL *mounts to the Seat of*

Judgment. The LEVITES *stand to right and left on the lower step. Twelve* ELDERS *of Israel enter, and bow themselves before him.* SAMUEL *remains silent, eyeing them sternly. There is a long pause: The* ELDERS *stand in obvious embarrassment; at last one of them speaks.*)

1ST ELDER Holiness, is it permitted that we speak?

SAMUEL Speak.

1ST ELDER Holiness, this is the voice of all Israel that thou hearest. We speak only as they have commanded us. Many years hast thou judged Israel, and hast been our help and stay – a leader and a guide to God's chosen People. But now thou art old; and because the burden has become too heavy for thee, thou hast given rule and judgment unto the men of thine own house. But thy sons walk not in thy ways, to do justly as thou hast done. They have turned aside to seek after lucre; with them the rich find favour, and the poor are defrauded, and in taking bribes they corrupt judgment. So now, because thou art no longer able to prevent these things being done, we require that thou give us a King to rule over us.

SAMUEL A King?

1ST ELDER Yes, Holiness.

SAMUEL Why do you ask for – a King?

1ST ELDER Other nations have Kings, Holiness; and we shall be stronger, and more feared, having a King, than with only Judges to rule over us. Also in war, we shall do better against our enemies – with a King to lead us.

SAMUEL In war? Have I not kept you in peace – many years?

1ST ELDER Yes, Holiness; but some of our cities are still held by garrisons of the Philistines, and we might soon be rid of them, had we a King to lead us.

SAMUEL You might, or you might not. Is it not better to

let sleeping dogs lie? Have ye considered what price ye must pay for – a King? Hearken, and I will tell you. To make himself great in your eyes, instead of peace he will give you war. He will take your sons from their labour in the fields to make for him instruments and chariots of war. He will have horsemen, and footmen, and men to run before him, and trumpeters to sound his coming wheresoever he goes. And he will appoint him captains over hundreds and over thousands, whose word you must obey. And he will take the best of your land, and make you be servants to ear his ground and reap his harvests. And he will take your daughters to be his cooks and confectioners, and the best of your vineyards and oliveyards will be for his servants; a tenth also of your harvest will he take, and of your asses and your flocks. So will ye be his bondsmen, and no longer a free people . . . And ye shall cry out in that day because of your King that ye have chosen; and the Lord will not hear you in that day, because ye would not hear His Word that I spake unto you.

AN ELDER   Surely, Holiness, if you entreat the Lord for us, He will not give us such a King to rule over us, but a better.

SAMUEL   Why should I entreat the Lord for a rebellious people? For He gave you Judges to be your rulers, to make of you a peple after His own heart – not like other nations serving strange Gods. Nay, heed not *me*: I am nothing! It is not *me* that ye have rejected; it is the Lord your God whom ye have rejected this day – asking for a King!

1ST ELDER   We are sorry, Holiness, that what we ask does not please you; but we speak not for ourselves. The Children of Israel have sent and commanded us that we ask of you a King.

THE ELDERS   Aye; a King, Holiness. We must have a King.

SAMUEL   Enough! I have heard you. It is the voice of a rebellious people. On your heads be it! The Lord lay not this sin to *my* charge . . . Go, every man to his own city and his people, and say to them what I have said to you. And when the Lord has spoken His Word to me, and made known His Will, I will send for you again . . . Go, all of you!

> (*They bow themselves out.* SAMUEL *watches them go; then speaks.*)

Aye, depart from me, ye men of stubborn mind! The Lord do so to me, and more also, if I make not His will known, and His judgment upon Israel.

> (*He descends from the Seat of Judgment. The* LEVITES *take off his vestments, and bear them away.*)

Jasher, find Abiah, and bid him come to me.

> (JASHER *goes.*)

A King! A King! O God, send down Thy Judgment upon this people! Yea, give me a sign that I may declare Thy wrath against them for having rejected me, Thy servant, this day, that I should not rule over them. A sign, O Lord, give me to declare a sign of Thy wrath, that, fearing Thee, they may fear me also.

> (*Enter* ABIAH.)

ABIAH Yes, Father?

SAMUEL (*angrily*) Abiah, this is your doing. You and Joel have done this.

ABIAH What have we done, Father?

SAMUEL The people are asking for a King.

ABIAH (*smoothly*) Well, why should they not?

SAMUEL 'Why not?' If they have a King, where am *I*; where are *you*? We judge Israel no more.

ABIAH (*quietly*) Lawgivers, Judges, Kings – they all have their turn and go. Prophets last longer. So long as the people believe in them, Prophets have more power.

SAMUEL What power shall I have – over a King?

ABIAH The same as over the people – if you make them believe in you. And as they have asked *you* for a King, you will have the choosing of him.

SAMUEL Whom *can* I choose?

ABIAH Why not one of us? Though judging is less trouble, I should rather like to be a King.

SAMUEL You! You that are the very cause of this evil that has come on me! Were I to name one of you to be King, they would spit you out at me like dirt, if what they say of you be true.

ABIAH What *do* they say?

SAMUEL That you, whom I made to be Judges in Israel, seek only after lucre, and sell judgment to the highest bidder – to the rich man at a price – to the poor man oppression.

ABIAH So, that's the tale, is it? Aye, surely these are a people who think to get something for nothing. Justice is a commodity – like everything else, and must be paid for. When a man wants food or raiment, sheep or oxen, house or land, you do not give it him – you ask a price for it. So also when a man comes to the Priest with a meat-offering for sacrifice, does not the Priest take part of it, though the offering be to God? And if the Priests are to be paid for their office, as was ordained by Moses, shall not Judges also receive their due, and be paid likewise?

(SAMUEL *is silent.*)

You see, Father. So, though I give judgment at a price, I do not sell the judgment which I deliver.

SAMUEL (*searchingly*) Is your price always the same, my son, for rich and poor?

ABIAH No, Father; for the poor man cannot pay the same price as the rich man; so the rich man pays more. And that is why – if I give judgment for the rich, those that expect something for nothing say that I have taken a bribe for it. Also, when two rich men come before me, I find out, from each separately, how much the matter is worth to him; and he to whom it is worth most pays most. Is not that fair, Father? So then – if I give judgment for him that paid most, the one that paid less is not pleased, and says that I take bribes, though I only take my due – even as the Priest takes *his* due. So you see, Father . . .

SAMUEL (*with a sigh*) Yes; I see, my son. But it likes me not. When I judged Israel, my judgments were free; and when all was done, the people brought me a free-will offering. It was the better way.

ABIAH Aye, so one of them told me the other day. 'Twas a man defrauded of his neighbour, who claimed judgment for nothing – said that, so long as you judged Israel, your way was his way.

SAMUEL Aye? What said you to that?

ABIAH Oh, he'd a clear case, so I gave judgment in his favour – had to.

SAMUEL Ah! So that time you met your match!

ABIAH Yes; but I got even with him afterwards. Next day he found that he had lost his father's asses.

SAMUEL Lost them?

ABIAH Yes. That night they were safe in the field; the next morning there was a break in the fence, and five of them were gone.

SAMUEL So I have a son who is also a thief!

ABIAH Legal distraint is the right word, Father. For what he owed me, I took no more than my due. So now he has gone seeking them; but he won't find them.

SAMUEL A good man that, and worth knowing. What was his name? Where dwells he?

ABIAH His name? Saul; he is of Gibeah, his father a man of substance named Kish, of the tribe of Benjamin. Aye, a fine-looking fellow he was too, and a leader of the people. I liked beating *him*. 'Twas worth it.

SAMUEL And you a Judge of Israel!

ABIAH A Judge has a right to his due like anyone else. But if I'd my choice, I'd sooner be a prophet.

SAMUEL You a prophet!

ABIAH Well, if I'm no longer to be a Judge, I must be something. Can you not teach me?

SAMUEL If you have not learned truth – if God's Voice has not spoken within you, *I* cannot make you a prophet.

ABIAH (*as he seats himself beside* SAMUEL) How did you come to be a prophet yourself, Father?

SAMUEL It was the Lord's doing – not mine. A day comes when you hear His Voice speaking to you.

ABIAH How – speaking? Is it a voice like a man speaking that you hear?

SAMUEL No; not like any voice – speaking. God's Voice comes to a man's heart. You hear Him not with the outward ear. But He speaks, and you know that it is *He* speaking.

ABIAH When did you first hear Him speak, Father?

SAMUEL When I was a child. It came to me suddenly one night; and it was a great thing that He called me to do then – to speak His Judgment upon Eli, the High Priest, and upon his sons for their evil doings – and I was but a child. I heard no Voice – only in my own heart 'twas the Lord speaking; and *my* wrath against Eli and his sons was *His* wrath.

ABIAH And did Eli believe you?

SAMUEL Aye, surely he did; for he knew that what I said was true. Nevertheless, had I not told him of – the Voice, he might *not* have believed.

ABIAH How came the Voice to *you*?

SAMUEL 'Twas this way. One day, I, a child, had seen with my own eyes the wickedness of his sons – how they took by force the offerings of the people, and lay with the women at the doors of the Tabernacle. And Eli rebuked them not. So that night I waited till Eli slept: then I went and wakened him. 'Here I am,' I said. 'You called me.' 'No,' he said; 'I did not call you. Go, and lie down.' I waited till he was asleep again; then I came a second time; 'Here I am,' I said. 'You called me.' 'No, I did not call you,' he said. I came a third time, saying the same words. Well, that set Eli thinking – no one else was in the house but we two. Whose voice, then, could it be but God's that I had heard? So he told me that when next I heard the Voice, I was to say: 'Speak, Lord, for Thy servant heareth.' Oh, I had heard well enough, for I knew what the Lord was telling me to do. But that was how I made Eli also believe that I *had* heard the Voice of the Lord speaking.

ABIAH And you thought it right to do that, Father?

SAMUEL Aye, surely; for often men are slow to believe the Lord's Word when it is spoken by others. But those that *do* hear His Word hear it in the secret places of the heart. That, my son, is to be a prophet – if you hear God speaking in your heart.

ABIAH What if the heart be evil, Father?

SAMUEL God would not speak to an evil heart.

ABIAH And did what you said come true?

SAMUEL Aye, it came true, though not so soon that I had not a fear that it might *not* come true. But of this, Abiah, man can always be sure – Evil brings evil upon itself. So when a prophet of the Lord sees evil being done, he can prophesy surely that more evil shall follow; and the Lord will fulfil his word – in His own time.

> (ABIAH *has listened with interest, but without much sympathy; and upon* SAMUEL *comes a feeling of failure and loneliness: a consciousness that he is the last of the old order.*)

But when I am gone, will there be a prophet left in Israel? Nay, I know not! I am lonely, and desolate, and old; and my sons are no comfort to me, for they walk not in my way. After me, who shall come to guide Israel? It is the Lord's will: The days of the Judges are ended.

ABIAH Why, then, Father, was it not God's will that the people *should* ask you for a King?

SAMUEL Why should they ask *me* – for a King?

ABIAH If you choose the right man, Father, you may judge Israel still . . . So it's not to be me, eh? Had you chosen *me*, I would have done your bidding . . . Farewell, Father. (*He gets up to go.*) Maybe the Lord will find you – a better.

> (SAMUEL *sits thinking.* ABIAH *stands looking at him, half pitying, half amused, then turns to go out. But as he goes* SAMUEL *calls him back.*)

SAMUEL Abiah . . . Where are Saul's asses?

ABIAH I have them no longer, Father.

SAMUEL Where are they?

ABIAH I sold them to Joel, for a good price.

SAMUEL Tell Joel he is to send them back to you.

ABIAH He will not – unless I repay him.

SAMUEL *I* will repay him! Go: send me Saul's asses.

> (ABIAH *goes out, repeating softly to himself, in curious bewilderment as to what it can mean,* SAMUEL'S *command, 'Send me Saul's asses!'* SAMUEL *sits– thinking.*)

(The same scene. JOEL *has now returned. He stands before* SAMUEL, *very conscious that his father is not pleased with him; but, like his brother Abiah, being accused, he defends himself.)*

SAMUEL So! 'Tis a fine pair of sons wherewith God has afflicted me! Abiah in the seat of judgment taking bribes; and now you – a Priest of the Tabernacle, seeking counsel of witches.

JOEL Who told you that, Father?

SAMUEL Ah! 'Tis well that I take means to know things that my sons would like better that I should not. That woman – where is she?

JOEL They are bringing her, Father; as you commanded.

SAMUEL She was brought before you for judgment. Why did she not have it?

JOEL I found no harm in her – so I let her go.

SAMUEL Has not the law of Moses commanded: 'Thou shalt not suffer a witch to live'?

JOEL A wise woman need not always be a witch, Father.

SAMUEL I never knew a wise woman that was not. For it was not God's will, when he made woman, to make her wise. Wisdom he kept for man.

JOEL But when a man has not that which he should have – may it not fall to others – aye, sometimes to a woman?

SAMUEL *(suspiciously)* What has this woman done for *thee*?

JOEL Let her tell that herself, Father. She is there, waiting.

SAMUEL Aye, and now here is judgment waiting for *her*. Let her be brought in.

*(*JOEL *goes to the door and signals.)*

JOEL She did no witchcraft for *me*, Father.

SAMUEL Stand aside, and hold your peace. We will hear what *she* says; nor shall she have thee for a defender. I will be judge now.

(*The woman enters with two men guarding her.*)

Thou evil woman, whence art thou? What is thy name?

WOMAN I have none, Holiness. The wise woman of Endor, men call me.

SAMUEL How com'st thou to be 'wise', woman?

WOMAN 'How' I know not, Holiness. The Lord has given me knowledge for the service of men.

SAMUEL What service is that?

WOMAN I look for signs, Holiness. I watch the rising and the setting of the sun, and the changes of the moon; also the stars in their courses. And from them I learn the ways of Heaven – whether there is to be rain or drought, heat or cold, hail or tempest, blight or blessing. Also when the sun is to be darkened, I know the time of it; and when a shadow is to fall upon the moon, I know the day of it and the hour. (SAMUEL *makes a gesture of holy horror at such evil knowledge.*) Does not God also tell you, Holiness, of things which are to come?

SAMUEL Not by hidden divination, nor by the power of darkness, do I come to know God's will; for those ways are evil. There are things it is not lawful that any man should seek to know: and for a woman to know them is sin worthy of death.

WOMAN If what I foretell be true, Holiness, how can it be evil?

SAMUEL If it is foretold by power of evil, how can good come of it? Out of thine own mouth I judge thee for that which thou hast done. It is not permitted for any so to do – and live.

WOMAN If I am judged of my life, I have that to say, Holiness, which only you may hear.

(*Their looks meet; there is a pause.* SAMUEL *looks at* JOEL; *he seems ill at ease.*)

SAMUEL Go, Joel; I will hear her alone.

(JOEL *goes out reluctantly; there is a furtive look about him – if he can, he is going to listen.* SAMUEL *makes a gesture of dismissal to the two men on guard. They go out. The* WOMAN *looks at* SAMUEL, *and smiles. There is a pause.*)

SAMUEL (*suspiciously*) What have you done for my son?

WOMAN Nothing but what was good. I did but tell him that, for the saving of his harvest, he should reap quickly.

SAMUEL Wherefor?

WOMAN I saw signs, which he did not . . . Why do you shut your eyes to signs, Holiness? Are they not from God?

SAMUEL *Signs*, you say?

WOMAN Aye; and they come not from evil spirits, nor by divination, nor by enchantment: but are there where God wills them to be – for man to be blind to.

SAMUEL You say that *I* am blind, woman?

WOMAN (*pointing upwards*) Holiness, see yon cloud.

SAMUEL I see it.

WOMAN And you see nothing in it? . . . Nothing? . . . If you had my eyes to help you, you'd see better. 'In three days,' it says, 'in three days.' Well, if you misjudge me for being what I am, and what God made me, I shall then be dead. But I shall be seeing it better from the other side . . . 'Tis pity you can't use these eyes of mine while they are still living. There's wisdom in them – for you, could you but know.

SAMUEL How would you have me to know, woman?

WOMAN You are a seer, Holiness; yet you see not what *I* see: because your God is not my God.

SAMUEL Who is your God?

WOMAN My God is Truth.

SAMUEL *My* God is the only True God. How then can Truth be your God?

WOMAN Your God says what you want Him to say – Samuel. My God hears no prayer of man to change His will, once He has made it.

SAMUEL Why are you saying this?

WOMAN Because *my* God can give you what you are asking of *your* God . . . You are wanting a sign, are you not, of God's wrath against this people, who are putting you away, so that they may have a King (*This makes* SAMUEL *sit up.*) Well, I can give you the sign – if you spare my life . . . Well? What about it, Samuel?

SAMUEL If I spare your life, how shall I know whether you will have told me the truth?

WOMAN 'Tis but three days. Hold me for three days, and if it be not the truth, then slay me.

SAMUEL What *is* the sign?

WOMAN Your oath first, Samuel – that if what I tell you be true – you will suffer 'a witch' to live.

SAMUEL (*after a pause*) Aye, speak, then!

WOMAN Your oath, Samuel.

SAMUEL I swear by the living God, that if the sign whereof you tell me come true in three days – I will suffer you to live – to your life's end.

WOMAN To *my* life's end? That's not good enough, Samuel. You are a clever man! . . . To *your* life's end would be better. Say it!

SAMUEL Aye: to *my* life's end, and further – if it be God's will: I swear it.

WOMAN Hearken, then . . . Yonder cloud is the sign. Its like came yesterday: it comes again today. Yesterday 'twas like a closed fist – so. (*She begins to make gestures – first of a closed fist then of a hand opening more and more*). Today it begins to open – so. Tomorrow it will be – so. The day after – so. *Then* – so! (*She turns her open palm and makes a swift downward stroke.*) And there will come thunder and lightning and rain upon the earth, *and the harvest will be destroyed!* – 'a sign of God's wrath upon this people – for asking of you a King' . . . Eh, Samuel?

(SAMUEL *sits thinking.*)

SAMUEL In three days?

WOMAN Aye, in three days.

SAMUEL It must not be sooner.

WOMAN It will not be sooner. If it be God's will that I should die – it might even be four. Nay, would that not serve you as well? Four days, Samuel?

SAMUEL If it come not till four days, you shall not be slain . . . And if what you tell come to be true, God also shall pardon you.

(SAMUEL *claps his hands and calls. The* GUARDS *enter.*)

Take this woman, and see that ye hold her safe, till I give command.

(*The* GUARDS *take hold of her and lead her away. As she goes, she turns and points up, and with a motion of her fingers she counts three. She looks back at* SAMUEL, *but he makes no sign.*)

Send me my servant Jasher. Bid him come quickly . . . .

(*They go.* SAMUEL *stands looking at the cloud.* JASHER *enters.*)

JASHER Yes, Holiness?

SAMUEL Jasher, call back the Elders of Israel! Bid them be here in three days.

JASHER Will that be possible, Holiness?

SAMUEL Aye: for they have not yet gone far. Send after them swift messengers. Say that the Word of the Lord has come to me; and His command to declare it to all Israel. So shall they know that I am His prophet, and that He speaks by *me*. Make haste, Jasher.

(JASHER *goes.* SAMUEL *again stands looking at the cloud.*)

Three days — and then — the sign! O Lord, I beseech Thee, make this Thy Word, that Israel may know and fear.

(*Enter* JOEL. *He has a knowing look.*)

JOEL Well, Father? What have you done with her? Is the woman to die?

SAMUEL If she have spoken truth to me, she dies not.

JOEL (*ironically*) So you also have suffered a witch to live.

(*To that bit of insolence* SAMUEL *makes no reply.*)

SAMUEL Joel, send a man whom you can trust to Gibeah; and bid him inquire there of a man named Saul, son of Kish, the Benjamite, and bring back word of all that he can learn concerning him.

JOEL Ah? Saul, the man whose asses Abiah sold to me. He said, Father, that you would repay me for the return of them.

SAMUEL (*impatiently*) I will repay you. Go, and do as I bid you quickly!

(SAMUEL *goes out, leaving* JOEL *alone.*)

JOEL So? It's going to be Saul, is it? God, do you hear that? You've chosen Saul.

(SAMUEL *is dictating to* JASHER *the story of Israel, in the days of Joshua. He moves slowly to and and fro, pausing now and then, as the writing goes on.*)

SAMUEL 'And it came to pass, as they fled from before Israel, that the Lord cast down great stones from Heaven upon them; and those which died of the hail-stones were more than those whom Israel slew with the sword.' And in your book, Jasher, write this, which was told me when I was a child. Whether it be true, I know not, but it makes a good story. 'Joshua cried unto the Lord and said, "Sun, stand thou still upon Gibeon, and thou, moon, in the valley of Ajalon." And the sun stood still, and the moon stayed – '

(*A while back a* SERVANT *has entered, and stands waiting to speak.* SAMUEL *sees him and stops.*)

Yes? What is it?

SERVANT A man is here, Holiness, asking that he may have a word with the seer.

SAMUEL The seer? He did not ask for me by name?

SERVANT No, Holiness.

SAMUEL Let him come in. (*The* SERVANT *goes.*) This will be the man, Jasher, whom those I sent will have taught the way . . . Go, now, and come again presently.

(*As* JASHER *goes out, he meets* SAUL, *turns and looks at him; and truly he is worth looking at – a man of noble bearing, tall and strong, and of a goodly countenance. And now* SAMUEL *is going to tame him to his purpose.*)

SAMUEL Your name is Saul.

SAUL It is, sir; but how come you to know it? For here I am a stranger.

SAMUEL You do not know who I am?

SAUL No, sir.

SAMUEL Then what has brought you?

SAUL There was one who met me in the way, and told me that here lived a seer of whom I might inquire concerning that which I have lost, and have been seeking.

SAMUEL Your father's asses?

SAUL Whence knew you that, sir?

SAMUEL Whence does a seer know anything? . . . How came you to lose them?

SAUL The fence of their field had been broken.

SAMUEL You did not know it was broken?

SAUL Not till, in the morning, I found they were gone.

SAMUEL So – having won your case – you lost your asses.

SAUL Sir, who *are* you that know all this?

SAMUEL I am Samuel, the prophet, whom the Lord made Judge over Israel.

SAUL Oh, pardon me, my lord, that I did not know. But I come from a small people, and among them only do I dwell.

SAMUEL Even so, yesterday the Lord spoke to me saying: 'Tomorrow I will send thee a man of the Tribe of Benjamin, to inquire of thee about that which he has lost.' Be not concerned about thy father's asses. They are here waiting for thee.

SAUL My Lord, how came they *here?*

SAMUEL Because, when the fence of their field was broken it was the Lord's doing; and when the asses strayed, He guided them in the way that they should go. So also He guided thee that thou shouldst come to inquire of me to whom the Lord has revealed His will concerning thee.

SAUL (*astonished*) Concerning *me?*

SAMUEL For He spake unto me saying, 'I will make this man Saul to be the Captain of my people, to make them a strong nation, and to save them from the hand of their enemies. For I have looked upon my people, because their cry is come unto me that they should have a King.'

SAUL Holiness! How can such as I be King? For Benjamin is the least of the Tribes; and what is my Father, or what am I, that I should rule over Israel?

SAMUEL The Lord sees not as man sees; nor does He choose by the hearing of the ear, or by the seeing of the eye; but by that which is within – even a man's heart. So has the Lord chosen thee to be His Anointed this day. Howbeit, let no man know of it, until I have declared God's judgment upon this people. For they have done very wickedly in asking for a King . . . But they shall have their wish.

SAUL But, Holiness, if what they ask is evil, is it well that it should be granted?

SAMUEL Nay, God has heard them. He is Judge, not I. On their heads be it! They shall have a King.

SAUL I would that He had chosen one wiser than I.

SAMUEL Fear not. Thou shalt not lack wisdom – so long as thou hearken to His voice.

SAUL How shall I know – His voice, Holiness?

SAMUEL Am I not His prophet? Though this people have rejected me, God has not. When thou art in need of counsel He will speak to thee – by *me*. So, in fear and obedience to His word, shalt thou rule Israel.

SAUL Holiness, there is one thing which yet troubles me.

SAMUEL Aye? Speak.

SAUL If, to fulfil God's wrath against Israel, I am to be King, what help to them am I? But if it be for good and not evil, shall He not hear my prayer for this people, over which I am to rule?

SAMUEL What prayer wouldst thou make?

SAUL That He forgive them for asking of Him a King.

SAMUEL He will forgive, so long as thou dost rule according to His will. Doubt not. Tarry with me this night; and tomorrow, when I have anointed thee King, return to thy Father's house, until the day when the Lord shall make known before the eyes of all Israel that thou art His chosen.

SAUL Shall Israel be willing for a man whom they know not to be King?

SAMUEL There shall be no King in Israel save him whom the Lord has chosen. Have no fear; for when I have anointed thee, the spirit of the Lord shall come upon thee, and thou shalt be turned into another man. And if in all things thou do as I bid thee, God shall be with thee, and keep thee in the way wherein thou shouldst go . . . Come, leave, here, all that thou hast brought with thee for thy journey, and follow me.

> (SAMUEL *goes out.* SAUL *lays aside his staff and scrip and is about to follow, when* ABIAH *enters. They look at each other in surprise; but do not speak.* SAUL *goes out after* SAMUEL. ABIAH *stands looking after him; he is evidently much puzzled. Along with his scrip* SAUL *has left five halters for his asses.* ABIAH *takes them up and handles them.*)

ABIAH What? Come to fetch his asses? Hm.

> (*He goes to the outer door and calls.*)

Joel!

> (JOEL *enters.*)

JOEL Yes?

ABIAH Yonder is Saul – the man whose asses I took. What brings him here? Has he come to complain?

JOEL You brought him, brother.

ABIAH I?

JOEL Oh, yes. You did him a good turn when you took from him his asses. What you told the High Judge of Israel about Saul seems to have pleased him . . . Saul is going to be King.

ABIAH Going to be King?

JOEL Yes. Why not? The Old Man won't have you or
me; but he's got to choose somebody, who, he thinks, will
suit him. So why not Saul?

ABIAH But how comes he here?

JOEL I don't know. Ask Father. Saul has come, I
shouldn't wonder, to have his first lesson in 'kingly obedience', shall we call it? He mustn't be too much of a King,
you know, if he's to please the Lord – and Samuel.

ABIAH I told him that the other day; a King needn't make
much difference to *him*, I said, so long as he chose the right
man . . . Saul? I wonder whether he *has*. In my dealings
with him, I didn't find him a very yielding character –
far from it.

JOEL I also have done the Old Man a good turn – or
tried to.

ABIAH Eh? What was that?

JOEL Got him to consult a wise woman; which is not
quite according to the Law of Moses. She's told him something – what, I don't know – but he's going to make use of
it; so her life is to be spared.

ABIAH Where is she now?

JOEL The Old Man is keeping her – safe. And if what
she's told him comes true, then it isn't witchcraft – it's
'the Word of the Lord'.

ABIAH You know, Joel, I think Father's a bit of a wizard
himself, but doesn't know it. You can call anything the
Word of the Lord, if you want to. And when my Lord
Samuel wants anything rather badly, that's what he calls it.
Well, where's the difference between that and being a
wizard?

JOEL (*smoothly*) The Lord God of Israel is the difference,
Brother. Who *is* the Lord God of Israel? – practically.

ABIAH Yes, you're right. Only the other day he was
telling me how first he became a prophet; and 'my wrath was
God's wrath', he said. And it's the same now when the

people are asking for a King. Because *he* doesn't like it, *his* wrath is *God's* wrath.

JOEL Aye. Of which presently he'll be wanting to give them a sign ... I wonder how he'll do it. (*He stands thinking.*) Look! Here's your man Saul coming back.

(*Enter* SAUL.)

ABIAH Ah! Saul of Gibeah, are you not?

SAUL (*stiffly*) Yes, I am.

ABIAH You remember me? I gave judgment in your favour when I was last in Gibeah.

SAUL You did, my lord.

ABIAH For which you offered no payment.

SAUL None being due.

ABIAH Well, I hear that your asses have now come back to you.

SAUL (*startled*) My asses? How do they concern you?

ABIAH *I* took them, as payment for that due which you denied me ... No, not theft; recovery of a legal debt ... I just wanted you to know.

(*This gives* SAUL *a shock.*)

SAUL Then how came they – here?

ABIAH The Holy One, hearing of what I had done, required that I should return them.

SAUL To *him*?

ABIAH Yes; in order, apparently, that he might return them to *you*. What I told him about you seems to have – interested him.

(SAUL *stands stupent.*)

SAUL God! What is here? What have I done that he should have so deceived and mocked me? ... Oh! my God!

(*He runs out.*)

JOEL You've given the Old Man away, Abiah. You shouldn't have done that.

ABIAH Well, he's taken the asses off us. He can't have it both ways.

JOEL But he has repaid us for them.

ABIAH He hasn't repaid *me*.

JOEL Oh, no? So he doesn't think the debt was a legal one; and 'just wanted you to know'.

(*He gives a spiteful chuckle.*)
(*Enter* SAMUEL.)

SAMUEL Where is Saul?

JOEL He's run away, Father. Abiah frightened him.

SAMUEL Abiah, what have you done?

ABIAH Told him the truth about the asses. It seemed to surprise him.

JOEL Yes; it quite startled him. So now – he's gone.

SAMUEL Gone! The man whom I had chosen to be King over Israel!

JOEL Finds it too great an honour, and has run away.

(SAMUEL *stands faced with a situation which he does not at all like. He begins to have his doubts.*)

ABIAH (*maliciously*) You think he was the right man, Father?

(SAMUEL *looks at him angrily, turns without a word, and goes in.*)

JOEL And the word of the Lord came to Samuel, saying – 'Samuel, you've made a mistake.'

ABIAH Yes, I think we saw it come. What's going to happen, Joel, if Samuel and the Lord cease to have trust in each other?

JOEL It will be very interesting.

(SAMUEL *stands looking very anxiously at the sky.*
JOEL *stands watching him.*)

JOEL (*meaningly*) What's the weather going to be
Father? . . . Is thunder about?

SAMUEL (*uneasily*) What do you think, Joel?

JOEL There are clouds; but I don't think they mean anything. I needn't have been in such a hurry over my reaping. What that woman told me hasn't come true – proving
that she's no witch, and that, in letting her live, I judged
rightly . . . What are you going to do about it, Father? Let
her go?

SAMUEL Send word to her keepers that she be brought
to me.

JOEL What? Now?

SAMUEL Yes. Now.

JOEL Holiness, you know the Elders of Israel are waiting?

SAMUEL What of it?

JOEL They have been waiting a whole day. This is not
the third, but the fourth day since you sent word for them
to return.

SAMUEL Well, let it be the fourth day.

JOEL They are getting impatient, Holiness.

SAMUEL Do as I tell you, Joel. Have that woman brought
to me. Quickly.

(JOEL *goes. Again* SAMUEL *looks at the sky; its
appearance does not please him.*)

O God, if I do not give them a sign this day, will they believe
in Thy wrath? Or that I am Thy prophet? Lord, if I have
served Thee faithfully, forsake me not now. The sign, O
Lord; give me the sign. (*He claps his hands, and calls.*)
Jasher!

(JASHER *enters.*)

JASHER Yes, Holiness?

SAMUEL Send word for the Elders to be here ready, when presently I send for them.

JASHER Yes, Holiness.

> (JASHER *goes. The* WISE WOMAN *enters, accompanied by two* GUARDS. JOEL *follows.*)

SAMUEL (*to the* GUARD) Leave her and go! (*They go out.*) You also can go, Joel.

> (JOEL *goes, not pleased at being thus dismissed.*)

Woman, this is the fourth day; and still there is no sign. (*He points skywards.*)

WOMAN The day has not yet ended, Holiness.

SAMUEL If this day it comes not – you die.

WOMAN Yes, Holiness.

SAMUEL You say that you can read signs in the heavens which others are blind to. Where is the sign now?

> (*There comes a very faint distant roll of thunder.*)

WOMAN There, Holiness . . . If it come not this day, so be it: thou art quit of me and of thine oath . . . But see! . . . Nay, it will not be long now.

> (*As she speaks the sky has already begun to darken.*)

The people are waiting, Samuel – for the Lord's Word to be spoken.

> (*Enter* JASHER.)

JASHER The Elders are here, Holiness.

SAMUEL Bid them come in. Go, Woman; but I will not have thee depart yet. I will call thee again.

(She goes. SAMUEL claps his hands. The two LEVITES enter, carrying the High Priest's robes. They open the curtain behind the Seat of Judgment. SAMUEL goes in. The ELDERS enter, followed by JOEL and ABIAH. Behind them presses a great crowd, which remains standing without.)

JOEL *(pointing)* Abiah, it looks as if the Old Man is going to get what he wanted.

ABIAH What is that?

JOEL A sign that Samuel's wrath is God's wrath. That woman was right after all.

(The two LEVITES enter, and part the curtains for the coming of SAMUEL. To give a touch of added importance, he keeps them waiting for a few moments; as he enters all bow. SAMUEL does not return their salute.)

SAMUEL Elders and men of Israel. They tell me that you have been waiting. I too have been waiting – for the Word of the Lord. His Word has come. This day He speaks – by *me*. Hear them, while I reason with you of that which ye asked of me. 'Give us a King to reign over us.' I have hearkened unto you in all that ye said, and ye shall have a King.

(This is received with loud applause; which does not please SAMUEL.)

And ye are glad because I have said ye shall have a King. For behold, now I am old and grey-headed, and the days of my judgment are over. And here I am whom ye have known all your days, having walked before you continually, fulfilling God's will for his people. Witness, then, against me, before the Lord – whose ox have I taken? . . . or whose ass have I taken? . . . Whom have I defrauded? . . . Whom have I oppressed? . . . or of whose hand have I received any bribe to blind mine eyes therewith?

(To this recital there is a rising murmur of protest: 'No no, Holiness! No.')

Let him speak now: and I will restore it to him.

ELDER Holiness, thou has defrauded none of us; nor hast thou oppressed any; nor hast thou taken ought of any man's hand.

(A voice from the crowd: 'But there be others, Holiness!' The voice is hushed down by general consent.)

SAMUEL So say ye all?

ELDERS We all say it.

SAMUEL The Lord is witness.

ELDERS He is witness.

SAMUEL Hear, then, the Word of the Lord, spoken by me, His prophet. It is the Lord who speaks now: not I.

(He makes a commanding gesture: they all bow themselves.)

Behold, I have hearkened unto the voice of my servant Samuel, that ye might have a King to reign over you . . . So shall it be. And I will appoint you a day; and ye shall come together in your Tribes and your families, and from among them, by the casting of lots, I will choose you a King.

(At this there is a murmur of applause, low and reverent. As SAMUEL continues speaking, he watches the weather for the coming storm.)

And if, hereafter, ye will fear the Lord, and serve Him, and rebel not against His commandments, it shall be well with you; and you and your King shall prosper in all that ye do, and he shall save you from the hand of your enemies. But if you obey Me not, then shall My hand be against you, as it was against your Fathers in the wilderness, when they rebelled against My servant Moses, and hearkened not to his word . . . Nevertheless, because ye have done very wickedly in asking for a King, now stand and see this great thing which I, the Lord, will do before your eyes this day. Behold it is now wheat-harvest, and the reaping of your fields has begun. But that which ye have reaped, ye shall not store, neither shall ye make bread of that which ye have sown.

> (*While* SAMUEL *has been speaking, darkness has gathered; and now a low muttering of thunder is heard.*)

For behold I will send thunder and hail upon you, and upon your harvest this day, that ye may perceive and know how great was your wickedness in asking for a King. Hear, O Israel, the Judgment of the Lord! I, Samuel, His prophet, have spoken it.

> (*There comes a sudden flash of lightning.* SAMUEL *raises his arms; his voice rises to meet the approaching storm.*)

Now, therefore, O Lord, send down Thy wrath upon this people, that, ere this day be ended, Thy Word which I have spoken may be made true.

> (*As he speaks, there comes a crack of thunder. Lightning, thunder and hail follow. As the fury of the storm increases, the people prostrate themselves with cries of terror; with loud babblings they protest their willingness not to have a King; but now their voices can scarcely be heard above the noise of the thunder and hail.* SAMUEL *strikes an attitude: like the conductor of an orchestra he beats time to the raging of the storm, making it seem as though each rolling thunder came at his bidding.*)

SAMUEL Lo! The wrath of the Lord! The wrath of the Lord, for the wickedness of His people!

(The curtain falls: the thunder goes on; then dies gradually away. When the curtain opens again, light is beginning to return. SAMUEL *still stands master of the situation: the people are on their knees before him.)*

JOEL That was very convincing, Abiah. I couldn't have believed it possible.

ABIAH 'Tis well that it should so – happen. King or no King, Samuel will still be ruler of Israel, now.

SAMUEL *(to the people)* Nay, fear no more! Though ye have done this wickedness, the Lord will not slay you, nor will His wrath be against you for ever, now that ye have repented of your sin. I will not cease to pray for you that He forsake not His people. And though from this day I am no longer Judge over Israel, hearken to me, and I will teach you the right way. But if ye continue to do wickedly, ye shall be consumed, both you and your King . . . Go now, return each to his own Tribe and City, and there wait till I send for you, on the day appointed for the choosing of your King.

(The ELDERS, *hushed with awe, make their obeisances and go.)*

JOEL You did that well, Holiness.

*(*SAMUEL *does not like the tone in which that is said. Without a word, he points to the door.* JOEL *and* ABIAH *go out, and* SAMUEL *remains alone: no, not quite alone. Behind him, unperceived, the* WISE WOMAN *has entered. She stands watching him. Distant thunder is still heard as the storm moves on its way.)*

SAMUEL O God, I thank Thee that Thou hast given me power this day to declare Thy Word, and to make known Thy Judgment upon this people.

WOMAN Your God, or *my* God, Samuel?

(SAMUEL *turns and stares at her angrily, yet with a touch of fear.*)

Aye; which was it, sent that storm? Was it yours or mine?

SAMUEL Mine, Woman! Aye, surely mine. For even as I spake the Word and called on His Name, He thundered to me out of heaven. It was He, He only, that answered when I called for the sign of His wrath against this people.

WOMAN Aye; you made a good story of it, Samuel, and chose your time well; came in on the minute, didn't you? But I gave you the day; had I not, would all the Elders have been here?

SAMUEL God's curse be on you, Woman! You tempted me; with fair words you tempted me, promising me a sign. And because I doubted whether God *would* hear me at the time appointed, I listened where I should have been deaf – to you, O accursed one! and took counsel of Evil. *Your* God is nothing – has no meaning, does not exist. Not from Him came the wonder which my God has wrought at my word before all Israel this day. It would have come, had I only had the faith for it, without your aid or telling.

WOMAN Aye, surely; it would still have come – even had I not spoken – aye, even had you slain me.

SAMUEL Therefore, to you I owe *nothing*.

WOMAN Your oath, Samuel.

SAMUEL I gave you life, when I should have given you death. Take it and go! And never let me see your face again.

WOMAN Nay, but hear me before I go. You have a dangerous God, Samuel – a God of vengeance and wrath – too much like yourself to be trusted. Try to lead Him by the nose, and some day He may turn on you for it. You say you doubted of Him, when you should have trusted. May it not be that His wrath is not against Israel, but against Samuel?

(*Distant thunder.*)

Ah! Hark!

SAMUEL No; for 'twas when *I* called on Him that He spoke the Word. Had His wrath been against *me*, He would not have so spoken then.

WOMAN Can you be sure of that, Samuel? . . . Nay, my God is a safer God for man to put trust in. For my God is Law; and in Law is no wrath, save against them that, being fools, are blind to it. What does the God of Law know or care whether you be Judge of Israel, or an outcast of the people? Whether you be alive or dead? The God of Law that is higher than the Heavens, cannot be moved or changed by man's will, nor canst thou turn Him from His course by prayer or supplication. But if a man break that Law, that Law breaks him. There is no wrath in thunder, or lightning, or hail, or tempest; but there's death in it. The lightning does not strike a man for the evil that he has done, but the fool that gets in the way of it . . . Hark! Here it comes again, though you thought it was over. What does your God say to that? Can He stop it? You, His prophet, go out among those hail-stones, and they'll slay you. Stay within, and they'll not harm you . . . Mine is the safer God, Samuel, for the man that is wise to learn His ways. But for the fool He has no mercy.

SAMUEL Go, Woman!

WOMAN Into the hail-stones to my death? No, Samuel, I'm not one of the fools. I'll bide here within awhile. It's not going to be long . . . This has been a good day for you, Holiness. Surely the people do well to fear one whose word God obeys. Did Samuel speak for Him? Or did He speak for Samuel? Well, well: some day we shall meet again.

(*She goes.*)

SAMUEL Oh! accursed woman! Why did I spare when

I should have slain? Oh, God, hear me! And if Thou hast pardoned my transgression, let not this evil woman live to triumph over me . . . and Thee. Give me, for sign . . .

(*He stops, startled.*)

A VOICE Your oath, Samuel.

(*Whether he has indeed heard it, or whether it is only his conscience speaking to him, he cannot tell. But he does not finish what he was about to say. There is a long low roll of thunder. He stands listening to it. For the first time in his life* SAMUEL *is in doubt, whether what he hears* is *the word of the Lord.*)

SAMUEL Who spoke then?

SCENE 5

JASHER (*speaking before the curtain*) And Samuel called the people together unto the Lord at Mizpah, and said to them, 'Though ye have rejected the Lord your God, which brought you forth out of Egypt, and delivered you from the hand of them that oppressed you, and have said unto Him, "Nay, but set a King to rule over us," now, therefore, present yourselves before the Lord that He may answer you according to the desire of your hearts.' And when the people were come to Mizpah, Samuel caused lots to be cast; and the lot fell on the Tribe of Benjamin; and when he had caused the Tribe of Benjamin to come near, the lot fell on the house of Kish; and when the house of Kish was taken, the lot fell on Saul . . . But when they sought him, he could not be found. And when they were about to inquire further, where the chosen of the Lord might be, there came one who said, 'Behold he has hidden himself in the fodder-house of his father's asses.' So they ran and fetched him thence; and Samuel said unto the people, 'Behold, here is the man whom the Lord hath chosen to be King over you.'

> (*Loud and prolonged shouting is heard. The curtain opens on a high-roofed chamber overlooking the place of assembly. At the back is a wide doorway to which steps lead up from below, where unseen by the audience, is a great gathering of the people, still shouting and cheering.* ABIAH *stands watching them with amusement.* JOEL *enters, carrying the bowl containing the lots, which rattle as he tosses them up and down. With a common understanding of the situation, the two brothers look at each other and smile.*)

ABIAH So the chosen of the Lord is now also the chosen of the people. He seems to have pleased them.

JOEL Yes, the casting of the lots went well, didn't it? (*Dipping into the bowl, he proceeds to demonstrate, picking out the three lots in turn.*) Benjamin . . . Kish . . . Saul! . . . Marvellous!

ABIAH None of which would have happened, if I hadn't taken Saul's asses. Where did they find him at last?

JOEL In the asses' stable, hiding under the hay.

ABIAH An appearance of unwillingness, which had, as was intended, I suppose, a good effect upon the people.

JOEL Saul's not that sort, Abiah. And, mind you, now that he *is* King, he *will* be King, or I'm much mistaken. Which are you going to serve?

ABIAH (*puzzled*) 'Which?'

JOEL You don't suppose the Old Man's going to give things up willingly, do you? – to Saul or anyone, King or no King . . . Well? The Lord's Prophet, or the Lord's Anointed; which are you going to stand for – now?

ABIAH We can't very well go against our Father, Joel.

JOEL Against him? No. But he is not going to last long. Even these last few days have aged him. And when he goes – where are we then?

ABIAH We are still Judges of Israel.

JOEL Yes, but for how long? . . . What's become of the Old Man?

ABIAH He came in – sharp and quick, just now – and went in yonder – as if something hadn't pleased him.

JOEL No. You saw what happened?

ABIAH No. What?

JOEL When the people started cheering the King, and went on cheering, and forgot to cheer Samuel, he came away . . . Nobody noticed . . . I was sorry for him then.

(*There comes a fresh burst of cheers.*)

ABIAH They are cheering still.

JOEL Yes. Saul's making himself popular. I don't want to get left. Do you?

(*Enter* SAMUEL.)

SAMUEL Joel, send Saul to me.

JOEL Send him? How am I to send him, Holiness?

SAMUEL What is your difficulty?

JOEL How does one give orders to a King – saying, 'You are to come!'

SAMUEL I bade him – after I had shown him to the people – to come here to me for further counsel. Tell him that I am waiting.

(JOEL *turns to go; then, at the sound of louder cheering, he stops.*)

JOEL Nay, here he comes. Look, with what great rejoicing the people are bringing him.

(SAMUEL *looks; but what he sees gives him no pleasure.*)

You have pleased them well, Holiness, in giving them a King.

SAMUEL (*bitterly*) Yes; in giving them a King, I have pleased them. Go, Joel . . . Go, both of you.

> (JOEL *and* ABIAH *go within.* SAUL'S *head appears; borne high on the shoulders of the people, he mounts the steps. Half-way up he dismounts; with a gesture dismisses the shouting crowd and comes forward alone.* SAMUEL'S *dignity of pose, and lack of any gesture of welcome, conveys the fact that he has been kept waiting.* SAUL'S *manner is courteous, but neither humble nor apologetic.*)

SAUL I should have been here sooner, Holiness; but the people so thronged on me, I could not get away.

SAMUEL (*coldly*) Surely. This is a great day for *them*; and for you also – to be their King.

SAUL It was not of my own will that I was made King, Holiness; yet so to be, surely *is* a great thing. I trust that I shall be found worthy.

SAMUEL The Lord God of Israel will guide thee in the way thou shouldst go.

SAUL So be it, Holiness.

SAMUEL My Son – for so surely thou art – since by this hand the Lord anointed thee King – why didst thou hide thyself when the lot fell on thee?

SAUL Holiness, because I was not then sure.

SAMUEL Of what?

SAUL Whether I was truly the chosen of the Lord, or only of my Lord Samuel.

SAMUEL What made thee to doubt?

SAUL If I was already the Lord's Anointed, why had the lots to be cast, Holiness?

SAMUEL For the better understanding of the people, my

Son. For they might have doubted my word – till the casting of the lots proved it true.

(SAUL *stands silent.*)

What causes thee still to doubt?

SAUL That which I learned concerning my Father's asses – that it was not the Lord who brought them to you, but another.

SAMUEL Nay, my Son, it was the Lord's doing; for He uses man to bring to pass that which He wills, though it be done in ignorance. Before ever they were lost, or found again, the Lord had spoken to me concerning thee . . . Dost thou now doubt, my Son, that it was the Lord's will to make thee King over Israel?

SAUL I will not doubt it, Holiness, when I have proof of it.

SAMUEL What further proof wouldst thou?

SAUL If the people obey my word in all that I command, so that by my hand they are delivered from their enemies, and become a strong nation, then shall I know surely that I *am* the Lord's chosen.

SAMUEL And by what way, and what commands, wouldst thou make them a strong nation?

SAUL I would do this, Holiness. I would make of them one people. For now they are weak, being divided, each tribe caring only for itself; therefore do they fall into the hand of the spoiler. And in our midst there are garrisons of the Philistines. Those garrisons I will drive out.

SAMUEL They are strongly placed and strongly held, my Son.

SAUL Aye. And because none came to our aid when the children of Benjamin went up against them, we were defeated. It shall be so no longer. The cause of one, even of Benjamin the smallest, shall be the cause of all.

SAMUEL Because Benjamin is your tribe, must all serve Benjamin?

SAUL Aye, even as Benjamin will serve them in like case. So shall we no longer be subject to the Philistines.

SAMUEL Have a care, my Son, that you take not too much upon you. Not till you have inquired of the Lord in all these things can they prosper.

SAUL When in doubt, Holiness, I will inquire. But the Lord himself commanded us to drive out the heathen before us. And to have them here in our midst is contrary.

SAMUEL (*coldly*) Well: what else would you do?

SAUL I will have from every tribe (save only in the days of the harvest) men trained in war to serve under me. So shall we be strong, and ready for battle, and the nations shall fear us.

SAMUEL Aye! It is as I spake unto them. 'Ye ask for a King; and instead of peace your King shall give you war; and shall take your sons from their labour in the field that they may serve him; so shall ye be no longer a free people.'

SAUL Without service, Holiness, where is freedom? For if the people will not serve their King, neither can the King serve his people. But already this day five hundred of the young men have offered themselves. Presently it shall be thousands.

SAMUEL The King speaks. What more does he require of his people?

SAUL I will have judges freely chosen of the people, from the men they know and can trust, each for their own city, so that justice be better served.

(*This gives* SAMUEL *a shock, which he endeavours to hide.*)

SAMUEL Are not my sons to be judges still?

SAUL If the people choose them, Holiness; but I do not

think they will. For it was because of them that they asked for a King.

SAMUEL Then am I and my house to be nothing in Israel?

SAUL You, Holiness, who are the prophet of the Lord, will speak His word to us.

SAMUEL Which you will obey?

SAUL The word of the Lord I will obey, Holiness.

SAMUEL When the word of the Lord came to Moses, he made it to be law. Wilt thou keep the law of Moses as the law of God for this people?

SAUL Make me to know it, Holiness, and I will keep it; for maybe I do not know all of it.

SAMUEL Even so it is now in Israel. For many have taken wives of the heathen, and come not to Shiloh to worship, nor do they bring their meat-offerings to the Priests, as Moses commanded. And many take usury of their brethren, which is forbidden; only of strangers may we take usury. Thus has Israel strayed from the right way.

SAUL So long as I am King, I will see that the law of Moses is obeyed, Holiness.

SAMUEL There is another thing. There are yet in this land many diviners, soothsayers, dealers in witchcraft, foretelling hidden things which it is not lawful for man to know – familiar with evil spirits, holding converse with the dead. Moses said, 'Thou shalt not suffer a witch to live.' Let the King see to it.

SAUL He *will* see to it, Holiness. Any that he finds dealing in witchcraft – shall die.

SAMUEL So; that is well.

(SAMUEL *is now feeling his way to safety.*)

There was one whom my son Joel set free, whom he should have slain . . . .

(And then a strange thing happens: SAMUEL *hears a voice, which* SAUL *does not — Is it the voice of conscience? Or is it an evil spirit speaking?)*

THE VOICE Your oath, Samuel.

SAMUEL *(after a pause)* Well, thou art King: and the King will do as seems good to him . . . And now, because I am old and weary, and am near my end, I cannot be with thee in all thy goings and comings, as I would wish to be. Therefore, I pray thee, take one of my sons with thee that he may bring word to me, when thou hast need of counsel, and I will send word by him of what the Lord shall say concerning thee and this people.

SAUL I will not take with me thy son, Abiah, Holiness: for him I do not trust. But thy son, Joel, I will take, if it please thee.

(Outside is a growing murmur of voices from the crowd.)

VOICES The King! Where is the King? Let the King show himself to his people!

SAUL Holiness, yonder the people are calling for me.

SAMUEL Go to them! Let them be satisfied, while they can be satisfied, in that which they have chosen.

SAUL Will not you come, too, Holiness, that we may stand before them together?

SAMUEL Nay! This is *their* day of triumph, not mine. The Lord has taken from me the Judgeship of His people. Go thy way! When thou hast need of me, come again.

SAUL Farewell, Holiness.

(He goes out. The people greet him tumultuously with shouts of 'God save the King!')

SAMUEL Aye! They rejoice, because I have given them a King; and I am forgotten! . . . Joel, Abiah, my sons! Where are you?

(JOEL *and* ABIAH *come in. They have but to look at* SAMUEL *to see that things have not gone well.*)

ABIAH What has he done, Father?

SAMUEL He has taken your judgment from you. Ye are nothing.

JOEL And you . . . Holiness?

SAMUEL I know not . . . Saul is King . . . The days of the Judges are ended.

ACT II

JASHER So Saul was made King, and reigned over Israel.
And Nahash, the Ammonite, came up and encamped against
Jabesh-Gilead to take it; and messengers brought word of it
to Saul. And the spirit of the Lord came upon Saul, and he
took a yoke of oxen and hewed them in pieces and sent them
throughout the coasts of Israel, saying: 'Whosoever cometh
not forth to fight for Jabesh-Gilead and to save his brethren
from the hand of Ammon, so shall it be done to his oxen
also.' And the fear of the Lord fell on the people, and they
came out with one consent, to follow after Saul to battle.

SCENE 1

(ABIAH *has remained with* SAMUEL *in his house at
Ramah. It is now a whole year since* JOEL *has been
away in the King's service, and all this time* SAMUEL
*has heard nothing from him; nor has he sent word
now of his coming, which takes* ABIAH *by surprise.
The year's separation has had a curious effect: the two
brothers have lost something of their old intimacy; it
would almost seem as though they have taken sides —
not quite; but each knows which side his bread is
buttered, and is prepared to act accordingly. In
attendance upon* JOEL *is* DOEG THE EDOMITE. *He takes*
JOEL'S *cloak and wallet and retires.*)

ABIAH So you've come at last, Joel. The Old Man's been
waiting for you. How goes it with Israel — and Israel's
King?

JOEL The King is accepted of the people, and the kingdom prospers.

ABIAH Is that what you've come to tell him? You should have come sooner.

JOEL Oh! Why?

ABIAH Things have been happening; and you brought no word of them.

JOEL I am now in the King's service, Abiah. And unless he sends me –

ABIAH We are to hear nothing?

JOEL What others have heard, did not you hear also?

ABIAH Aye! We heard that the King had made war upon Ammon. And did not send first to inquire of the Lord by the voice of Samuel, His prophet. The Old Man took to his bed when he heard of it.

JOEL Of the victory?

ABIAH Yes.

JOEL Would defeat have pleased him better?

ABIAH Maybe.

JOEL What's the matter with the Old Man? Does nothing please him?

ABIAH He's losing his teeth, Joel: can't bite any longer; so it makes him vicious. All his life he's loved power; now he's lost it. The people have found one whom they like better.

JOEL You mean Saul?

ABIAH Whom else should I mean? Our father made a mistake, Joel, when he chose Saul to be King.

JOEL The people don't think so.

ABIAH No; that's why. Too much of a King, too little of a servant – that's *his* trouble. I'm sorry for him, Joel – to see his old fingers twitch, and his limbs shake, when word comes of things done that he's had no hand in – wasn't even consulted. Life to him doesn't mean much now. But, mark my word, if he gets the chance, he'll do – someone a mischief; and if a big enough one, he'll die happy . . . What brings you now?

JOEL (*dryly*) The King has sent me to inquire of the prophet Samuel.

ABIAH Well, that's better . . . Pity he didn't do it before.

JOEL It's an inquiry that my Lord Samuel won't like.

ABIAH Oh?

JOEL It's that woman again.

ABIAH What of her?

JOEL One telling's enough. Tell his Holiness, Abiah, that I am here on the King's service.

ABIAH No need; here he comes.

> (SAMUEL *enters. He has aged, and walks now with a stoop. Seeing* JOEL, *he halts and grunts.* JOEL *is evidently out of favour.*)

SAMUEL Oh, so it's Joel. I thought it was his voice . . . What brings you here?

JOEL (*keeping his end up*) The King's command, Holiness.

SAMUEL Oh? 'The King's command'! Has he commands for *me* also?

JOEL He seeks to learn something that you may know, concerning the intentions of the God of Samuel – Holiness.

SAMUEL (*suspiciously*) Was that said to mock me?

JOEL Indeed, no, Holiness. The King knows – only too well – that about God's ways you know far better than he.

SAMUEL (*tetchily*) Well? What is it?

JOEL A certain woman, charged with witchcraft, was brought before him for judgment – Holiness.

> (*This makes* SAMUEL *sit up.*)

SAMUEL Aye? Did you . . . know this woman?

JOEL Yes, Holiness.

SAMUEL Well?

JOEL He heard the witnesses against her. If what they

told was true, it meant death . . . by the law of Moses. (*He pauses*.)

SAMUEL Death, aye, death . . .Well? Is she *not* dead?

JOEL No, Holiness . . . not yet.

SAMUEL Wherefore *not*?

JOEL Before he judged her, he asked – had she anything to say . . . She answered: 'If you slay me for what I am, the curse of Samuel's God be upon you!'

(*This is a hard one for* SAMUEL – *something he didn't expect.* JOEL *waits for him to speak.*)

SAMUEL (*warily*) Well? . . . What said he to that?

JOEL Nothing. But I saw the King's countenance change as though he doubted what judgment to give. He ordered her to safe keeping, and has sent me to require that you tell him what she meant.

SAMUEL (*angrily*) How do I know – what she meant? Let the King give his own judgment. Why should he spare one whom Moses said slay?

JOEL Did you not, Holiness, spare one whom Moses said slay?

SAMUEL I spared her on that for which she was brought to me. What she has done since concerns not *me*. Let him do as Moses commanded.

JOEL He cannot do that now, Holiness.

SAMUEL Why not?

JOEL Her keepers say – as truly they believe – that she has escaped by witchcraft: when they came to seek her, she was gone . . . I thought but to do right, Holiness, lest the curse of the God of Samuel should fall upon . . . my lord the King.

SAMUEL (*weighing his words*) So . . . you have let her live! . . . Well, you shall tell your lord the King . . . nothing. Let him answer his own question. But I also have a question for *him*. Answer for him if you can.

JOEL Yes, Holiness?

SAMUEL When he made war upon Ammon, why did he not send first to inquire of the Lord?

JOEL Had he waited, Holiness, Jabesh-Gilead would have fallen into the hands of the Ammonites, and all would have been slain.

SAMUEL If he had time to call Israel to battle, he had time to call *me*.

JOEL But what was there to inquire about, Holiness?

SAMUEL Am I not the voice of the Lord to this people? Does He not still speak by me? And if there is to be war, must not sacrifice be offered for the blessing of God to be on it?

JOEL The King did make sacrifice, Holiness.

SAMUEL The King? What right had he to make sacrifice, that is neither priest nor prophet?

JOEL Nevertheless, when he so did, the Lord prospered him.

SAMUEL Are you standing up for Saul against your own father?

JOEL You gave me to his service, Holiness. Shall not the servant speak as his master would have him speak?

SAMUEL I gave you to his service to keep watch on him, and bring word to me of all that he purposes: for that and for that only . . . What next has he a mind to do that I am not to know?

JOEL Nothing, Holiness, that you are not to know. The King is about to make war on Amalek; so would have you appoint a day to come and offer sacrifice before the army goes forth.

SAMUEL Oh! He would, would he? So this time he sends for me.

(*He sits thinking.*)

What strength has he now?

JOEL He has already with him three thousand of the tribe of Benjamin; others are coming.

SAMUEL What others? Whence come they?

JOEL All the rest of the tribes from north to south.

SAMUEL How does he get food for so many – coming from far?

JOEL They bring it with them, Holiness, by the King's command – each man enough for himself.

SAMUEL Enough for how long?

JOEL Seven days.

SAMUEL And then?

JOEL When the Amalekites are beaten, and the spoil taken, there will be enough for all.

SAMUEL And if they are not beaten?

JOEL Will not the Lord give victory to His people? . . . So, with all speed, the King bids thee come to offer sacrifice.

SAMUEL He bids me, eh? The King bids the Prophet of the Lord to a war of his own making, and sets him a time! . . . Well, I will come in . . . in seven days.

JOEL Seven days, Holiness, for what is but a day's journey?

SAMUEL I will come when I choose to come – that is, when God tells me to come. I am not this King's servant as thou art. What cause had he to be in such haste? Why did he not send for me first, before this gathering of the people? Bid him tarry till I come.

JOEL In seven days?

SAMUEL Yes: in seven days. And hark you! Tell him this. He is to destroy Amalek utterly – there shall be no sparing of Amalek after that which he did to Israel when he laid wait for him in the way, as he came up from Egypt. Therefore shall all be slain; man and woman, infant and suckling . . . sheep also, and cattle, camel and ass.

JOEL But Holiness!

SAMUEL The Lord has spoken it. If the King is of a mind

to know what the Lord would have him do, tell him that! (JOEL *makes as if to speak.*) Say no more! I have set him a time. Let him see that he keep to it . . . and wait till I come.

JOEL I will tell him . . . what you say.

(SAMUEL *sits thinking, while* JOEL *waits. There is something that yet troubles him.*)

JOEL Anything more, Holiness?

SAMUEL Why did you let that woman live, Joel! Nay, it was not the Lord's will that I should hearken to her voice . . . Say to Saul that the curse of Samuel's God will *not* be on him, if upon any found guilty of witchcraft he do as Moses commanded.

JOEL I will do so, Holiness. Farewell, Father.

(SAMUEL *looks at him but makes no answer. Exit* JOEL.)

SAMUEL There goes one – that is my own son, my first-born, whom I can no longer trust. Saul has stolen him from me . . . He let that woman live! To save Saul from the curse of the God of Samuel . . . It shall not! . . . Listen, Abiah! I will give the King a lesson. Is Samuel, the Prophet of the Lord, to be of no account because Israel has a King? Who made him King? I – by the Word of the Lord. And if he obey not His Word, when I speak it, he shall be King no more.

(ABIAH *does not respond.* SAMUEL *eyes him suspiciously.*

Well? What have you to say against that?

ABIAH That it will be difficult, Holiness. Saul is no fool: he knows how to make his will pleasing to the people. When he fetched them away from their fields to fight for Jabesh-

Gilead, many of them murmured, and said – why should
they fight for Jabesh-Gilead when their own borders were
safe? But when Saul gave them the spoil – and all the
sheep and oxen that were taken, they sang differently then.
They went back richer than they came. So now that he
sends for them again, they come gladly.

SAMUEL What right had he to take and divide the spoil?

ABIAH It is always done, Holiness.

SAMUEL It shall be done no more. All that is Amalek's
shall be had in abomination. They shall take no spoil of
Amalek.

ABIAH The people will be disappointed, Holiness.

SAMUEL Let them be! The word of the Lord has been
spoken.

> (*He sits thinking; and now it is with a more set pur-
> pose that he speaks.*)

In seven days, did I say? Well, should it be more than seven
days, the Lord will appoint some other time for the slaying
of Amalek. Maybe it is not His will that *Saul* should destroy
Amalek, but some other. For surely he that destroys
Amalek will be great in the eyes of all Israel; and the
people will follow him – not heeding the word of the Lord.
Abiah, I have an errand for thee. Joel I can no longer trust:
he stands now for Saul. Go to Shiloh, to Ahimelech, the
High Priest, and to all the Priests that are there with him;
and say to them – from me – that Saul is to be King no
more. The Lord shall raise up another in his stead; and
the Kingdom shall be taken from Saul, and given to another.

ABIAH To whom will it be given, Holiness?

SAMUEL I know not yet. When it is the Lord's will to
make it known, He will tell me.

ABIAH But, Holiness, if Saul hear of it –

SAMUEL How shall he hear of it . . . unless thou tell him
of it?

ABIAH How shall he *not* hear of it, if another King be chosen? And if he hear of it, will he not slay?

SAMUEL Slay whom? Think you that any dare slay the Priests of the Lord? If he did, in that day his kingdom would be over. For as the Lord has set Prophet above Priest, so has he set Priest above King, for the ruling of Israel. Therefore, when I say to Ahimelech that Saul is King no more – he *is* King no more . . . Dost thou doubt?

ABIAH No, Holiness. But for this would it not be better for Ahimelech to come to you himself? For my word, in so great a matter, he might doubt.

SAMUEL Well, so be it. Send Ahimelech to me. Bid him come . . .

(SAMUEL *pauses. Across the doorway goes* DOEG, *moving swiftly and furtively*.)

ABIAH (*artfully*) In . . . seven days, Holiness?

SAMUEL Aye, seven days will be time enough. Saul can wait.

(*A sound of galloping is heard.* SAMUEL *turns to look*.)

Who is yonder man, riding away?

ABIAH (*looking*) That? That is Doeg, the Edomite, one of Saul's servants. He came with Joel.

SAMUEL I will not have any of Saul's servants brought here. Tell Joel that!

ABIAH Yes, Holiness: better that Saul should *not* know that you have sent for Ahimelech.

SAMUEL It were well he should not. Bid him come – secretly.

ABIAH (*dryly*) Yes, Holiness.

(SAMUEL *looks at him suspiciously*.)

SAMUEL Are *you* faithful, Abiah? Have I one son left to me for comfort in my old age, whom I can yet trust?

ABIAH Surely, Holiness! Why should you doubt *me*?

SAMUEL Nay, I know not whether of all who served me while I judged Israel, there be one left to me. But the Priests of the Lord . . . aye, them I can trust. Go, then, send me Ahimelech.

> (ABIAH *goes. The day is now near its end; the air grows dark.* SAMUEL *stands silent for a while; then speaks.*)

Aye; surely when I let her live I did ill. She has brought a curse upon me. Because I trusted not the Lord Himself to give me the sign of His wrath against Israel, He has shut His mouth at me. I took counsel of Evil; and He has cursed me with a King who heeds not my word. The people follow him. I am forgotten. The shadow of death is round about me; the pains of Hell have got hold upon me . . . Yonder comes darkness of the Heavens (*distant thunder*) and a sound. And I know not the meaning of it – whether it be of good or of evil. (*There comes a faint flash of lightning, followed by distant thunder.*) Lord, if it be Thy voice, speak! Let me hear Thee again. (*Thunder.*) Surely, it is a voice of wrath . . . Against whom? Is it against Saul, the King? (*He pauses.*) Or is it against Samuel, that was Thy prophet? (*Thunder. He trembles and bows himself in fear.*)

> (*While he has been speaking the* WISE WOMAN *has entered, and stands watching him.*)

WOMAN What is thy fear, Samuel? (*He starts and turns.*) Is it of me? . . . Or of thyself? . . . Or of thy God?

SAMUEL Woman, whence art thou?

WOMAN From the folly of them that fear wisdom, and would have me dead.

SAMUEL Why hast thou come to me?

WOMAN Thou didst promise me life. Why, then, does Saul seek to slay me?

SAMUEL I know not I am not in the King's counsel.

WOMAN Who made him King, Samuel? He that makes Kings – do they not heed his word, and take counsel of him?

SAMUEL He heeds not mine . . . When I promised thee thy life, in that day I had power for life and death. I have it no more. Go, trouble me not. Thy life is in thine own hands. I cannot save thee.

WOMAN So! Thy God has failed thee at last: He believes in thee no more.

SAMUEL Thou blasphemest, Woman!

WOMAN Why therefore shouldst thou believe in *Him*? Nay! what has His wrath against Israel done for thee? It has not given thee back thy power. Thou art become as a dead man. Slay thy God, Samuel! Slay thy God! And thou shalt live again . . . His name? . . . Samuel! Aye, truly, His name is Samuel.

SAMUEL What mean you by that, Woman?

WOMAN Truth; but hard for thee to believe. Yet will I show it thee; and thou shalt see, or be blind, as pleaseth thee best . . . When thou didst seek a sign of God's wrath against Israel, asking for a King – was it the wrath of God, or was it the wrath of Samuel? And if it was Samuel who so visited his wrath on Israel, was not Samuel his own God?

SAMUEL Surely, I was cursed in the day when I first saw thee, and hearkened to thy word!

WOMAN It was thine own curse, Samuel. I cursed thee not. Nevertheless a curse is on thee now. Thou fearest Saul. *I* also fear him – because of thee. Well, keep thy God; and see that thy God keep *thee* in safety. But I will tell thee a thing ere I go. Saul is become too strong for thee. Thou hast raised up one whom thou canst not pull down. He is King. Thou art forgotten. Hast thou called on thy God to curse him – to give thee another storm? Is this an answer to thy prayer? Or is it . . . nothing? Is this the voice of *thy* God, or . . . of mine? (*Thunder.*)

SAMUEL There is but one God . . . though I hear Him no more.

WOMAN How far outside Israel does thy God rule? Among the Gods of the nations, what power has He? Does He show signs and wonders among them? Do they fear Him, that have never heard His name? There is one God that rules all. Him only do I worship and fear. His name? He has no name. He will never be named, for He will never be known. But He is there . . . He is here . . . in thee, and in me; but we know Him not . . . though by Him we are known. Farewell, Samuel. Beware of Saul, lest . . . He slay thee also.

(*She turns to go.*)

SAMUEL Stay . . . Hark, Woman . . . Can thou put a curse upon a man?

WOMAN Can I? No. What need? He puts it upon himself.

SAMUEL How?

WOMAN By fear . . . If a man fear thee enough, thy curse is on him. If he fear thee not, he is free. For where the sight of a man's eye goes, he goes with it. Where the hearing of his ear can reach, or the sound of his voice, there goes the man also. So, too, the thoughts of a man's heart; where he sends them they go; and he goes with them. For man is not made of flesh and blood only – but of mind and spirit; and from these comes power – whether it be for good or ill. There be evil spirits, and the world is full of them – anger, fear, jealousy, hatred. Wherever they go, they seek to enter and take possession. Dost thou fear Saul? Nay, fear him not! But if Saul fear thee, he is in thy bonds. If he fear thee not – then is he free of thee; and thy day of power is over . . . Farewell, Samuel.

(*She goes.*)

SAMUEL So . . . it is Saul that is mine enemy. Surely it repenteth the Lord that He made Saul to be King. Speak, Lord! (*Distant thunder.*) Nay, I know not what Thou sayest! O God, if Thou have cursed me with this King because I trusted Thee not, pardon now Thy sorry servant. Let Thy curse be now on him: make him to fear the God of Samuel, and let an evil spirit from the Lord trouble him!

(*Thunder.* SAMUEL *stands listening. He is still not sure whether he does hear the word of the Lord so as to understand it.*)

SCENE 2

(*The fight with Amalek is over.* SAUL *stands in his tent clad in full armour; before him, under a guard of armed men,* AGAG, *King of the Amalekites, crouches and fawns.*)

AGAG My life! My life! Grant me my life, and I will serve thee faithfully all my days. Oh, King! Only to live is all I ask.

SAUL (*with a gesture of disgust*) Thy life! Thy life! Take him away! . . . This is no King, but a sheep that I have spared! Oh, God, were I such a King, let me be slain!

(AGAG, *struggling feebly, is led out. Saul's armour-bearer begins to disarm him. An attendant offers him a cup of wine: as he drinks a distant blowing of horns is heard. He pauses to listen.* JOEL *enters.*)

JOEL My lord, it is the Holy One.

SAUL (*hotly*) Nay. What purpose brings him now? It is too late. Let him go back: we have no use for him.

JOEL See him, my lord.

SAUL I will not! Why tarried he so long – would you know?

> (*At a gesture from* SAUL, ARMOURER *and* CUP-BEARER *go out.*)

JOEL I *do* know, my lord.

SAUL Ha! So you are of his counsel still?

JOEL No, my lord, No! But I know this man that is my own father. My counsel is for my lord, the King. Hear me, my lord!

SAUL Speak, then!

JOEL My lord, for forty years he was Israel's Judge and Ruler. Of all that were before, none was so great: and bitter has it been to him to give up power and rule to another. And now he is old and near his end. Satisfy him this once, my lord, that he may leave you in peace.

> (SAUL *is hard to convince.*)

SAUL How – satisfy – him?

JOEL My lord, give him, this last time, that for which he craves – a show of power and authority in the eyes of the people . . . Nay, is he not still the Prophet of the Lord?

SAUL So he says. Comes he with good intent, think you? Or to reprove me – that I did not wait his coming?

JOEL Accept his reproof, my lord; for he has yet power to divide Israel.

SAUL And the will?

JOEL It may be so, my lord.

SAUL If he so wills, he has no part in Israel – not while I am King.

> (*And now from a nearer distance, again comes the blowing of horns, followed by sounds of cheering. A* MESSENGER *enters.*)

MESSENGER My lord, the Holy One.

SAUL Let him come! (*To* JOEL.) I will deal with him as he deserves.

JOEL I beseech you, my lord!

SAUL Go, Joel. He is your father; what I have to say to him, I will say to him alone . . . If he be honest, he has not to fear.

> (JOEL, *who has his doubts of Samuel's honesty, makes a forlorn gesture, and goes.* SAUL *stands waiting. Outside are heard the excited murmurs of a great crowd.*)
>
> (SAMUEL *makes an impressive entry, borne high in a litter upon the shoulders of four* LEVITES; *and though age and infirmity may be his excuse, it is not his reason: now, as he comes face to face with the King, he occupies the dominating position which he considers to be his right.*)

SAUL You come late, Holiness.

SAMUEL I come in the Lord's time, and in the Lord's name, to do the Lord's will, and speak His judgment before Israel.

SAUL You stay too high, Holiness. Come down to earth, that we may meet as man to man.

> (SAMUEL, *very much upon his dignity, ignores the request, which* SAUL *proceeds to enforce.*)

Levites, set down your load!

> (*They hesitate.* SAMUEL *opens his mouth indignantly, as if to speak.* SAUL *makes a commanding gesture. The* LEVITES *set down* SAMUEL, *who, as the litter comes to ground, rises angrily to his feet.*)

SAUL (*to the* LEVITES) Enough. You can go.

(The four LEVITES, *unable to withstand the King's command, indicate their higher allegiance by making their bows not to* SAUL *but to* SAMUEL. *They go out.)*

Again I say – you come late.

SAMUEL The Prophet of the Lord has not to excuse himself to any man.

SAUL Even the Prophet of the Lord should be true to his word, in the service of Israel.

SAMUEL I serve not Israel, but Israel's God; His Word only do I obey.

SAUL I also have obeyed His Word – spoken by you. Amalek is smitten, and destroyed utterly: and Agag, their King, I have taken alive.

SAMUEL Aye, alive! Was that what the Lord commanded thee to do? What means, then, this bleating of sheep in mine ears, and this lowing of oxen that I hear?

SAUL It means that when the people go to war they must also be fed. Because we waited your coming, of that which they brought with them nothing was left. Therefore have they spared the best of the sheep and of the cattle for their own need, which was great. Your doing, Holiness. – Also for a sacrifice and a peace-offering to the Lord our God. The rest they have utterly destroyed as I commanded them.

SAMUEL Hath the Lord as great delight in burnt offering and sacrifice, as in obeying the Voice of the Lord? Behold, to obey is better than sacrifice, and to hearken than the fat of rams.

SAUL How could I obey your broken word? Had I waited, when you came not, Israel would have been scattered before the face of the enemy.

SAMUEL Aye, till the Lord chose for Himself another and a better time – and – a better man. Thou hast rebelled against the Word of the Lord; and thy rebellion is as the sin of witchcraft, and thy stubbornness is iniquity and idolatry. And because thou hast gone thine own way, rejecting the Word of the Lord, He also hath rejected thee from being King.

SAUL That is a hard saying, Holiness, and hard to believe. What is your proof? Was it truly the Lord's will that Israel should be scattered – or was it *yours*? If I am no longer the Lord's Anointed, let Him declare it. Aye! Stand now with me before this people, and tell them that I am no longer their King. Will they believe you? No! Will they not say 'This is no Prophet of the Lord that speaks, when the Lord has given our King victory'?

SAMUEL Aye! So, making thyself great, wouldst thou steal the heart of my people from the Lord their God. I will not! I will hear thee no more. Go thy own way, Saul; and I will go *mine*. Aye, surely this is thy day; and the people follow thee and are glad. But a day will come when they shall *not* follow thee. . . .

(*He turns to go.*)

SAUL Dost thou go to divide Israel? Thou shalt not!

(*He catches hold of Samuel's mantle; it tears in his hand.*)

SAMUEL See! As thou hast lifted thy hand against the Prophet of the Lord, and rent from him his mantle, so hath the Lord rent the Kingdom of Israel from thee this day, and given it to one who is better than thou.

SAUL His name?

SAMUEL Thou shalt know his name in the day when the Lord hath set him over thee to be the strength of Israel.

SAUL Time enough. I will know then.

(SAMUEL *again turns to go.*)

Nay, you go not yet. I have more to say to you.

SAMUEL (*furiously*) I will not hear it! Nay! I will not hear it!

(*But* SAUL *stands in his way; he cannot go out.*)

SAUL Old man, be silent! It is the King speaks now. Aye, the King! You called me to be God's Anointed: you told me that I was. If I was, I still am: and there is none over me but God Himself. If I am not – then whose? Yours? The Lord God of Israel deliver me from your hand. For your mind towards me is evil, and your hand is against me. Yea, I know well how you have sought to divide Israel from me. But I am King still. If they would have some other I will know of it, and will be King no more. But they shall have no King of *your* choosing. You raised me up in the name of the Lord – truly or falsely. If falsely, *you* shall not cast me down – *not while I live*, saith the Lord!

SAMUEL Is Saul also among the Prophets?

SAUL Aye! For on that same day when you anointed me King, the spirit of the Lord came on me, and I prophesied. And I prophesy again that I will live and die a King, *after you are dead* . . . Nay, be not afraid; *you* I do not slay – for truly the Lord spake by you while yet you judged Israel. But if you teach others to conspire against me, them I will slay without mercy. I will have no traitor in Israel, not while I am King – be he priest or no. I know what you have done. You sent your son Abiah to Ahimelech; and Ahimelech came to you secretly, and secretly returned. Was it for that you waited and came not on the day appointed, and would have scattered Israel from before the army of Amalek had I not done your office, and myself offered sacrifice?

SAMUEL What right hadst thou – that art not of the priesthood – to offer sacrifice?

SAUL The same as thou; for neither art thou of the priesthood, nor of the tribe of Levi. But if prophet be priest, then

also King is priest when he must lead his people to battle
. . . and the prophet came not. But if thou wouldst now –
though so late – make sacrifice and peace-offering for the
people, and thanksgiving for victory – so be it. Take what
thou wilt of that which they have spared of the sheep and
the oxen, as many as it may please thee . . . And I will
come with thee to the sacrifice.

> (*This offer does not please* SAMUEL, *who no longer
> has any desire to share honours with* SAUL; *but now
> he sees his chance and takes it.*)

SAMUEL No; I will not; for that which they have spared of
Amalek is abomination to the Lord; and no offering shall
be made of it . . . But I will take from thee Agag, their
King; and him I will slay. So shall the wrath of the Lord
be turned from His people this day, because they and their
King obeyed not the Word of the Lord – as spoken by me.

> (*There is a pause.* SAUL *sees clearly that* SAMUEL *is
> going to score: but he does not take back his offer.*)

SAUL So be it. Thou shalt have thy desire. I give thee
Agag.

> (*He claps his hands. A* GUARD *enters.*)

Bring Agag. And bid in again those Levites that stand
without.

> (*The* GUARD *goes.*)

My part is done – Holiness; the rest of this matter is for
thee. I come not to thy sacrifice – a poor offering to the
Lord thy God is this sheep which calls itself a King. There,
yonder he comes.

> (SAMUEL *instinctively strikes an attitude of dignity for
> a scene in which he is to be the principal figure. The*

four LEVITES, *followed by* JOEL, *have entered, and
stand waiting for orders.* SAUL *makes a gesture.*)

SAUL Resume your eminence, Holiness. Levites, take up
your load.

(SAMUEL *seats himself in the litter. The* LEVITES
*hoist him into a position which once more satisfies him.
He is now master of a situation which is greatly to
his liking. Guarded to right and left,* AGAG *enters,
walking delicately; not yet confronted by the high
majesty of* SAMUEL, *he advances towards* SAUL.)

AGAG Now surely the bitterness of death is past.
SAUL Ask yonder man. He will tell thee.

(AGAG *turns, and sees now, for the first time,* SAMUEL
*raised up for judgment. Before that Presence all
spirit goes out of him.*)

SAMUEL Ask not thy life of me, I speak for the Lord God
of Israel. This is His Judgment upon thee, and thy doom.
As thy sword hath made women childless, so shall thy
mother be childless among women.

(AGAG *utters a quavering cry, and falls on his knees
before* SAMUEL.)

AGAG No! No! No!
SAMUEL Lift him! Bind him, and let him be brought
after me straightway to the place of sacrifice. There will I
hew him in pieces before the Lord.

(AGAG, *struggling desperately, is raised and bound.
On the shoulders of his* LEVITES, SAMUEL *makes a
stately exit.* AGAG *and his* GUARD *follow. As* SAMUEL
*appears before the people, horns are again blown.
The shout of welcome increases and becomes tumul-
tuous.* SAUL *stands looking after him.*)

SAUL There goes the show, Joel. Well, I have given him that for which he craved – as you begged of me – to stand great in the eyes of the people. For a great thing it is to have a King for sacrifice. And hark how it pleases them! Aye, I have given him Agag; but he would have liked better had it been Saul.

JOEL (*horrified*) Oh, my lord. No!

(*But* SAUL *is sure of it.*)

SAUL He goes to divide Israel.

SCENE 3

(SAMUEL *has come back to Ramah. It is the third day since his return; no longer wearing his robe of ceremony, he sits wearily waiting for the news which* ABIAH *has for him.* ABIAH, *as he lays aside his travelling gear, seems in no hurry to begin.*)

SAMUEL You have come back soon, Abiah. You have seen Joel? Did he send me any – message?

ABIAH No, Holiness.

SAMUEL When is he – coming again?

ABIAH He is not coming again.

SAMUEL Why not?

ABIAH He says the King will not send him.

SAMUEL So it is only the King's word now that he obeys . . . I have done with Joel. You only are left to me . . . What are the people saying, Abiah – about me and the King?

ABIAH There is much talk, Holiness, but little is known. They say that you and the King were at high words together; but nevertheless, that before parting, it pleased the King to give you Agag for sacrifice.

SAMUEL That it pleased him, eh? It did *not*. He came not to the sacrifice. Had it pleased him, would he not have done so?

ABIAH Yea, Holiness – surely. For 'twas a great thing to see a captive King slain by the Prophet of the Lord for a sacrifice. It pleased the *people*.

SAMUEL Aye. I knew well it would.

ABIAH And for having so done, you are held greatly in honour.

SAMUEL Aye . . . Well, what else have you to tell?

ABIAH After you were gone, the King gave a great feast to all his captains from the spoil that had been taken; and another feast to the people. They feasted till they could feast no more. (*Samuel gives a grunt of disapproval.*) But while he was at the feast, they saw the King's countenance change, as though an evil spirit troubled him. And suddenly, full of wrath, he cried 'Where is that man who would make himself King in my stead?' (*At this Samuel's interest becomes keen.*) They were all astonished, and they said 'There is no such man among us, my lord.' The King said 'If there be such a man, let him see to it: he shall die.'

SAMUEL Oh? He said that, did he?

ABIAH And he went forth alone from the feast. And all wondered what it might mean.

SAMUEL They shall know what it means – some day . . . some day. And how stands the King now, with the people?

ABIAH He also is held in great honour, Holiness. They say – now that he has destroyed the Amalekites, he will destroy the Philistines also; and give Israel peace.

SAMUEL (*angrily*) There shall be no peace for Israel while Saul is King . . . (*He sits thinking.*) Call Jasher to me. There is that which must be written, as the Lord would have it written – ere I die – that Israel may know hereafter of Saul's disobedience, and of how the Lord judged him for it – by me.

ABIAH Holiness, has it been also with Saul as it was with Eli?

SAMUEL What mean you?

ABIAH That your wrath was God's wrath . . . You heard no Voice?

SAMUEL I heard – no Voice.

ABIAH (*quoting*) 'Nevertheless, had I not told him of the Voice, Eli would not have believed me.' Did you tell Saul, Holiness?

SAMUEL What I told Saul, you shall hear. Call Jasher.

(ABIAH *goes, and presently returns followed by* JASHER.)

Aye, Israel shall know how the Lord has spoken by me . . . Sit down, Jasher. Take your tablets and write. Write it in brief, and copy afterwards.

(JASHER *sits down, and makes ready with his tablets.* ABIAH *stands attentive to what follows; and presently one perceives that he knows a good deal more of what actually happened between* SAUL *and* SAMUEL, *when they were alone together, than* SAMUEL *suspects. Possibly* JOEL *was his informant – a tent not being sound-proof when voices become loud. And so, when* SAMUEL *reshapes the story to his better liking,* ABIAH'S *eyes turn on him curiously – and knowingly.*)

SAMUEL (*dictating*) Then came the word of the Lord to Samuel, saying 'It repenteth Me that I have set up Saul to be King, for he hath turned back from following Me, and hath not performed My commandments.'

(*This gives* JASHER *a shock; for, since their first meeting, he has loved* SAUL *greatly; and as he continues to write at Samuel's dictation, his grief and consternation become greater.*)

'And it grieved Samuel; and he cried unto the Lord all night'. . . . Yes, it gave me a sleepless night, Abiah.

ABIAH (*smoothly*) I can well believe it, Holiness.

SAMUEL Yes: I wore myself out, praying that the Lord would repent Him. But He would not. Go on, Jasher. 'And Samuel rose up early, and went to meet Saul that had gone before to Gilgal. And Saul said unto him – ' . . . When I came before Saul, Abiah, your brother Joel was with him – with others; but Saul made them all go forth from before him – fearing, I doubt not, what the Lord would have me say to him. . . .

'And Saul said unto him' . . . (Go on, Jasher) . . . 'Blessed be thou of the Lord; I have performed the commandment of the Lord.' . . . (Yes, that's what he said, Abiah) . . . 'And Samuel said 'What meaneth, then, this bleating of sheep in mine ears, and the lowing of oxen that I hear?' And Saul said 'They have brought them from the Amalekites, and have spared the best of the sheep and oxen to sacrifice unto the Lord thy God. Also they have brought Agag their King captive, and the rest we have destroyed utterly.' (*To* ABIAH) – They had not. They had not – 'And Samuel said, 'Hath the Lord as great delight in burnt offering as in obeying the voice of the Lord? Behold, to obey is better than sacrifice, and to hearken than the fat of rams. Now, because thou hast rejected the Word of the Lord, He also hath rejected thee from being King' . . . Go on, go on, Jasher What are you stopping for? . . . (*To* ABIAH) I doubt not Saul was glad then that he had sent all forth from before him, ere that word was spoken. And mark you, now, his answer – heard only by *me*; but this shall make it known – hereafter . . . 'And Saul said unto Samuel, 'I have sinned, and have trangressed the commandment of the Lord, spoken by thee, because I feared the people, and obeyed their voice.'

(*This is so out of character for* SAUL, *that* ABIAH *and* JASHER *both open their mouths in astonishment. But*

it is only his own character that SAMUEL *cares about;*
and he continues to dictate:)

'Now therefore, I pray thee, pardon my sin, and turn again
with me that I may worship the Lord thy God, and be held
in honour before the people.' And Samuel said 'I will not
turn with thee.' And as Samuel turned about to go, Saul
laid hold of the skirt of his mantle, and it rent. And Samuel
said 'So hath the Lord rent the Kingdom of Israel from thee
this day, and given it to another that is thy better.' (*Then
to* ABIAH) And when he would have me tell him who that
might be, I would not – for I do not yet know. The Lord
will show it me, when the time has come to declare it.
'Then,' said Samuel, 'bring hither to me Agag, the King
of the Amalekites.' And Agag came unto him delicately.
And Agag said 'Surely the bitterness of death is past.' And
Samuel said, 'As thy sword hath made women childless, so
shall thy mother be childless among women.' And Samuel
hewed Agag in pieces before the Lord in Gilgal.'

(*Having finished his piece, Samuel rises, and as he
turns to go, says to* ABIAH *in a tone of great satis-
faction:*)

SAMUEL There, Abiah; What do you think of that?
ABIAH Fine, Holiness! Fine!

(SAMUEL *is about to go out, when he sees Jasher, his
head bowed with grief, and his hand faltering as he
writes. He pauses, returns, and then, laying his
hand gently on Jasher's shoulders, he says:*)

SAMUEL And now you may add this, Jasher: 'And Samuel
came no more to see Saul, until the day of his death.
Nevertheless Samuel mourned for Saul, that the Lord
repented that He had made Saul King over Israel. . . .

(*He goes out.* JASHER *ceases to write, and bows his head over his tablets in a passion of weeping.* ABIAH *goes up to him, and slapping his back with kindly jocosity, says:*)

ABIAH The Word of the Lord, Jasher! The Word of the Lord! Is it not written in the book of the Prophet Samuel?

ACT III

JASHER (*speaks before the curtain*) Now after Samuel had parted from Saul, an evil spirit from the Lord troubled him. And Saul's servants said unto him 'Behold now, an evil spirit from God troubleth thee. Let our lord command, therefore, that we seek out a man who is a cunning player on the harp, so that when the evil spirit is upon thee, he shall play with his hand, and thou shalt be well.' And Saul said 'Where wilt thou find me such a man?' Then answered one of his servants, and said, 'There is a son of Jesse, the Bethlehemite, named David that is cunning in playing – a valiant man, and a man of war, prudent in speech, and of a goodly countenance; and the Lord is with him.' And Saul said 'Send him to me.' So David came to Saul, and stood before him; and Saul loved him greatly; and he became his armour-bearer. And it came to pass, when the evil spirit was upon Saul, that David took a harp and played with his hand; and the evil spirit departed from him.

SCENE 1

(*The curtain opens, and discloses* SAUL *seated in a large tent: with his armour lying beside him. The sides of the tent are of dark red. There is no light; only from a brazier at his feet comes a dull red glow: For a while there is dead silence; then from a distance comes the sound of marching; it is the guard. At the word of command, it halts outside the tent; the guard is changed; the pass-word is given and repeated: 'Let the King live.' At the word of com-mand the marching is resumed, and dies slowly away; and again there is dead silence. The flap of the tent is lifted softly; DAVID enters; he carries a harp in his hand. He stands looking at SAUL.)*

SAUL Who is there?

DAVID Your servant David, my lord.

SAUL Come in . . . Come nearer . . . Stand by me.

(DAVID *goes and stands beside* SAUL.)

See you yonder man?

DAVID I see no one, my lord.

SAUL An old man . . . with eyes of wrath . . . he stands looking at me. And in his hand he holds a mantle that is rent.

DAVID No, my lord: there is no such man here.

SAUL You do not look in the right place. Come! Look at me! Look! Look! Into my eyes . . . Can you not see him now?

DAVID No, my lord.

(*But his voice has faltered.*)

SAUL (*searchingly*) What did you see?

DAVID Pardon, my lord . . . I saw . . . Fear.

SAUL Of what?

DAVID I know not, my lord.

SAUL (*violently*) Nay, tell me! Of what? Of what?

DAVID I know not whether it be of yourself, my lord, or of another. A King should fear only God.

SAUL Aye! But if *he* speaks for God, then is God my enemy.

DAVID God is the enemy of no man who trusts Him, my lord.

SAUL I did trust . . . I did trust. But if Israel be divided

245

and fall a prey to the enemy – whom then can I trust? Neither God, nor man . . . God nor man. See there! He is beckoning to you with his hand. (*Challengingly.*) Are *you* faithful, David – to your King?

DAVID My lord! My lord!

SAUL Look me in the eyes! Show me your face!

> (SAUL *takes hold of him and draws him close – eye to eye.*)

SAUL You look honest. Oh, were you to deceive me, you my sweet singer and comforter, there would be none left whom I could trust. (*A sort of convulsion takes hold of him.*) Death! Death! For all that rise up against me, it *shall* be death.

> (DAVID *leaves him; sits down at a little distance, takes up his harp and plays. At first* SAUL *seems to take no heed; he sits staring wildly into vacancy; but gradually relaxes; slowly his head sinks, his clenched hands fall to rest, all his fear and wrath have gone out of him. Presently, in a low voice,* DAVID *begins to sing:*)

DAVID The Lord is my shepherd; therefore shall I lack nothing.

He maketh me to lie down in green pastures, and leadeth me beside the still waters.

He shall restore my soul, and bring me into paths of righteousness for His Name's sake.

Yea, though I walk through the valley of the shadow of death, I will fear no evil;

For Thou art with me; Thy rod and Thy staff comfort me.

Thou preparest a table before me against them that trouble me.

Thou anointest my head with oil, and my cup runneth over.

Thy goodness and mercy shall follow me all the days of my life; and I will dwell in the house of the Lord for ever.

(*Slowly* SAUL *raises his head, and rises to his feet. A soft faint light streams over him. He makes a gesture.* DAVID *comes forward and kneels at his feet.* SAUL *reaches down and lays his hands upon David's head.*)

SAUL Oh, thou voice of my comfort, thou light to the darkness of my soul! What is this thou hast done for me? The pit that had opened before me has shut its mouth. And him that I feared, I fear no more. . . .

(DAVID *takes Saul's hand and kisses it. Slowly the curtain closes.*)

SCENE 2

(*In the dim light of his chamber* SAMUEL *lies sleeping. In a dream he sees the* WISE WOMAN *of Endor, and hears her speaking.*)

WOMAN Art thou still sleeping, Samuel?

SAMUEL Oh, cursed woman! Why have you come here to trouble me again?

WOMAN Maybe, I am not here. Maybe, I am only a dream sent to thee – by the Lord.

SAMUEL Nay! Wherefore should He send *thee*? For surely thou art an evil thing, and hast been a curse to me since the day when I took counsel of thee.

WOMAN Does not the Lord thy God send evil as well as good? Cannot He that blesses curse also? Is not that evil spirit which is now upon Saul – also from the Lord – and thee? . . . Aye! didst thou not pray that the Lord should send it? Well, He has sent it: To what end? That Saul should fear the God of Samuel. 'Twas a wise prayer, Samuel; for if Saul fear *thy* God, he fears thee also . . . You made too much of a King when you made Saul, Samuel. Yet would he be more of a King — and thou so much the less — did he *not* fear thee. . . .

SAMUEL Why does he fear me?

WOMAN Because he is an honest man — more honest than thou art. And there has come to him a doubt whether he was truly the chosen of the Lord, or only the chosen of Samuel . . . Which was he? . . . Look yonder! See how he sits, throned, and crowned. With the weapons to his hand wherewith he has fought valiantly for the strength of Israel . . . What is that shadow that has fallen upon him? Why is his face darkened and his heart troubled? The curse of Samuel's God — whom he fears — is upon him.

(*Faint music is heard.*)

SAMUEL Who is that — sitting at his feet, and playing upon a harp?

WOMAN A man named David, that has come to take thy curse from him . . . Have a care for David, Samuel: — have a care! For if David serve Saul faithfully, and take thy curse from him, Saul will fear thee no more.

(*As she speaks, her form begins to fade and grow dim.*)

SAMUEL Where art thou going, Woman?

WOMAN To mine own place, the rock wherein I have hid myself from them that seek after my life to slay me . . . Was it for *that* that you made Saul my enemy? . . . Farewell, Samuel.

(*She disappears.* SAMUEL *lies for a while without motion, still sleeping. Then he stirs, rouses himself, and calls:*)

SAMUEL Caleb . . . Caleb.

(*His old servant* CALEB *enters; and through the open-ing door comes a gleam of daylight.*)

CALEB You called, Holiness?

SAMUEL Caleb, get me up. Help me to rise.

(CALEB *raises him from the bed,* SAMUEL *sits up.* CALEB *brings a cloak, and lays it over his knees.*)

Let in the light, Caleb.

(CALEB *throws back the shutters, letting in the cold light of early day.*)

Send Abiah to me.

CALEB Will you not now have something to eat, Holiness?

SAMUEL Presently; not yet.

(CALEB *goes.* SAMUEL *sits waiting.* ABIAH *enters.*)

ABIAH Have you had a good night, Holiness?

SAMUEL A good night? I know not . . . No. I have had a dream which troubles me.

ABIAH Why should a dream trouble the Holy One of Israel? Are not all dreams from God?

SAMUEL No . . . not all. There be dreams that come of Evil . . . Who is this man – David?

ABIAH (*surprised*) David? From whom have you heard tell of him, Holiness?

SAMUEL The Lord has bid me inquire concerning him. Who is he?

ABIAH He is Saul's chosen servant and armour-bearer; also his musician. And when Saul's trouble is upon him –

SAMUEL His trouble?

ABIAH That evil spirit which now afflicts him –

SAMUEL Aye?

ABIAH — This man David goes in alone to him, when no one else dare, and plays to him . . . Also they say that Jonathan, the King's son, loves him greatly.

SAMUEL Whence comes he?

ABIAH He is of the tribe of Judah, a son of Jesse, the Bethlehemite.

SAMUEL What brought him to Saul? How came he to know of him?

ABIAH First it was but by report, for the healing of the King's malady, by his playing upon the harp. Till then he was only a keeper of sheep; but already a mighty man of valour — by his own account. One hears tales of him which are hard to believe.

SAMUEL Is he young?

ABIAH Yes, Holiness. A year ago he was hardly more than a boy; but now he is a full man, and wise beyond his years.

SAMUEL (*suspiciously*) How come you to know so much of him, while I know nothing?

ABIAH I had it from Joel.

SAMUEL (*ill-pleased*) So you have been to see Joel?

ABIAH Yes, Father.

SAMUEL Why? I did not send you.

ABIAH No, Father. But is not Joel still my brother? And from him I hear things that it is well you should know, Holiness.

SAMUEL What should I know?

ABIAH Because he believes that you are of a mind to divide Israel, the King has set a watch upon you. I was to warn you of that, Holiness.

SAMUEL So, it has come to that! — The man whom I made to be King thinks to set a watch on me. Well, that also shall go to his unmaking — when the Lord hears of it.

ABIAH I think you came to the making of him too late, Holiness.

SAMUEL What mean you?

ABIAH To shape a King as you would have him be, you must catch him young. Saul was already too much his own master when you first took measure of him . . . I warned you, Father.

SAMUEL How did you warn me?

ABIAH When I told you how he had withstood me in the seat of Judgment, you praised him for it. Well, you have learned better since.

SAMUEL Go to! Are you daring to teach your Father?

ABIAH (*dryly*) No; only *learning* him.

SAMUEL Tell me more of this – David.

ABIAH It could be better told, Holiness, by those that are better able to believe what he tells of himself. But if what the boy has told be true, and if out of the boy comes the man, David is like to become the light of Israel.

SAMUEL Aye?

ABIAH While yet a keeper of his father's sheep he did – so he says – what no living man has yet done: took a lion, and a bear, by the throat (not on the same day, maybe) and tore the life out of them. Even Samson could not do that: he needed the jawbone of an ass to do it with.

SAMUEL You are wrong, Abiah; it was with the jawbone of an ass that Samson slew – not the lion, but a thousand Philistines.

ABIAH Was it so? Then, like enough, with his own jawbone David will some day do the same; for he seems able to make people believe whatever he chooses to tell them. And that, surely, is a gift which comes only from the Lord – Eh, Holiness?

SAMUEL Abiah, you have an evil mind. You mock at things which are holy. If the Lord is with David, He *is* with him. Aye! God works wonders in them whom He has chosen – to raise up.

ABIAH Did He so, when He raised up Saul, Holiness?

SAMUEL Whom He raises – if he do ill – He shall also cast

down . . . So now Saul is troubled of an evil spirit, eh? Doubt not it comes from God.

ABIAH Does God send evil on men, Holiness?

SAMUEL On them that do evil – yes.

ABIAH Then is David doing the will of God, Holiness, when he drives it away?

SAMUEL What is it that he does? How does he – drive it away?

ABIAH How, I know not. He seems to have a gift of enchantment. When Saul's trouble is upon him he plays and sings to him, and presently the evil spirit departs, and Saul's mind comes back to him.

(SAMUEL *sits thinking.*)

SAMUEL Is David always with him?

ABIAH No, Holiness. When the King no longer needs him, he goes back home to the care of his father's sheep. He is there now, so Joel tells me.

SAMUEL At Bethlehem?

ABIAH Yes, Holiness.

(*And now* SAMUEL *has an attack of plenary inspiration. Usually he has these in private; but on this occasion* ABIAH *is the privileged witness.*)

SAMUEL Abiah, the Word of the Lord has come to me. He has told me what He would have me do. I will take David from Saul. For surely it is not the Lord's will that Saul should be free from that evil spirit which now troubles him . . . Fetch me my horn, and fill it with oil. Also tell Caleb to saddle the ass, and to be ready himself to go with me. Bid him prepare food for the journey.

ABIAH Where are you going, Holiness?

SAMUEL Where the Lord sends me. You also, Abiah, shall go to Ahimelech and tell him to come to me – quickly.

ABIAH Again, Holiness?

SAMUEL Aye, again. For what the Lord had not then shown me of that which He purposed, now He has declared it. Say to Ahimelech that Saul is King no more. The Lord has chosen another in his stead; and the Kingdom is taken from Saul, and given to him . . . My horn, my horn, Abiah!

(ABIAH *goes out.*)

Yes, Lord, now plainly I do hear Thee again — speaking to me as of old. Thou hast pardoned my unfaithfulness, and the curse of the wicked one thou wilt take from me. I go to do Thy will; to anoint David to be King.

SCENE 3

(*The same scene.* ABIAH *and* JOEL *are alone together.*)

ABIAH You should not have come, Joel. Our Father is now so bitter against you, that when I told him I had been to see you, he was angry.

JOEL Why?

ABIAH Because now you are the King's man, and his no longer.

JOEL I have more cause to be bitter against him. If he goes on the way he is going, my life will no longer be safe to me.

ABIAH Not safe?

JOEL No. That I am my Father's son is now cause enough for the King to suspect me. Why does he still so itch for power that he cannot leave well alone? He has had a full life; and for what he did for Israel in his day men hold him in honour. But his day is over. Why cannot he gather up his old feet, and die in peace? . . . What is he doing now?

ABIAH Nothing that I am supposed to know.

253

JOEL Is it nothing that between him and Ahimelech there are comings and goings? – for what cause, think you?

ABIAH May not Priest take counsel of Prophet, Brother, to know the Lord's will concerning Israel?

JOEL Why so secretly? Why by night?

ABIAH (*startled*) Does the King know that?

JOEL Yes: and charges it to *me* that I know also.

ABIAH How comes he to know?

JOEL As I told you – because he no longer trusts me, he has taken others to his service, who bring word to him . . . You also, Abiah, may not be as safe as you think yourself. That is why I have come.

ABIAH What is it the King knows – or thinks to know?

JOEL Only that he is out to divide Israel.

ABIAH Aye, that is true. By what way?

JOEL Why do you question of that which surely you know? To the Priests at Shiloh has not word gone that, sometime, there is to be – another King?

ABIAH Is to be?

JOEL Yes! What do you know about that, Abiah?

ABIAH (*deciding to make a clean breast of it*) Is –

JOEL Who? Who?

ABIAH David.

JOEL Oh! but impossible!

ABIAH Why?

JOEL David is the King's right-hand man; Saul loves and trusts him . . . He brings him comfort in his affliction.

ABIAH (*smoothly*) Yes?

JOEL He is to marry the King's daughter. And he and Jonathan, the King's son, are as brothers – so great is their love for each other.

ABIAH Yes: very like; all that you say is true. And that is *why*. You do not know our Father as well as I do, Joel. When he heard of David, and of how greatly Saul loved and trusted him, he said: 'I will take David from Saul.'

JOEL But — does David know?

ABIAH I have already told you: David is King.

JOEL So Samuel the Prophet has chosen David, the Giant-Killer, for the dividing of Israel! . . . Had I known *that*, I should have feared to come, Abiah.

ABIAH Joel — how big, really, was that man, Goliath, whom David slew?

JOEL Not so big as they say: but big.

ABIAH Taller than Saul?

JOEL Oh, yes: he was taller than Saul. But he was a great fat fellow, and broad; and that made him look much bigger. And now that he's dead, rumour has done the rest, adding as many cubits to his stature as it can get people to believe . . . It wasn't quite fair, you know, the way David killed him: didn't give him a chance. But it was clever . . . Tell me, Abiah; was he *then* already Samuel's and the Lord's anointed?

ABIAH Yes.

JOEL He kept his secret well! And well for him that he did. If ever Saul comes to know of it, David is a dead man — and deserves to be!

ABIAH Our Father was right: you are all for Saul now, Joel.

JOEL I'm all for my own skin; and you had better be for yours. Can you not see the peril we stand in? I had no hand in it; but *you* — you knew of it. And if you knew of it, will Saul believe that I did not know also.

ABIAH Are you going to tell Saul?

JOEL No. And therein lies my danger if he hears of this day's meeting. I would that I had not come. Oh, what a fool a wise man can be! Does our Father think that he can now take back the Kingdom from Saul — a King loved by the people? Can you not persuade him to cease meddling in things which no longer concern him, and from troubling Israel?

ABIAH No, Joel; he can't be persuaded of anything, except that he is the Prophet of the Lord, and that those who do not obey his word must be cast down and destroyed.

(JOEL *sighs angrily.*)

JOEL How long has he yet to live, Abiah?

ABIAH As long, maybe, as he has the will for it. For though now so feeble that scarcely can he rise from his bed, his will is as strong as ever.

JOEL What does he do with himself now?

ABIAH He is still writing, by the hand of Jasher, his Book of the Judges. When that is finished, maybe he will have the will to depart in peace.

JOEL If it is to be in peace, it were well for him that he goes soon: – for you and for me also. I'm going, Abiah. You were right, I should not have come. If the King does find out, I will send word to you – if I am spared to do it . . . Pity, Abiah, that you and I could not also have been prophets of the Lord.

ABIAH Why?

JOEL It would have been safer.

(*And now, very feebly, on stumbling feet, and cling-ing to the door-post for support,* SAMUEL *enters. At the sight of* JOEL *he trembles with rage.*)

SAMUEL So your master has sent you to spy on me! Go! Go! You are no longer my son! The curse of the Lord God be upon you!

(*He can say no more; he makes a gesture of dismissal.* JOEL *stands looking at him for a moment in a silence which is eloquent. It is to* ABIAH *he speaks at last.*)

JOEL Farewell, Abiah.

(*He turns abruptly, and goes out; and presently the galloping of hoofs is heard.*)

ABIAH Holiness, you do Joel a great wrong. He came only to warn you.

SAMUEL Of what?

ABIAH Of your peril, when Saul comes to know of what you have done – making David King.

SAMUEL If I do the Lord's will, whom shall I fear? . . .

(ABIAH *does not answer.* SAMUEL *looks out to watch* JOEL'S *departure.*)

Who is that man – following after Joel?

(ABIAH *looks, and starts, for he sees danger.*)

ABIAH That is – Doeg, the Edomite.

SAMUEL The man who came with him before; and that I said was not to come again?

ABIAH Yes: but this time he did not come with him; nor have they gone back – together.

SAMUEL So! This is the watch that Saul has set on me. H'm!

ABIAH And now also on Joel, Holiness; because he has come to warn you.

SAMUEL I need no warning of Joel. The Lord is my Keeper.

(*He sits thinking.*)

Abiah, send word to David – 'Beware of Doeg, the Edomite.'

ABIAH Yes, Holiness.

SAMUEL Take me back to my bed, Abiah. Maybe this is the last time . . . the last time that I shall rise from it – now that I have done the Lord's Will.

(ABIAH *supports him back to his bed, from which he will not rise again.*)

ACT IV

SCENE 1

(SAUL *sits in his tent, not in full state, but it is as a warrior-King that one sees him: to right and left stands his shield-bearer and sword-bearer; and by his side piled armour and a stack of javelins. Before him stand* JOEL, *and* DOEG, *the Edomite.*)

SAUL Answer me! Who is it that now you serve – King Saul or King Samuel?

JOEL My lord, you only do I serve.

SAUL This man tells me that, two days since, he followed you to your Father's house at Ramah.

JOEL It is true that I went there, my lord. I did not know that he had followed me.

SAUL Nor were you meant to know.

JOEL But I did know, my lord, that you no longer trusted me. Therefore – for my own safety – I should not have gone.

SAUL Why did you go?

JOEL For *his*, my lord. For though I no longer serve him, he is yet my father.

SAUL And was that to do *me* service?

JOEL Yes, my lord. I went to warn him that he should no longer meddle in matters which concern only the King.

SAUL You ask me to believe that?

JOEL You will believe it, my lord, when I tell you that he would not hear me, ordered me away – never to see his face again. Aye! cursed me bitterly for being your servant – not his . . . He is dying, my lord; he can do nothing more than what he has done already. Let him die in peace.

SAUL Peace? . . . Let that wait . . . (*to* DOEG) What more have you to report?

DOEG My lord, that there is now one whom he has already chosen to be King – in your stead, my lord.

SAUL (*to* JOEL) What say you to that?

JOEL (*doing the best he can for himself*) I heard it, but I did not believe it, my lord. No, my lord.

SAUL 'Chosen' you say?

DOEG And *anointed*, my lord.

SAUL (*controlling his rage*) Who is the man?

DOEG I fear to tell you, my lord. Let him tell you (*pointing to* JOEL); he knows.

JOEL I did not believe it, my lord.

SAUL (*furiously*) His name! His name!

DOEG David, my lord.

SAUL (*springing to his feet*) You lie, Devil! You lie! (*He seizes* DOEG *violently*.) Swear to me that you lie, and I will not slay you for it.

DOEG No, my lord, no! I speak truth. It *is* David, my lord.

JOEL (*still saving himself*) It cannot be true, my lord.

SAUL What proof have you? What proof? You saw it done?

DOEG No, my lord. But I heard him tell my Lord Abiah, when he returned, that David was to be King. Also, my lord, he had sent word to Ahimelech and the Priests, telling them. And by them the people are to be taught that presently the Lord will send them another King.

(SAUL *stands searching for the truth. He turns to* JOEL.)

SAUL And *you*. Were *you* told that it was – David?

JOEL I was told, my lord; but I could not believe it.

SAUL . . . 'Another King' . . . When was this done?

DOEG Ten days since, my lord.

SAUL Where?

DOEG At Bethlehem, at his father's house, my lord.

SAUL Aye. He asked leave of me to go . . . I gave him leave . . . Three days later he returned . . . Said nothing. . . . He sang to me; aye, sang, and played, even as before; and as I heard him, I was refreshed and comforted . . . (*then, furiously*) Oh! It cannot be true! Prove it to me! If you cannot prove it, you die!

DOEG My lord – that it is true there is *one* that knows.

SAUL Who?

DOEG Your own son, the Prince – Jonathan.

(*This is too much for* SAUL *to believe.*)

SAUL Jonathan! Jonathan *knows* that over him, David is to be King! How should *he* know? *He?*

DOEG My lord, so great is the love of the King's son for David that he denies him nothing; and between them nothing is hid. I saw him – three days since – take the gold circlet from his head and set it upon David's. Also he stripped off his robe, and sword and bow and girdle, and put them upon David. Surely, in so doing, he knew. I speak truth, my lord.

(SAUL *signs to an Attendant standing without. He enters.*)

SAUL Send Jonathan to me.

(*The Attendant goes. There is a long pause.* SAUL *waits, saying nothing.* JOEL *and* DOEG *look at him with fear; his face is terrible. Presently* JONATHAN *enters.*)

When did you last see David?

JONATHAN But now, my lord.

SAUL Send him to me.

JONATHAN He is no longer here, my lord. He has gone.

SAUL Where?

JONATHAN To Bethlehem.

SAUL Again?

JONATHAN Yes, my lord; for the day of the yearly sacrifice at his father's house. He asked that he might go.

SAUL He did not ask leave of me that he should go.

JONATHAN No, my lord, he asked leave of me. I gave it.

SAUL (*to* DOEG) Saw you David, as you came in hither?

DOEG Yes, my lord.

SAUL Did he speak to you?

DOEG No, my lord. He looked at me, turned quickly, and went.

SAUL (*to* JONATHAN) And that he might get himself safely hence, came not to me, but to *thee*! Oh, thou son of a blind father, born of evil; now I know surely that thou hast taken this son of Jesse to be thy lord, and hast made thyself his servant, that he may take the Kingdom from thee when I am gone. Not while I live shall he live to do it: or thou! Send! Fetch him back to me, that this day he may die – and Israel be saved from the hand of Samuel.

JONATHAN Nay, my lord! What has he done that he should die?

SAUL For this – for this! That thou and he are so much one, that slaying thee, I slay him also. Die!

> (SAUL *snatches up a javelin and is about to hurl it at* JONATHAN. *His* ARMOUR-BEARER *beats it aside.* JONATHAN *runs out.*)

ARMOUR-BEARER No, my lord, no! Slay me, but not your son! Not my Lord Jonathan!

> (SAUL *throws him down, takes up another javelin, and hurls it after* JONATHAN.)

SAUL After him! Seize him! Let him not escape!

(*He staggers; seizes shield and sword from the two* BEARERS, *as they run out, followed by* JOEL *and* DOEG. *A red darkness begins to fall upon the scene. He lets shield and sword fall, strength goes out of him.*)

SAUL Oh, God, why hast thou smitten me where I am weakest, in them that I love? . . . Jonathan, my son . . . David, my comforter.

(*And now, as the Evil Spirit takes hold of him, we see, as* SAUL *sees. Darkness gathers round him; and in the darkness come flashes of light; and in those flashes figures move before his eyes and vanish. He sees Samuel, Agag, David – hears confused voices from the past: Agag pleading for his life: Samuel speaking the 'Word of the Lord': the Wise Woman of Endor: 'If you slay me for what I am, the curse of Samuel's God be upon you.'* SAMUEL: *'Be not concerned for thy father's asses. The Lord has rent the Kingdom of Israel from thee, and given it to another.'* DAVID: *'The Lord is my Shepherd, therefore shall I lack nothing.' And along with these mixed visions and voices, comes a sound of rising wind, that wails and shrieks as the darkness closes down deeper and deeper. Suddenly, out of the darkness, comes Saul's voice.*)

SAUL Ahimelech! Send me Ahimelech.

(*There comes a roll of thunder, and a sudden flash of lightning. In it* SAUL *is seen standing, sword lifted, a figure of wrath and vengeance. The darkness closes !own again.*)

CURTAIN

SCENE 2

(*In Samuel's house at Ramah, night is falling.* ABIAH *is seated at a table on which stands an unlighted lamp.* JASHER, *with a large scroll in his hand, stands before him.*)

JASHER The Book, he says, is finished. Here is the last of it. When I had written so far, and was yet waiting (I waited a long time, my lord) 'That is all,' he said. 'You need write no more. The days of the Judges of Israel are ended.'

(ABIAH *has taken the scroll, and is reading it.*)

ABIAH It ends strangely, Jasher.

JASHER I think, my lord, he would have written more, had he been able.

ABIAH Well, the Book of Judges is written; but who is going to write the Book of Samuel? . . . You, Jasher?

JASHER (*with a curious coldness*) No, my lord. I could not write it as my Lord Samuel would have it written. What he would have me write for him is done. Is it your wish, my lord, that I should come again tomorrow?

ABIAH There will be no need, Jasher. Light the lamp before you go.

(JASHER *lights the lamp.* ABIAH *takes up the scroll, and is about to read it; as* JASHER *opens the door to go out, he pauses.*)

What is the night going to be, Jasher?

JASHER A dark night, my lord.

(ABIAH *turns back to the reading of the scroll.* JASHER *looks back at him, then goes without speaking.*)

ABIAH (*reading*) 'And in those days there was no King in Israel; and every man did that which was right in his own eyes . . . Here endeth the Book of the Judges, written from the mouth of my Lord Samuel by the hand of his servant Jasher' . . . Yes, surely, the days of the Judges *are* ended. And now there are two Kings in Israel . . . Which of them are you going to serve, Abiah?

(*He gets up, and closes the shutters.*)

Aye, a dark night – when the light of Israel goes out.

(*From the inner room, from which there comes a faint light,* CALEB *enters hastily.*)

CALEB My Lord Abiah, will you come? The Holy One calls for you.

ABIAH What? Already awake again?

CALEB No, my lord. It is in his sleep that he calls for you.

ABIAH Then what use my coming?

CALEB Oh, my lord, in his sleep the Holy One says things which frighten me.

ABIAH Frighten you? Why?

CALEB It is as if in his sleep, some evil spirit troubled him . . . I fear to be alone with him, my lord.

ABIAH What is it you hear him say?

CALEB It is not his own voice that speaks, my lord. Yet out of his mouth I hear it – 'Where is the God of Samuel? Where is the God of Samuel?' And then – 'Your oath, Samuel!' – And then his own voice comes back to him, and he cries out for you, and for my Lord Joel to come to him.

ABIAH For Joel, you say?

CALEB Yes, my lord.

ABIAH Well, go back to him. I will come presently.

CALEB Come soon, my lord.

ABIAH (*impatiently*) Yes, yes. Go! I will come.

(CALEB *goes.* ABIAH *stands in thought for a while.*)

ABIAH So he calls also for Joel? Strange! 'Tis well, then, that I have already sent for him . . . 'Where is the God of Samuel?' Aye, where? Has he begun to have a doubt? . . . 'Your oath, Samuel.' What oath?

> (*A sound of galloping is heard; it comes to a halt. The door is flung open.* JOEL *enters in great haste and agitation.*)

Joel! Here already? I did not think my message could have reached you so soon.

JOEL I got no message. I came to save myself – my life!

ABIAH From whom?

JOEL The King. He is mad, mad, mad!

ABIAH Mad!

JOEL Aye – for blood! Never was such madness known! All tremble that hear of it. It cries to God that such a thing could be done in Israel, and the doer thereof – live!

ABIAH What has he done?

JOEL He has slain the Priests. Ahimelech is dead, and all with him, save one.

ABIAH Oh, horrible!

JOEL Aye, horrible, most horrible!

ABIAH Have you seen the King?

JOEL Nay, for when I heard of it, I fled. For my own life I feared, being Samuel's son: for if Ahimelech and the Priests be slain, what life can be safe?

ABIAH This will kill our Father, when he hears of it.

JOEL It may well! – for it is his doing.

ABIAH His? What mean you?

JOEL Who else made David King; and sent word of it to Ahimelech? Doeg has told of it . . . David, fleeing from Saul, sought help of Ahimelech; and the old man gave him shelter and food, and armed him with the sword of Goliath, and sent him safely away – to King Achish of Gath. When

the King heard that, madness came on him; he ordered
Ahimelech and the Priests to be brought before him. And
what does Ahimelech do? Withstands Saul to his face – and
praises David as a faithful servant of the King! That was
enough! The King gave command, and Ahimelech and the
Priests are slain.

ABIAH Who did the slaying?

JOEL Doeg, the Edomite. There was no other would do it.

ABIAH Did you *see*?

JOEL I saw Ahimelech fall. Then I fled. As I fled I heard
the slaying – go on. There was one that escaped and fled
with me – the only one. We parted – well for me! For hard
after *him* goes death . . . What about our Father? Does he
live still?

ABIAH Only just; but – not for long.

JOEL 'Twere well he should not. 'Tis better he should
die ere the vengeance of Saul fall on him.

ABIAH Would he dare?

JOEL One so mad will dare anything . . . Abiah, if Saul
slays him, he will slay us also. Are you going to wait for
that?

ABIAH We can't leave him to die alone, Joel.

JOEL What good will it do that we should die also? 'Tis
to this he has brought us. 'Tis his doing . . . Who now is
with him?

ABIAH Old Caleb; the only one left, now that Jasher has
gone.

JOEL Is not one enough? What more can we do. When
Saul finds me gone, he will send after me. *I* have no call to
be here. Our Father sent me from him. *You* he kept.

ABIAH Of late he has been asking for you. 'Twas but
yesterday he sent for you to return.

JOEL Why – having cast me off?

ABIAH The reasons of a dying man are hard to know,
Joel. . . .

Nay, will you not see him before you go?

(*But already* JOEL *is making ready to go.*)

JOEL What good? He does not know that I am here. And, why should I wait? Saul's messengers may soon be here . . . I'm going, Abiah.

ABIAH Maybe that is wise.

JOEL Farewell, Abiah – *farewell.*

(*He goes. That last word was said with so ominous a meaning that* ABIAH *is moved by it. He feels very much alone. Fear takes hold of him. At the sound of galloping of hoofs he starts; but they are going, not coming. He has yet time to save himself.*)

ABIAH Aye, what use? What use? Is not one enough?

(*He looks out.*)

Truly a dark night!

(*He wraps himself hurriedly in a cloak, puts out the light, and goes, leaving the door wide.* CALEB *enters.*)

CALEB My lord, my lord! He calls for you!

(SAMUEL'S *voice is heard faintly calling for* ABIAH. CALEB *sees* ABIAH *running away.*)

He's gone. He has left me alone!

SAMUEL (*His voice*) The curse! The curse! Take it from me!

(CALEB *is seized with panic. He wavers between fear and faithfulness. A cry from* SAMUEL *finishes him. He runs away.* SAMUEL *is alone. The* WISE WOMAN *comes slowly in. As she crosses to the inner room, she sings in a low voice:*)

WOMAN   Rat-a-tat-tat! 'Twas a rat in the house,
That wanted to kill the old grey mouse.
But the old grey mouse, for all that,
Has come to see the death of the rat.

As she reaches the inner room, the voice of SAMUEL *is heard calling 'Abiah . . . Joel'. The stage darkens: the scene changes.* SAMUEL *is seen lying on his bed, half-conscious. With twitching hands he clutches at the bedclothes. The* WISE WOMAN *enters, stands looking at him, and speaks:)*

WOMAN   The old man is full of sorrow,
Here today, and gone tomorrow.
Kings come up, and Judges go down;
All alike when the Gods frown.

SAMUEL Who's there? . . . My sons, where are you? . . . They've left me – alone!

WOMAN Aye! alone – all alone, at last.

(Hearing the voice he most fears, SAMUEL *starts to full consciousness.)*

SAMUEL Woman, what brings *you* here?

WOMAN *You* brought me. I've a word for you, 'twill be good for you to hear. Will you hear it? . . . or will you have it not said?

SAMUEL Speak.

(She sits down by him.)

WOMAN You asked me once, Samuel, whether I could put a curse upon a man; and I answered, 'He puts it upon himself'. Aye, it's your own curse that's upon you now, Samuel. For though you still live, all your power has gone from you. Who cares for you now? Oh, yes; you thought to break Saul – to do it, you broke Israel. What good has it done you? Over Saul's head you anointed David to be King. You won't

live to see David King — *you* won't, Samuel. Has David
come back to you for a last blessing? No. David has fled
away from Saul, and gone to give service to the foes of
Israel — to Achish, King of Gath. Aye, you've been a sore
trouble to Saul — the two of you. And I helped you to do
it when Saul became my enemy. *Your* doing, Samuel; you
didn't break your oath to me, eh? You set Saul to do it for
you. I know it now.

SAMUEL Oh, cease, cease, Woman, from troubling me!
Let me die in peace.

WOMAN Peace! What peace have you given to Israel?
David was Saul's servant, his friend. Saul loved and trusted
him. But behind Saul's back you anointed David to be
King. Did David tell Saul? No; Saul was not to know. So
at your bidding David became a traitor to his King. For if
Saul *was* truly the Lord's Anointed — what was David? Was
he the Lord's, or was he only Samuel's? Who can tell? A
prophet can always speak the 'Word of the Lord' as seems
good to him; but we've only *his* word for it. And if there
be evil in his heart, the word he speaks will be evil also.
And *your* heart was evil.

SAMUEL Go, Woman, go from me! You have cursed my
life from the day when first I hearkened to you, and took
your counsel for the sign, and did not wait for the Lord.
You took the Word of the Lord from me — tempting me;
and I heard His Voice no more. Though I called upon Him,
He heard me not.

WOMAN Call on Him again, Samuel! Make thy peace
with Saul, and maybe He will yet hear thee.

SAMUEL I will *not* make peace with Saul.

WOMAN Therefore has this come to pass; that because
you also made Ahimelech and the Priests of the Tabernacle
to conspire with you for David against Saul, therefore has
Saul slain them. The Priests are dead, Samuel.

SAMUEL The Priests are dead!

WOMAN Your doing, Samuel. So now is Israel broken and divided, because Samuel loved himself more than he loved Israel, and was wroth when power was taken from him and given to another.

SAMUEL Ah! God, why hast Thou made me live to see this day?

WOMAN For the better knowing of thyself, Samuel, and of the man thou art.

SAMUEL Oh, God, send down Thy curse upon this Woman, whose life I spared, when I should have slain.

WOMAN You did your best, Samuel, you did your best. 'Twas a fine oath you took that day – took and kept; eh, Samuel? – that I should live to *your* life's end – and further – if it were God's will. Well, it has been – God's will. Now die! and your God – go with you.

    (*She turns to go.*)

> Rat-a-tat-tat! 'Twas a rat in the house,
> That wanted to kill the old grey mouse.
> But the old grey mouse, for all that,
> Has lived to see the death of the rat!

    (*She goes out.*)

SAMUEL (*feebly*) Help, help! Joel, Abiah! My sons, where are you? Oh, God, Thou hast emptied me out, and cast me away; and there is none left to succour me – none to regard me. Abiah! . . . Abiah! . . . Joel!

    (*He goes on calling. Slowly the curtain falls.*)

(The WISE WOMAN *of Endor's house is built against a wall of rock, which gives it the appearance of a cave. In a hollow of the rock is a fire. She sits bent over it, stirring a pot. From outside comes the sound of wind and rain. As she stirs the pot, she croons a song:)*

WISE WOMAN   Rain and wind, wind and rain,
                Fall and blow, fast or slow;
                Hours, and days, and years go:
                None of them ever comes back again.

(A SHEPHERD LAD *enters. He has a sack over his head as a cover from the rain.)*

SHEPHERD Old One, have you heard? Did you know?

WOMAN Know what?

SHEPHERD Away yonder there's going to be a battle.

WOMAN Aye, aye, surely. There'll always be battles so long as there's men left to fight them.

SHEPHERD Ah! There's the Wise One talking!

WOMAN One doesn't need to be wise to know that. What's this one about? Who are they fighting?

SHEPHERD The Philistines. King Saul, with ten thousand or more, is camped yonder on Mount Gilboa; and the Philistines are coming up against them, with a bigger army — two to his one, so they say.

WOMAN Aye, like enough — now that Israel is divided; some being for David; others for Saul.

SHEPHERD Which are you for, Wise One?

WOMAN Neither. What use would I be to either of them? As for Saul — he would have had my life long ago, could he have found me. Why should I help him?

SHEPHERD Isn't he the Lord's Anointed, Gammer?

WOMAN He was — once on a time. But when there's two

Lord's Anointed, who's to say which is the true one?
Samuel's doing, that was. What for? Who knows? — now
that the old Grey-beard is dead.

SHEPHERD He was a great Prophet of the Lord, wasn't he?

WOMAN Aye; of *his* Lord he was. Well and truly did he
prophesy for *Him* — both of 'em dead now.

SHEPHERD But a God can't die, Gammer!

WOMAN Can't he? There's many Gods'll die yet — when
men cease to believe in 'em . . . Here! You'd better get
home. This storm's going to be worse.

SHEPHERD You don't mind being here all alone, Gammer,
miles from anywhere?

WOMAN I'm never alone. Off with you!

(*He goes. She closes the door after him and bolts it.*)

WOMAN No; never alone, while I've a mind to remember.

(*She sings.*)

> Wind and rain, hail and snow,
> The hours, the days, and the years go.
> The past is past, and wishing is vain:
> The dead shall never come back again.

Aye! Dead — I've outlived you, Samuel.

(*There comes knocking, and a voice calling.*)

VOICE Ho! Is anyone within?

(*She gets up, goes slowly to the door, and opens it.
SAUL enters, cloaked and hooded, so that his face is
hidden.*)

WOMAN Who are you? What do you want — here?

SAUL Shelter from this night of storm, and the wrath of
Heaven.

WOMAN I can give you shelter from the night: but I cannot shelter you from the wrath of Heaven . . . Sit down, and

warm yourself . . . What brings you here of all places – and to me?

SAUL Are you not that one whom men call the Wise Woman of Endor?

WOMAN Was it that which brought you?

SAUL Of a truth, yes. I have come because men say you are wise.

WOMAN Not now. Such I was once, but my wisdom has gone from me.

SAUL Do not lie, Woman. If God ever gave you wisdom, you have it still.

WOMAN God? What God gave me put me in peril of my life . . . to be taken from me if I used it. Wise? What is it to be wise? Here – here's food for you.

(She puts a bowl into his hands.)

SAUL To have knowledge of hidden things – that surely is to be wise.

WOMAN One may have knowledge – and use it foolishly. Where men are fools, 'tis better to be silent.

SAUL If you have knowledge, and do not speak it – of what use can it be?

WOMAN Had I not been silent these many years, I would have been dead. Because I was wise, the King, who feared Samuel, feared me also. Had Saul's men found me out they would have slain me. Aye, many of us has he harried and slain, that for their wisdom were called witches; I only am left. Let me die in peace. Ask me nothing.

SAUL Have no fear of King Saul, Woman. He has no wish to harm thee now, or to take thy life from thee.

WOMAN How will you make me sure of that?

SAUL By my own head, and the King's, I swear it.

WOMAN Oh, if but a while ago I could have used my wisdom that has been shut up in me all these years, I might have saved Israel – and the King also.

SAUL From what?

WOMAN From the curse of one that is dead – but in the evil that he did lives still.

SAUL (*startled*) Truly, thou has said it: for that am I come.

WOMAN (*suspiciously*) Did the King send thee?

SAUL There was no need for the King to *send* me. This matter concerns me – alone.

WOMAN Speak, then! What wouldst thou?

SAUL Woman, canst thou raise up the dead?

WOMAN The dead? I know not. They raise themselves, if there be anything left of them. If not, it is only their shadows that we see. Aye, if they have ears to hear a voice calling to them, they come. If they hear it not, they come *not*. Whom of the dead dost thou seek?

SAUL One that was mine enemy, and devised mischief against me.

WOMAN Thine enemy, eh? Wherefore?

SAUL Because I took from him that which he loved more than life – his power over others – therefore he put his curse on me, hated me, and went about to destroy me.

WOMAN Well; if his hate has gone with him, he will not come back to bless thee. Why dost thou seek him? Has he not cursed thee enough?

SAUL I would know whether he has power yet to curse me to my end. For now things go hard with me, and I am in sore straits because of him. Surely – if the dead *are* dead, his curse should not be on me now. Call him, so that I may know.

WOMAN His name?

SAUL Samuel.

WOMAN Nay, who art thou that seekest after Samuel that is dead? – Thy name?

SAUL Call him. Bid him speak: *he* will tell thee my name. So shall I know that thou art wise.

WOMAN I would know better first whether it were well that I should be – wise for thee. Show me thy hand.

(She takes SAUL'S *hand, and studies it.)*

Aye! 'Tis the hand of an honest man that has been crossed by evil . . . simple, truthful . . . a man of power . . . one having authority.

(She starts.)

Show me thy face!

(He turns his head away.)

Why dost they hide thy face from me? What dost thou fear?

(He turns back and faces her.)

Ah! It is the King! Surely this is an ill thing thou hast done – to lure me to my death!

SAUL Have no fear of me; I came not here to slay thee. Nay; nor was it of my own will that I ever sought thy life. It was Samuel's bidding.

WOMAN I should have known it! I should have known it! The oath which Samuel took to spare my life, he set thee to break for him. Aye, truly! That was Samuel!

SAUL Call him to me – that I may know the truth.

WOMAN What truth, living or dead, wilt thou get from Samuel?

SAUL His spirit haunts me.

WOMAN An evil spirit – a lying spirit. What wouldst thou ask of him?

SAUL This only: whether, after he has slain me, he will cease to divide Israel. To know that, ere I die, would be well.

WOMAN So . . . thou fearest him still? Well, I can show him to thee; for that which is in a man's mind I can make him see. But the dead are dead: no wisdom comes from them; only that which thou hast in thine own mind concerning them – neither more nor less. In man's fear of evil lies the power of evil. Fear him no more, and Samuel shall depart from thee into death; and his curse will go with him, like an evil dream when a man awakes out of sleep.

SAUL I dream still; and in my dream my fear of him is great. Call him!

WOMAN Well, thou shalt see thy fear! If thou fear him enough, he will come to thee . . . Call! . . . Call 'Samuel'!

SAUL Samuel!

(*There is a single faint echo: then a long pause.*)

WOMAN So heavily he sleeps. Call louder!

SAUL (*louder*) Samuel!

(*Two echoes die faintly away.*)

WOMAN He hears thee not; or comes not to thy call. I will call for thee. He shall hear *me*. Samuel! Wake! Wake! Samuel!

(*The echoes that follow go on, and multiply, as though other voices were taking up the call.*)

Aye, aye! The dead awake. Now through the House of Death goes the cry . . . Is he so far away? Hark! They are still calling him . . . Nay, here he comes.

(*At that coming from the other world, the fire of the hearth sinks down and dies. In the hollow of the rock, surrounded by a dull red light, the ghost of* SAMUEL *appears.* SAUL *utters a cry of terror, and falls senseless to the ground.*)

SAMUEL What power is it that calls me?

WOMAN The powers of that oath which you broke, Samuel – to her that gave you the sign of the wrath of Heaven – to whom you promised life, and sent death . . . The old grey mouse is still alive, Samuel. The rat is dead.

(SAMUEL *makes a gesture, and opens his mouth to speak.*)

Shut thy mouth! My power is upon thee! Be dumb! Now will I take thy curse from one that was thy better. He shall fear thee no more.

(*She turns to* SAUL, *and raises him to his feet.*)

Nay, nay, this is no place for a King to lie! Stand up, man, and look thine enemy in the face – what is left of him. Yonder stands the man that made me your enemy – you mine. You sought my life; I sought yours. Came a day when he took counsel of me for your destruction; and when my counsel seemed good to him, he called it the Word of the Lord.

(SAUL *raises his head, and sees the ghost of* SAMUEL. *Slowly he masters his fear and speaks.*)

SAUL Aye: there I see him; 'tis the old Samuel; death has not changed him . . . He looks at me; he does not speak . . . Speak, Samuel! I am Saul.

(*Behind his back the* WISE WOMAN *raises her hand in a gesture of command.* SAMUEL, *about to speak, stays dumb.*)

WOMAN He does not hear thee, or see thee. This that thou seest is but the face of thy fear. Let it trouble thee no more. They that did evil in their lives, when they die, they die – having neither ears, nor eyes, nor voices; nor is any understanding of life left in them. They are dead; and what thou seest here is but a mist rising from the grave, a shadow of the life that is gone. Thy reproaches reach him not, neither does he know to what pass thou art come through the evil he devised for thee. He remembers no more what he did to thee, nor why he was thine enemy.

To this end has he come . . . Go thy way, Saul! Put off thy fear of the curse he laid on thee, and thou are free from Samuel.

SAUL Because of him, I go now to my death.

WOMAN We all go to our death – some day. Whether thy death be today, or tomorrow, or the day after, what matters it? Die as a King should die, and thy reward shall be with thee. And thy name shall be had in honour hereafter when men tell of thee . . . See now, he fades away before thine eyes; and thy mind also is free of him, because thou fearest him no more. Thou art still Saul: and Samuel is nothing but a name.

(The ghost of SAMUEL *grows dim; but does not quite vanish.)*

SAUL O Woman, thou hast taught me wisdom, and given me strength. I came to thee in fear. Without fear I go to my death.

WOMAN Aye, now truly thou art thyself again; and the evil spirit troubleth thee no more. Go thy way: yonder is storm; but in the Heavens there is no wrath. Farewell . . . Saul!

*(*SAUL *goes. She stands at the open door looking after him. As she comes back she sees the ghost of* SAMUEL*; he also is looking after* SAUL*, watching his departure.)*

What? Still hungry for that which thou hast lost? I have taken Saul from thee; he fears thee no more. Aye, there he goes – the better man whom thou hast slain. There is no blood on thy hands, but there is blood on thy heart. Thou slewest him – not with sword, but with hatred and jealousy, because he took over the power of the Kingdom, and ruled Israel well. I told him that thou wast nothing, and sent him away a free man, no longer fearing thee.

But thou canst still hear *my* voice, and my word . . . Dead
rat! Get back to your hole!

> (*As she speaks* SAMUEL'S *ghost changes colour; all
> semblance of life goes out of it; it takes on the hues of
> death and corruption, and fades slowly away.*)

EPILOGUE

JASHER I am Jasher, the writer of history, servant of my Lord Samuel. What he bade me write I wrote for him in his books. What he did not bid me write I wrote in my own book, the Book of Jasher. But after that Samuel was dead, my own book was taken from me, because there was truth in it which was not to be told. I served Samuel, and feared him; but I loved Saul. Now Samuel is dead, and Saul is dead also; Saul whom Samuel slew, dividing the Kingdom against him. Ye Mountains of Gilboa, let there be no dew nor rain upon you, neither fields of offering. For there the shield of the mighty was vilely cast away – the shield of Saul as though he had not been anointed with oil. Ye daughters of Israel weep over Saul, who clothed you in scarlet with other delights, who put ornaments of gold upon your apparel. How are the mighty fallen and the weapons of War perished. Also he taught them the use of the bow. Behold, it is written in the Book of Jasher.